Creating the Discipline of Knowledge Management

The Latest in University Research

Creating the Discipline of Knowledge Management

The Latest in University Research

Editor

Michael Stankosky, D.Sc.

ELSEVIER
BUTTERWORTH
HEINEMANN

AMSTERDAM • BOSTON • HEIDELBERG • LONDON
NEW YORK • OXFORD • PARIS • SAN DIEGO
SAN FRANCISCO • SINGAPORE • SYDNEY • TOKYO

Elsevier Butterworth–Heinemann
30 Corporate Drive, Suite 400, Burlington, MA 01803, USA
Linacre House, Jordan Hill, Oxford OX2 8DP, UK

♾ Recognizing the importance of preserving what has been written, Elsevier prints its
books on acid-free paper whenever possible.

Library of Congress Cataloging-in-Publication Data
Application submitted.

British Library Cataloguing-in-Publication Data
A catalogue record for this book is available from the British Library.

ISBN: 0-7506-7878-X

For information on all Elsevier Butterworth–Heinemann publications
visit our Web site at www.books.elsevier.com

Printed in the United States of America
05　06　07　08　09　10　　10　9　8　7　6　5　4　3　2　1

Contents

1

Advances in Knowledge Management: University
Research Toward an Academic Discipline 1
Michael A. Stankosky, D.Sc.

2

The Early Pathways: Theory to Practice—A Continuum........15
Francesco A. Calabrese, D.Sc.

3

Developing A Foundation For A Successful Knowledge
Management System 51
Charles H. Bixler, D.Sc.

4

An Empiric Study of Organizational Culture Types
and their Relationship with the Success of a Knowledge
Management System and the Flow of Knowledge in
the U.S. Government and Nonprofit Sectors...........................66
Juan Roman-Velazquez

5

Building a Knowledge-Centered Culture: a Matter of Trust

6

7

8

9

10

11

12

Preface

"Knowledge assets determine success or failure, but you will search in vain to find them in a company's books."

—*Thomas A. Stewart*

This is a critical juncture in the life of Knowledge Management (KM). KM is over ten years old. Should it continue to grow and age as KM, should it be abandoned, or should it morph into the many paths of management and information technology science? Should anyone really care, except a handful of practitioners and scholars who deal with this on a daily basis? Why would anyone care if we still don't have a globally accepted definition of KM; let alone universally accepted frameworks, principles, and best practices. Many executives and managers don't even know that KM exists, or that it is the solution to many issues concerning improving organizational efficiency, effectiveness, and innovation. There are many KM failures to point to; perhaps more failures than successes. Does KM then have, or even need, a future?

My answer is a resounding yes! When this author is asked, why KM? you will hear one answer time and time again: It's all about KM. It is an answer that bears constant repetition and reaffirmation. Many try to justify a KM initiative by searching for a value proposition, which is a good and necessary thing. The fact of the matter is we exist in a knowledge-based economy, however, where knowledge assets are the principal factors of production; just as physical assets, like coal and steel, dominated the manufacturing/industrial economy. If you have a difficult time grasping this notion, I recommend that you read *Wealth of Knowledge* by Tom Stewart. Tom lays this out in most direct and eloquent terms.

If nations and organizations want to attain a competitive advantage, they have to deal with knowledge assets. They are in the balance sheets of national and organizational wealth and value, although not in the explicit terms and figures that accountants need for calculation.

This book is about trying to establish a solid scientific background for KM, not only as an academic discipline, but also as a recognized essential element in all management research and practices. We often say that practice makes perfect. In fact, theory makes perfect; practice makes permanent. We need a theoretical construct for KM, so that practitioners can practice with confidence.

What makes this book unique is its dedication to using the scientific method, which underlies the basis for doctoral-level research; to obtain a doctorate, a candidate must follow century-tried methods of disciplined research, and subject themselves to the scrutiny and judgments of scholars, peers, and practitioners. This is not to say that there are no other like-KM research activities. What makes this unique is the "brain-trust" of faculty, doctoral candidates, and individuals—over 100 in number—working as a team against a research map, under the auspices of a nationally recognized university which has established the first master's and doctoral programs in KM. Only a university can ultimately legitimize an academic discipline.

What you will see in this book are the research results of eleven Doctors of Science, who combined the best of research with their own practical experiences in KM. They are remarkable individuals, completing a degree recognized as the ultimate in an educational experience. They represent the less than one percent of the population which has such an accomplishment.

Up front, however, I ask you to be patient with reading their works. This is a book of research, not readings. Look for the golden nuggets which we have highlighted. While they have attempted to modify their research works for general reading, a dissertation is not like the easy flowing prose that one finds in the best mystery novels. However, this collection is important enough to the knowledge economy to find a place in a more accessible publication such as this book. No one finds reading Newton's principles of mathematics and energy easy, yet they have defined and sustained the industrial age as no other written works have. We also see this book as a first installment, for we have 35 more doctoral candidates in some stage of KM research and education. In some ways, the research findings contained in this book are but the springboard for new research. You too can also play a key role by communicating with us; thereby adding your own research and practical insights to the KM body of knowledge.

Finally, if asked again if KM should have a future, I respond: If the current KM language and practices are not working, then we better find a way of making them work, or invent new ones. For the knowledge economy is in motion, and we need to not only stay with it, but also to get ahead of it to remain competitive. It is a fast-moving train, and we need to renew our knowledge assets at the same speed of our businesses and activities. In other words: Knowledge at the speed of business.

Michael Stankosky, D.Sc.
Washington, D.C.

Acknowledgments

No person lives and works alone. I have had the blessing to not only work with the following people, but also have gained insights and inspiration from them. They are the reason why we have this book and the vibrant KM academic and research programs at the George Washington University. I want to thank them all. I know in doing this list that I risk leaving out so many who have touched me and this program. You know who you are, and you have my gratitude: Howard Eisner, Charlie Bixler, Carolyn Baldanza, Bill Schulte, Vincent Ribiere, Charles Despres, Daniele Chauvel, Claude Bensoussan, Sue Hanley, Bill Halal, Steve Ruth, Art Murray, Lile Murphree, Julie Ryan, Mike Duffey, Jack Harrald, Gabriele McLaughlin, Kent Greenes, Dan Holtshouse, Annie Green, Geoffrey Malafsky, Alex and Dave Bennet, Hugh McKellar, Jim Watson, Dave Cheseborough, Debra Amidon, Rudy Garrity, Bill Millward, Giora Hadra, Tom Beckman, John Starns, French Caldwell, Steve Newman, Francesco deLeo, Mirghani Mohamed, Betty Kelley, Patsy Murphree, Elsa Rhoads, Bill Kaplan, Richard Wallace, Peter Engstrom, Diane Sandiou, Bill Cross, Sylviane Toporkoff, Steve Wieneke, Doug Weidner, Tom Paulsen, Bob Shearer, Ed Paradise, Donna Stemmer, Andreas Andreou, Niall Sinclair, Michael Kull, Theresa Jefferson, Denis Cioffi, Vittal Anantatmula, Maria Romanova, Po-Jeng Wang, Scott Shaffar, Linda Kemp, Connie Mokey, Mona Yep, Dave Britt, Mary Shupak, Cynthia Gayton, Steve Denning, Ramon Barquin, Pat Brislin, Lynne Schnider, Harriet Riofrio, Mike Dorohovich, Andy Campbell, Shahram Sarkani, Jon Deason, Zoe Dansan, Tom Davenport, George Brier, Gideon Frieder, Bob Buckman, Juan Pablo Giraldo, Hans Jerrell, Patrice Jackson, Belkis Leong-Hong, Cathy Kreyche, Juan Román-Velázquez Perry Luzwick, Mickey Ross, Cynthia Odom, Kanti Srikantaiah, Werner Schaer, Ken Slaght, Karla Phlypo-Price, Doug Tuggle, Kevin O'Sullivan, and Karl Wiig.

I especially want to thank George Washington University. In the past six years they have provided me a venue to live my vocation. I have received incredible support from all levels of the university, especially Bob Waters, my first boss and former Chair, (Department of Engineering Management), Tom Mazzuchi, my current boss, and Chair, Department of Engineering Management and Systems Engineering, Erik Winslow, Department Chair of Management Science, Deans Timothy Tong (School of Engineering and Applied Science) and Susan Phillips (School of Business), V.P.s Carol Siegleman and Craig Linebaugh, Associate Deans Jeff Lynn and Doug Jones, and finally, Don Lehman, Executive V.P. for Academic Affairs. They made things happen, and proved that a university is truly a place to innovate and learn. I owe all of them a debt of gratitude.

Finally, special thanks to Francesco Calabrese and Joanne Freeman. Frank has kept this program on a "managed" basis, capably picking up my pieces and ensuring we have the right agenda, the meetings scheduled, the right people notified, etc. Clearly he is the most capable of leaders and administrators and indispensable. He also brings that special wisdom that makes anyone look good. And Joanne has been the heavy duty typist, organizer, do-it-all, etc. She has kept this manuscript and us moving. If you're thinking about it, she's already doing it.

It truly does take a global community of practice!

To my twin grandsons, Michail Anthony and Joseph Archer, expected to be born in 2005; who will represent a generation of knowledge workers in the 21st century.

Advances in Knowledge Management: University Research Toward an Academic Discipline

1

Michael A. Stankosky, D.Sc.

How It Started: Knowledge Management as an Academic Discipline

When I was in business, it bothered me that my company had not taken advantage of what it knew. We had people scattered throughout the United States, and few knew the company's full potential. We chased new business opportunities, not really knowing what we had already developed and sold. We were always proposing new solutions, without taking advantage of those we had developed in the past. Moreover, how could we, when we did not know what they were?

I left industry and joined academia in 1998, having accepted a full-time faculty position at the George Washington University (GW). I was appointed as an associate professor of Systems Engineering in the Department of Engineering Management and Systems Engineering, School of Engineering and Applied Science. I chose to seek a position in this department because it was both multi- and interdisciplinary, reflecting the realties of the complex world one has to work in. One of the largest departments of its kind in any university, it included nine academic concentrations built on the premise that engineers eventually become managers and need the necessary management competencies to function in the modern world. On the other hand, it helped managers understand better the engineers who work in their domains, and thus provided some engineering skills to managers.

In addition to responsibilities for teaching systems engineering, I also inherited the oversight of courses in marketing of technology, technologic forecasting and management, law for engineers, artificial intelligence, and decision-support systems. These two latter courses got me interested in knowledge management (KM). When the chair of the department asked me if I wanted to delete these courses from the catalogue, I asked him to let me evaluate whether there was any interest and determine the state of these fields. As a result of that investigation, I was impressed with the quality and quantity of works in KM. Had I known about these when I was in industry, I could have used them to the profit of the company. I was surprised that KM was not part of a core curriculum in any degree program at GW.

So began my journey on creating an academic discipline for KM. In my new position, I had inherited several graduate and doctoral students and asked them to help me with KM research. This research revealed that many universities had some research and elective courses on KM, but none at the time had a graduate program, especially at the doctoral level, dedicated to the field. Even at GW, we had several noted writers, but certainly no major thrust at examining all the aspects of KM and subjecting them to the rigors of scientific exploration.

In our early research, two things became clear to me: (a) knowledge was the prime currency in our national and global economy, and (b) knowledge directly provided value to the bottom line. We still lacked a common language to deal with it, and consequently, we borrowed some of the language of the information revolution. While the United States officially reached the information age in 1991, we have always been a knowledge-based economy. What that means is quite simple: Our economic well-being and competitive advantage are dependent on knowledge resources—our knowledge, experiences, education, training, professional networks, collaborative, and innovative skills. Other names and categories for these resources include knowledge assets, intellectual capital, human capital, structural capital, customer capital, and market capital. In sum, these knowledge assets are the prime factors and resources of production in a knowledge-based economy. In the words of Jack Welch, former chief executive officer of General Electric, "Intellectual capital is what it's all about. Releasing the ideas of your people is what we're trying to do, what we've got to do if we're going to win."

The facts described in the preceding paragraphs have spawned a new way of thinking about and managing these assets: KM, which was popularized around 1995 by many authors, practitioners, and advocates of intellectual technology (IT). Since that time, KM has been both a wild success and a wild failure. KM represented an evolution from the data and information eras to that of the knowledge economy, as depicted in Figure 1-1. The same figure shows how each era spawned their corresponding management disciplines and technologic elements.

Figure 1-1

Timelines leading to the knowledge age.

The Past, Present and Future

MANAGEMENT CONCEPTS	**SYSTEMS THINKING / APPROACH**	**SOFTWARE ENGINEERING MANAGEMENT**	**SYSTEMS ENGINEERING MANAGEMENT**	**KNOWLEDGE MANAGEMENT ENGINEERING**
	Systems / Project Management	**CMM**	**CMM**	**KMA/EE**
SYSTEMS	**DATA PROCESSING SYSTEM (DPS)**	**MANAGEMENT INFORMATION SYSTEM (MIS)**	**DECISION SUPPORT SYSTEM (DSS)**	**KNOWLEDGE MANAGEMENT SYSTEM (KMS)**
TECHNOLOGY ELEMENTS	**DATA**	**INFORMATION**	**ARTIFICIAL INTELLIGENCE**	**KNOWLEDGE**
AGE	**INDUSTRIAL**	**TECHNOLOGY**	**INFORMATION**	**KNOWLEDGE**

Many organizations such as BP/Amoco, Ford, Xerox, Cemex, Siemens, and Cisco have mastered the practices of KM and have shown how they contribute to the bottom line. However, many others have abandoned it, because it did not deliver on the promises, or worse yet, because they see no relevancy for it in their strategies and operations. To many, KM is a fad, not to be bothered with. Many studies have looked at KM and found numerous obstacles to its success, yet none have looked at them in the light of prime resources for the organization.

Why Knowledge Management? It Is All About Knowledge Management!

Which led me to the conclusion that KM has significance and that it must be elevated to its own academic discipline, with the accompanying theoretical constructs, guiding principles, and professional society to serve as an evolutionary thrust. KM certainly is not a fad, because the knowledge-based economy is here to stay. In addition, fads normally hang around for 5 years, and KM has been in existence for at least 10 years. If the current language and practices of KM are not the right ones, then we must find them: Our knowledge-based economy leaves us no choice. Knowledge assets are the tools with which today's industries need to function. Consequently, KM must be given a priority position in our educational and training systems. It must be relegated to its own academic discipline, with guiding principles based on scientific research. We cannot afford the hit and miss of anecdotes and so-called best practices, even so called when they led to failure. Besides, it is not best practices that will give you the competitive advantage; rather, best practices-to-be.

So, what is an academic discipline? Webster defines it as a "field of study." Fields of study are what universities create on the basis of their importance to society. Only a university can legitimize an academic discipline. If KM were to be given such a status, it had to go mainstream, which meant, in university terms, that it had to be a degree-granting program. Without that, no one would be seriously attracted to it. While many individuals come to a university to learn, their principle objective is to get a degree. A degree is the calling card in our world and the first requirement for acceptance and advancement in the workforce. The challenge, however, was on what theoretical construct could I base KM. There were no KM degree—granting programs in America at that time—perhaps none in the world—as determined by our limited research at that time. I had to find some basis to present a proposal to the faculty and university. The sell would have been easier at GW if I could have identified other universities with KM degree–granting programs. Such programs would have also provided some basis for a proposed curriculum.

Theories are developed from top down or bottom up. The latter method was chosen because of the numerous writings and practices already in existence. The bottom-up method was used by Sir Isaac Newton in developing his theories for motion and physics that accelerated the industrial age: collecting falling apples and developing theories (i.e., validating, by scientific method, relationships among them). He often said that he could see further because he stood on the shoulders of giants. KM had such giants in Peter Drucker, Karl Wiig, Ikujiro Nonaka, Larry Prusack, Tom Davenport, Tom Stewart, Hubert St. Onge, and Karl-Eric Sveiby, to name just a few. I asked one of my doctoral students, now Dr. Francesco Calabrese, to help me in looking at not only their works, but also as many works and practices that we could find. We relied heavily on the KM research by Gartner et al. We benefited by the KM summary work of Charles Despres and Daniele Chauvel [1]. What emerged from this research was

Figure 1-2

List of knowledge management study impact areas.

Knowledge Management— Multidiscipline

❖ Systems Theory
❖ Risk Management Assessment
❖ Intelligent Agents
❖ Management of R&D
❖ Decision Support Systems
❖ Modeling and Simulation
❖ Data Mining / Data Warehousing
❖ Enterprise Resource Planning
❖ Business Process Engineering
❖ Systems Analysis
❖ Systems Engineering
❖ Leadership
❖ Ethics

❖ Communications Theory
❖ Organizational Psychology
❖ Visualization
❖ Groupware
❖ Virtual Networks
❖ Strategic Planning
❖ Management-by-Objectives
❖ Total Quality Management
❖ Management Theory
❖ Management of Information Systems
❖ Database Design / Database Management Systems
❖ Data Communications and Networks

an initial collection of the "KM apples" in existence—over 40 at that time, as shown in Figure 1-2. We also examined some of the barriers to KM success (Figure 1-3), and focused in on the research done by KPMG, which seemed to capture and summarize all the other efforts at examining this aspect. Our goals were to identify the key apples or ingredients necessary for a KM system and to ensure we designed into the equation the prescription to overcome the barriers to KM success.

The Four Pillars: The DNA of Knowledge Management

There were many statements gleamed from the KM works and writings, including a proliferation of definitions that sometimes disagreed with each other. Many attempts dealt with the definition of knowledge itself, a kind of epistemologic approach. These latter attempts never addressed the issue of managing these knowledge assets; they merely discussed the question of the definition. Other works dealt with learning and all its facets. Although I had some interest in these aspects, my main issue was to determine the critical elements, a *DNA* if you will, of KM. To me, the operative work in KM was the <u>management</u> of these assets. The company already had these assets; it just did not know how to articulate them and, consequently, had little to no guidance on how to manage them.

There were many formulations also, such as KM is all about people, and not technology. Communities of Practice were the main application for this group. For others, it was all about technology, such as a "portals and yellow pages" of knowledge workers. Some said it was about people, technology, and process. Everyone had his or her favorite silver bullet or saying/taxonomy.

Figure 1-3

Knowledge management barriers to success.

Barriers to Knowledge Management Success

Results From International Survey:

❖ **Organizational Culture**	**80%**
❖ **Lack of Ownership**	**64%**
❖ **Info/Comms Technology**	**55%**
❖ **Non-Standardized Processes**	**53%**
❖ **Organizational Structure**	**54%**
❖ **Top Management Commitment**	**46%**
❖ **Rewards / Recognition**	**46%**
❖ **Individual vice Team Emphasis**	**45%**
❖ **Staff Turnover**	**30%**

Earnst & Young KM International Survey, 1996
(431 senior executive responses)

In laying out all the so-called models, elements, definitions, pronouncements, cautions, and approaches, it became apparent that there were four principle areas or groupings, each containing many elements. The challenge was to find names for these four groupings and to validate them through some scientific approach. The clock was also ticking on my going before the faulty to introduce the proposal for KM as its own concentration in our master's and doctoral programs. I decided to take a stab at it, and the four pillars were born: All the KM elements were grouped under the following: Leadership/Management, Organization, Technology, and Learning (Figure 1-4). Names and groupings could change later on, on the basis of further research. The challenge now was to make deadlines to get a KM program in the academic calendar, if even that was possible given the necessary layers of approval and the many people involved (department, school, and university) to implement a graduate-level course of studies.

The Four Pillars

- Leadership/management: Deals with the environmental, strategic, and enterprise-level decision-making processes involving the values, objectives, knowledge requirements, knowledge sources, prioritization, and resource allocation of the organization's knowledge assets. It stresses the need for integrative management principles and techniques, primarily based on systems thinking and approaches.
- Organization: Deals with the operational aspects of knowledge assets, including functions, processes, formal and informal organizational structures, control

Figure 1-4

Four pillars of knowledge management.

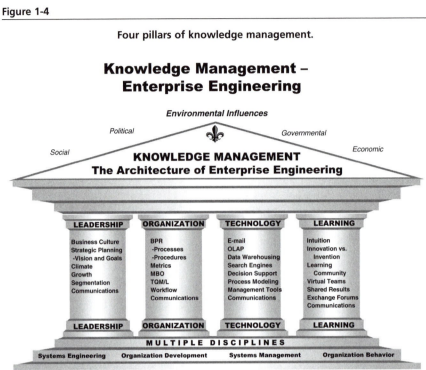

Knowledge Management – Enterprise Engineering

Environmental Influences

Political   *Governmental*

Social   *Economic*

KNOWLEDGE MANAGEMENT
The Architecture of Enterprise Engineering

LEADERSHIP	ORGANIZATION	TECHNOLOGY	LEARNING
Business Culture	BPR	E-mail	Intuition
Strategic Planning	-Processes	OLAP	Innovation vs.
-Vision and Goals	-Procedures	Data Warehousing	Invention
Climate	Metrics	Search Engines	Learning
Growth	MBO	Decision Support	Community
Segmentation	TQM/L	Process Modeling	Virtual Teams
Communications	Workflow	Management Tools	Shared Results
	Communications	Communications	Exchange Forums
			Communications
LEADERSHIP	ORGANIZATION	TECHNOLOGY	LEARNING

MULTIPLE DISCIPLINES

Systems Engineering	Organization Development	Systems Management	Organization Behavior

Stankosky / Calabrese / Baldanza, 1999

measures and metrics, process improvement, and business process reengineering. Underlying this pillar are system engineering principles and techniques to ensure a flow down, tracking, and optimum utilization of all the organization's knowledge assets.

- Learning: Deals with organizational behavioral aspects and social engineering. The learning pillar focuses on the principles and practices to ensure that individuals collaborate and share knowledge to the maximum. Emphasis is given to identifying and applying the attributes necessary for a "learning organization."
- Technology: Deals with the various information technologies peculiar to supporting and/or enabling KM strategies and operations. One taxonomy used relates to technologies that support the collaboration and codification KM strategies and functions.

Knowledge Management Curriculum

The curriculum proposed was based on the four pillars, each having its own course, bordered with introductory and capstone courses (Figure 1-5). The curriculum was based on a simple definition for KM and emphasized KM's management/operational aspects: leveraging relevant knowledge assets to improve organization performance, with emphasis on improving efficiency, effectiveness, and innovation. If KM did not deliver, then we needed to discover why, and fix it.

I was able to recruit a world-class part-time faculty, who had experience in KM programs; extensive business, nonprofit, and government experience; and teaching expertise. Collectively, they helped design the courses and ensured not only quality

Figure 1-5

Knowledge management curriculum map.

Subject	KM I (270) – Intro	KM – LDR/MGT	KM – ORG/Processes	Learning Enterprise	Knowledgware Technologies	KM II (370) – SE/CASES/KMS
Module	I	II	III	IV	V	VI

E C
X O
A N
M T
P E
L N
E T
	♦ Survey of KM
	♦ Definitions
	♦ 4 Pillars Model
	♦ Functions
	♦ Methods
	♦ Pay Offs
	♦ Strategies
	♦ Intro to Systems Thinking/Approach
	♦ Intro to Systems Engineering & Management.
	♦ An "As Is" State: Processes, Gaps, Opportunities, Risks
	♦ KM Map
	♦ KM Mental Construct(s)
	♦ KM Evaluation Criteria
		♦ Enterprise
		♦ KM.
		♦ Requirements
		♦ Strategic Plan
		  – Vision
		  – Goals
		  – Objectives
		  – Initiatives
		  – Actions
		♦ Functions
		  – Ldr: Roles, Motivation, Resource Allocations, Political Engineering
		  – Mgt: Plan, Staff, Organize, Monitor
		♦ CKO: Roles
			♦ Functions
			♦ Processes
			♦ Metrics
			♦ Organizational Structure:
			  – Formal
			  – Informal
			  – Centralized
			  – Decentralized
			  – Hierarchical
			  – 'Flat'
			♦ Organizational Tools
			♦ Applications
				♦ Org. Behavior
				♦ Motivation
				♦ Org. Change
				♦ Learning
				♦ Innovation
				♦ Social Engineering
				  – COP's
				  – COI's
				♦ Culture
				♦ Knowledge Sharing
				  – Recognition
				  – Rewards
				  – Etc.
					♦ Built Around KM Functions
					♦ Enabler(s):
					  – Data Mining
					  – Visualization
					  – Decision Spt Systems
					  – Search/Retrieval
					  – Collaboration
					  – Communication
					  – Group Support Systems
					  – Portals
					  – Web Links
					  – Knowledge Warehouses
					  – Etc.
						♦ System Management
						♦ Systems Engineering
						♦ Summary of Case Studies
						♦ A 'To Be' State:
						  – Knowledge Map
						  – KMS Architecture
						  – KMS Implementation
						  – KMS Performance Measures
						  – Political Engineering
						♦ Project Management
						  – Activities
						  – Timeline(s)
						  – Resources
						  – Milestones
						  – Investment(s)

Output(s)	♦ Theories ♦ 4 Pillars Model ♦ KM Life Cycle ♦ KM Framework	♦ Define KM Goals/Objectives in Measurable Terms, and Follow Through Techniques	♦ Derive Alternative Enterprise-wide KM Based Business Model(s)	♦ Create Plan(s), Timelines, and Profiles to Evolve a K Learning Enterprise	♦ Assess Technical Architectural Framework(s) for a KM Enabling Environment	♦ Design and Implementation of Integrated KMS ♦ Measurement Criteria and Processes

FOUR PILLAR CONSTRUCT

The George Washington University:
KM CERTIFICATE Curriculum Map

KM I = INTRO
II - KM LDR/MGT
III - KM ORG/PROCESSES
IV - LEARNING ENTERPRISE
V - KNOWLEDGEWARE TECHNOLOGIES
KM II = REAL WORLD (VI)

GWU KM CERTIFICATE:
"Your HOW-TO Portfolio":
Basics
Functions
Processes
Roles
Systems
Tools/Methods

teaching, but also relevant applications. Our goal was to create and bridge theory with the practice.

Because of their quality work, the proposal was endorsed at all levels of the university. GW had a new master's and doctoral program, which included a graduate certificate program (based on 18 graduate credits or half a master's degree). We had a program and faculty. Now the challenge began: Would students come? I needed not only master's level, but also doctoral applicants, for they were the basis on which KM research would validate the current curriculum and advance KM as a global academic discipline. Another question: Would other universities follow suit and create KM as a degree-granting area of study? If many students came, there would be competitive pressure to do so.

Knowledge Management: Research Map

The rest is history—many came. We were signing up classes in numbers of 20 and 30 each semester. These people were mostly working professionals, who brought a high degree of interaction with the faculty, as well as much needed feedback for course improvements. Other universities now have KM as a degree-granting program; there is even a consortium of KM doctoral candidates in Canada.

More important, I had doctoral applicants from all over the world. Although the average faculty had a handful of doctoral researchers, I knew I had to collect as many as possible, because we were at the beginning of a new area of research. Numbers became important: There is a certain quality to quantity. However, I needed people who not only had work experience in all sectors of the economy, but who also represented the many areas that make up the four pillars.

I also felt the importance of creating an institution that would create a community of KM enthusiasts dedicated to the field of KM. This institute would be based at GW, but would include interested people and groups from around the word; thus, it had to be global to succeed. It would have at its principal mission the bridging of KM theory and practice and advancing KM as an academic discipline, thereby augmenting the educational and research work for KM at GW. My colleague at the School of Business and Public Management, Dr. William Halal, a noted expert in forecasting and KM, cofounded and codirects the Institute with me. His leadership, vision, and energy made it all possible. This year, the School of Education and Human Development is also joining as a full partner. The Institute, formerly named the Institute for Knowledge Management, and recently renamed the Institute for Knowledge and Innovation (IKI) [www.gwu.edu/~iki], has attracted many prominent individuals and organizations: businesses, governmental agencies, academic institutions, professional groups and multinational organizations—all dedicated to the advancement of KM as an academic discipline. They serve as a brain trust for all members of the Institute as well as to the community at large.

It was truly necessary then to create a research framework upon which we could not only base decisions for choosing the doctoral students, but also oversee the many participants wanting to do work at the Institute. Dr. Art Murray, a long-standing expert in KM, part of the adjunct faculty in KM, and managing director of the Institute, created a KM research conceptual framework, which is based on the four-pillar construct and incorporates the various functions of KM: knowledge assurance, knowledge capture, knowledge retention, knowledge transfer, and knowledge utilization (Figure 1-6). As shown in Figure 1-7, each function was further divided into various categories.

Figure 1-6

Top-level conceptual framework for knowledge management.

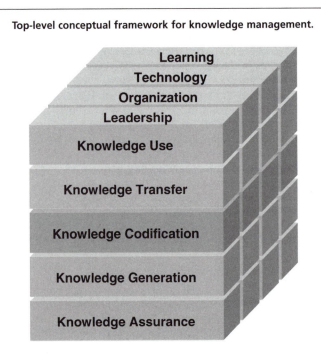

Figure 1-7

Levels of the knowledge management conceptual framework.

Conceptual Framework
For KM Research

Knowledge Use	Culture & Behavior	Metrics & Valuation	Implementation		Feedback & Control		Application
Knowledge Transfer	Social Structures	Sharing & Dissemination	Communication Infrastructure		Transfer Protocols		Presentation
Knowledge Codification	Conceptual Models	Ultra-Structure	Linguistics	Ontology		Artifacts	Retention
Knowledge Generation	Perception	Applied Semiotics	Visual-ization	Reasoning & Inference	Discovery & Innovation		Trans-formation
Knowledge Assurance	Confiden-tiality	Non-Repudiation	Identification & Authentication	Avail-ability	Integrity		Trust

Thus, having an initial basis for selection, we added one more selection criteria: To choose as many diverse people from around the globe, thereby ensuring we addressed regional cultural aspects. Now that we had a framework, again the question: Would students come? Come they did, from Korea, Taiwan, India, Africa, the Middle East, Mexico, Europe, and America. So many in fact that we had to start turning down many applicants. Currently, we are capped at 35 doctoral students from around the world, all with various work experiences and academic backgrounds, collaborating and using the research conceptual framework as a placement guide. We continually receive more applicants, but must delay them until further resources are available to guide their progress through the rigors of the dissertation. Fortunately, we have the generous support of the part-time faculty and other faculty members of IKI. Monthly meetings during the academic year facilitate research discussions and progress. Seminars and conferences also keep the group current, as well as challenged. They not only test their own hypotheses, but also collect resources for validation. We have KM technologies in place, thanks to the generous support of leading KM technology vendors, to maintain virtual collaboration and administration. We also use the KM technology laboratory as an educational tool.

Some Results: Laying a Foundation for An Academic Discipline

What follows, in the subsequent Chapters, are the results of 11 doctoral dissertations, dating from May 2000 to May 2004. Table 1-1 is a matrix of the writings, indicating their major objective and findings. They cover a range of KM areas, addressing frameworks, culture, technology, organizational value/metrics, and knowledge asset valuation. While dissertations are not the ultimate word, they must pass scholarly tests of research and examination, contributing to a body of knowledge. They are based on extensive literature reviews, research questions, and issues deemed significant. Their purpose is to define and enhance a body of knowledge.

Table 1-1

Matrix of Doctoral Research and Findings		
Name	**Topic**	**Guiding Thought**
Dr. Francesco Calabrese	Key elements for a KM initiative	Integration and balance
Dr. Charles Bixler	Conditions and drivers for KM success	Upfront recognition
Dr. Juan Roman-Velazquez	KM in government and nonprofit sectors	Streamline
Dr. Vincent Ribiere	Interpersonal trust in KM	Trust to share
Drs. Po-Jeng Wang and William Schulte	National culture impact on KM	National culture has impact
Dr. Juan Pablo Giraldo	Learning and KM technologies	Support knowledge flows and context
Dr. Kevin O'Sullivan	KM technologies support to intellectual capital management	Organization size is important factor
Dr. Heejun Park	KM technologies and organizational culture	Promote product and people orientation
Drs. Mickey Ross and William Schulte	KM in industrial-military organization	Agree on strategic objectives
Dr. Vittal Anatatmula	Criteria for KM success	Need hard and soft metrics
Dr. Annie Green	Framework for KM valuation	Knowledge assets are strategic
KM, knowledge management.		

The research described in this section is about creating the building blocks for the design and implementation of KM. Some may call these frameworks or models. In any event, these are some of the building codes and principles knowledge architects need for laying out the design for a knowledge management system (KMS) *(Note: "System" throughout this book is used in the larger sense and does not represent an IT system.)*

There are no single point solutions in KM, and while each chapter may look at only one aspect, it is important to regard each as a piece of a large, complex puzzle. I often use the analogy of the four pillars to that of the juggler. The juggler has four balls in the air and loses when he or she drops any one of them. While one may be higher than the others, they must all continuously stay in play. Management may focus more attention on any one at a particular moment, due to the demands of the moment or the stage in their life cycle, but they cannot drop any of the others. They may only be in their peripheral vision, but they still must be watched.

Each chapter attempts to not only codify their findings, but also may include some additional insights by each author, based on their own experiences. Each author offers *"golden nuggets" (italicized after each dissertation summary)*, which could be regarded as guiding principles for KM practitioners. While these are not the end game for KM (for one dissertation does not make a body of knowledge), they certainly represent solid advances for KM as an academic discipline. It is our intent to replicate these dissertations with new participants and to explore other ones to meet the growing demands and needs of the community. The chapters are grouped under the following: Frameworks, Learning/Culture, Technology/Environment, and Organization Metrics/Valuation. *(This grouping is solely the editor's choice, and recognizes that there is an overlap with other areas of study.)*

Frameworks

This section treats the necessary foundational building blocks in designing and implementing a successful KMS.

Dr. Francesco A. Calabrese (fcalab@gwu.edu) validated the four-pillar framework, suggesting key elements defining effective enterprise KM programs. His research is based primarily on reviewing and synthesizing the scholarly works and published practices of KM up to the year 2000. The results were validated from questionnaires to more than 240 industry and government personnel participating in KM programs. He and Dr. Arthur J. Murray then collaborated in creating an artifact of guidelines for applying KM principles to achieving improved business performance in the students' organizations.

> (KM requires the integration and balancing of leadership, organization, learning, and technology in an enterprise-wide setting.)

Dr. Charlie Bixler (bixlerc@utanet.com) examined the drivers for, and value delivered from, KM to an enterprise. He indicates what are the requirements and conditions for success, as well as ranking the benefits and expectations of this system. His research surveyed more than 100 enterprise managers. The results are expected to serve as a foundation for developing a KM capability maturity model, which can be used to assess the design and implementation of a KMS.

> (KM must not only recognize requirements and conditions for success, but also support the desired benefits and expectations of the enterprise.)

Learning/Culture

This section describes various aspects of how an organization addresses the dynamics of social relationships. Topics addressed include the impact of culture, both organizationally and geographically, on KMS; trust as a key ingredient for sharing knowledge; differences in the approach of government, nonprofit, and profit organizations to KM; and the impact of national culture on KM implementation.

Dr. Juan Roman-Velazquez (juan.roman@nasa.gov) examined the enterprise culture in government and nonprofit sectors vis-à-vis their strategic approaches for knowledge flows at the different hierarchical levels. Using a four-culture—type taxonomy, he questioned more than 340 employees. He concluded that government and nonprofit organizations that implement KM in a "hierarchical" culture had the lowest chance of success.

> (Streamlined organizational structure with strong cultures has a higher chance of KM success.)

Dr. Vincent Ribiere (vince@vincentribiere.com) examined the impact of interpersonal trust on knowledge-centered organizational culture. In 100 organizations, he explored the relationships between interpersonal trust and the likelihood of success of a KM initiative, the level of involvement/participation in communities of practice, and finally, the choice of the primary source of problem-solving information.

(An atmosphere/culture of trust is necessary to sharing knowledge.)

Drs. Po-Jeng Wang and William Schulte (wschulte@su.edu) examined the impact that national culture has on implementing a KM system. They used a highly regarded national cultural model as a baseline and studied the dynamic nation of Taiwan, which has a knowledge-based economy. They had access to more than 800 people and concluded that national culture plays a significant role in KM implementation.

> (National culture affects the values and practices of every organization in KM implementation, especially at the lower levels.)

Technology/Environment

This section discusses what KM technologies are appropriate for a particular KM system and environment and complex social systems and their impact on technology choices. The section also describes several taxonomies and frameworks of these technologies and provides design criteria when making buy-decisions.

Dr. Juan Pablo Giraldo (giraldo@us.ibm.com) examined the relationship between KM technologies and the learning actions of global organizations. He developed a framework that balances technologies, flow of knowledge, context of knowledge, and critical actions that support technology investments. After examining more than 60 people from 21 organizations, he concluded that KM technologies improve organizational learning, especially when learning actions are adapted to their environment.

> (KM technologies contribute to organizational growth only if the flow and context of knowledge are supported.)

Dr. Kevin O'Sullivan (kosulliv@nyit.edu) examined the extent to which KM technologies are used to manage intellectual capital. He grouped these KM technologies into eight major categories. He studied 145 organizations of different sizes, dispersed around the globe, and operating in different industry sectors. He concluded that the size of an organization is a factor in determining which technology is best suited for managing intellectual capital.

> (KM technologies are useful in managing and leveraging intellectual capital, but the size of the organization is a major variant.)

Dr. Heejun Park (hjpark@ssu.ac.kr) examined KM technologies from an organizational cultural impact focus. He developed a typology for KM technologies and used it to ascertain the ideal organizational structure for each KM technology. He concluded that cultural issues have a direct impact on technology selection and thus must be taken into account. Specifically, he noted that organizations most successful in KM technology implementation have identified an organizational culture that embodies a mixture of both product and people orientation.

> (Successful KM technology implementation requires an organizational cultural that promotes a blend of product and people orientation.)

Drs. Mickey Ross and William Schulte (rossmv@supship.navy.mil) examined an industrial-type military organization, comprising military, civil service, and contractor personnel. Their objective was to determine which among several factors, such as culture, processes, organization, and technology, were the more important for successful KM initiatives. Their findings indicated that technology was the least important, and viewed primarily as an enabler.

(KM success factors are dominated by management ones, such as culture, process, and organization; with technology as the least important.)

Organizational Metrics/Valuation

This section analyzes the impact of organizational functions, processes, controls, metrics, and organizational structures on KM. One of the main issues highlighted is the difficulty, but necessity, of valuing and leveraging knowledge assets. There are suggestions on taxonomies and methods for describing, measuring, and valuing these assets.

Dr. Vittal Anantatmula (vsa@gwu.edu) examines the establishment of criteria for measuring the success or failure of KM efforts in government, nonprofit, and for-profit organizations. Results from more than 153 responses, and a list of 26 criteria, show that improving communications is a common criterion for both government and nonprofit organizations, while enhanced collaboration is common for both for-profit and nonprofit organizations. Businesslike metrics were not high on any favored-criteria list. The research revealed that most KM efforts result in soft measures, which are not directly tied to end results.

(KM criteria for success should include both soft and hard measures if top leadership is to support KM initiatives.)

Dr. Annie Green (annie.green@att.net) proposes a framework that represents a dynamic relationship between strategic objectives of KM and the value drivers of intangible assets. She lists a common set of business dimensions, which support measurement and performance indicators of knowledge assets.

(Knowledge assets are strategic, and must be accounted for and valued accordingly.)

Summary

In summary, we have the results of 11 research efforts that address various aspects of KM, all with the intention of adding to the KM body of knowledge. These efforts examined correlations between and among key factors and perhaps more important, tried to verify cause and effect where possible. What makes a KM initiative successful? What are the strategic and operational things one must do? How do you value knowledge assets? What role does culture, both national and organizational, play? Their intent is to provide the theoretical construct for KM applications—bridging practice with theory. Without a sound theory, the best practices, and best practices-to-be, tread on weak grounds. Our goal is to build a body of knowledge and an accompanying academic discipline, with attendant guiding principles and theorems. The following golden nuggets, derived from their research, are only the beginning of this quest:

- *KM requires the integration and balancing of leadership, organization, learning and technology in an enterprise-wide setting.*
- *KM must not only recognize requirements and conditions for success, but also support the desired benefits and expectations of the enterprise.*
- *Streamlined organizational structure, with strong cultures, have a higher chance of KM success.*
- *An atmosphere/culture of trust is necessary to sharing knowledge.*

- *National culture affects the values and practices of every organization in Knowledge Management implementation, especially at the lower levels.*
- *KM technologies contribute to organizational growth only if the flow and context of knowledge are supported.*
- *KM technologies are useful in managing and leveraging intellectual capital, but the size of the organization is a major variant.*
- *Successful KM technology implementation requires an organizational culture that promotes a blend of product and people orientation.*
- *KM success factors are dominated by management ones, such as culture, process, and organization, with technology as the least important.*
- *KM criteria for success should include both soft and hard measures if top leadership is to support KM initiatives.*
- *Knowledge assets are strategic, and must be accounted for and valued accordingly.*

The Early Pathways: Theory to Practice— a Continuum

Francesco A. Calabrese, D.Sc.

In the fall and winter of 1998/1999, the label and concepts surrounding the discipline of knowledge management (KM) had not yet registered as doctoral dissertation material in American universities. In fact, there was no clear indication that postgraduate programs in the discipline had been accredited in this country. There was a report that one university in the United Kingdom did offer an accredited graduate degree in the subject, but that had little impact on those of us striving to earn doctoral degrees at the George Washington University's (GW) School of Engineering and Applied Sciences (SEAS). But, then a visionary emerged in the person of Dr. Michael A. Stankosky, associate professor for systems engineering in the Department of Engineering Management and Systems Engineering (EMSE). Dr. Stankosky assembled, defended, and acquired accreditation approval for graduate studies at the certificate, master's, and doctoral degree levels in KM—the first such program in the United States. He then set about "recruiting" some of EMSE's doctoral candidates to undertake directed research and ultimately to complete and publish their dissertation research findings in the field of KM.

So it happened that on a crisp winter Saturday morning early in 1999, I found myself in a working session with Dr. Michael A. Stankosky, Dr. Arthur J. Murray, and Dr. Geoffrey P. Malafasky. I was a student in Dr. Murray's pilot course in KM at the time, completing my doctoral course work and casting about for a dissertation focus in systems or software engineering. That morning session set me on a different path. The subject was a directed research effort that I should undertake as an exploration of the potential utility of applying a four-pillar KM model as a "blueprint" that could be used to create an optimal, enterprise-wide, results oriented, collaborative knowledge-sharing environment in support of an enterprise's vision (mission), goals, and objectives. The four pillars were intended to embrace the vast domains of leadership, organization, technology, and learning, and all of their underlying traditional disciplines. The results of the directed research effort were encouraging enough to spawn the full dissertation research summarized in the first half of this chapter, and subsequently leveraged into expanded research by other doctoral candidates as reflected in the following chapters. As the body of knowledge about KM grew at GW, the results were also harvested to form the curriculum for the program's six core courses discussed in Dr. Stankosky's introductory chapter.

Over time, others have speculated that there should be three or five pillars or that there should be eight or more "domains" to best describe a "framework." The fact is that on the continuum from theory to practice, many erudite voices have been raised but no consensus reached on a universally accepted framework, model, construct, or standards document. In my opinion, the "four-pillar framework" conveniently groups the 40-plus disciplines that comprise the foundational levels supporting the four-pillar construct into easily understood and communicated "domains." The multiplicity and breadth of the disciplines involved project the true complexity of seeking to create systems, processes or structures to manage ". . . knowledge . . . that intuitively important but intellectually elusive . . ." attribute of humankind (Despres & Chauvel, 2000).

This chapter first describes the exploratory research that formed a piece of the theory end of our continuum and helped to define the early stages of the GW KM program. Since the fall of 2000, the crucible of the classroom and the demands of busy, fully employed professionals who comprise a major segment of the graduate student population have led us to developing methods and guidelines to assist our students in experiencing the practice end of our continuum. Dr. Murray and I collaborated in the creation of an "8-step approach to applying the principals of KM to improve business performance"(Drs. Arthur J. Murray and Francesco A. Calabrese, September 2000). The lecture materials for that approach are contained in the second half of this chapter, with minimal guideline narratives pending publication of a full paper on the subject.

Introduction

Karl-Erik Sveiby, the founding father of KM, says,

> Knowledge management is not about yet another operational efficiency fad . . . It suggests that knowledge is an object that can be handled like a tangible good. It is not. Knowledge is a human faculty. (Wah, 1999, pp. 17, 26.)

Despite increasing endorsements from enterprises worldwide, many serious managers still believe that KM is the latest management sciences fad. However, experienced practitioners of KM believe this skepticism is fueled by the failure of numerous programs based on hasty "me-too practices" that lack the understanding required for an effective enterprise-wide solution. Numerous KM models exist and continue to proliferate. The problem is that they immediately focus on detailed mechanisms for identifying types and sources of knowledge and the means to capture, codify, and disseminate it, but do not address managing that knowledge across the full spectrum of organizational decision needs to achieve more efficient, effective and innovative results for the enterprise.

At GW, we undertook a dual-track approach to achieving a credible solution for use by KM practitioners and in response to the skepticism of many "nay sayers." First, we sought to validate the existence and applicability of the four-pillar model to be used as a blueprint to consistently guide the creation of effective enterprise-wide KM programs. To succeed, these programs must have the visible support and follow through by the *leadership* of the enterprise to manage the timely collaboration and sharing of pertinent knowledge with the correct decision makers throughout an *organization*, and to do so in concert with the enterprise's strategic vision and operational goals. The enterprise must nurture an environment of open knowledge sharing, collaboration, and *learning*, facilitated by and enabled by the power of leading-edge *technology* tools and methods. Second, we sought an extension of Senge's "systems thinking" element, which he describes as the "discipline for seeking wholes." Validation of the approach for meeting this need for systems thinking is derivative from years of practice in the disciplines of systems analysis, systems management, and systems engineering, all part of the GW EMSE curriculum.

Ultimately, as stated by Svieby, knowledge cannot be handled like a "tangible good." Rather, it is necessary to conceive, plan, architect, design, test, implement, evaluate, modify, and seek to perfect KM programs composed of systems for identifying, acquiring, storing, disseminating, communicating, maintaining, updating, modifying, and staying abreast of knowledge—to be used with the "human faculty" for taking intelligent and timely action on behalf of enterprise goals and objectives. Such a system solution is consistent with Senge's "framework for seeing interrelationships using a set of general principles distilled over the course of the twentieth century spanning fields as diverse as the physical and social sciences, engineering and management" (Senge, 1990, pp. 68–76). It is also consistent with the need to create a blueprint for use of the study's postulated four-pillar framework that can be applied in a systematic and replicable manner to produce high-quality, effective enterprise-wide KM programs. With these dual objectives as targets, we began the journey to traverse our theory to practice continuum.

Early Research Efforts

The merits of Stankosky's "four pillars critical to KM: technology, organization, leadership and learning" were explored further through several workshop sessions in the spring of 1999. Those sessions included Dr. Michael A. Stankosky; Dr. Geoffrey P. Malafsky, manager, R and D Concepts and Technology Transition, Science Applications International Corporation (SAIC); Dr. Arthur Murray, director of executive programs and professional lecturer, EMSE, GW, SEAS; and the author. The participants sought to identify defining key subelements (KSEs) within each pillar and traditional disciplines that could be readily accepted as relevant to some or all of the pillars and many of the specific subelements. An early conceptual schematic of the four-pillar concept is shown in Figure 2-1.

Initial Literature Reviews

A limited literature review was undertaken (Calabrese, 1999) seeking to identify the existence of the four pillars in the writings available at that time. This early research hypothecated that the four pillars would be found to coexist "harmoniously" in relatively equal parts as depicted in Figure 2-2.

Each of the literature samples was analyzed for the discernible presence of any of the pillars. Once the identification of pillar(s) had been reasonably satisfied, a subjective weighting from zero to ten (least to most dominant, respectively) was assigned to each pillar appearing within the particular piece of literature being evaluated. The literature analysis, while confirming the existence of the four pillars, also exposed a strong *imbalance* heavily weighted toward the availability and use of technology/tools (software) as the equivalent of KM programs and practices for the organization described. The results of those evaluations are assembled in Table 2-1.

The total score per pillar was then translated into a value of relative areas for each pillar. The resulting trapezoidal configuration shown in Figure 2-3 contrasts sharply with the "harmoniously balanced architecture hypothesized" in Figure 2-2.

The research concluded that the technology pillar was much more readily identified as the equivalent of KM systems/programs, with little regard for the postulated

Figure 2-1

Four pillars—conceptual construct.

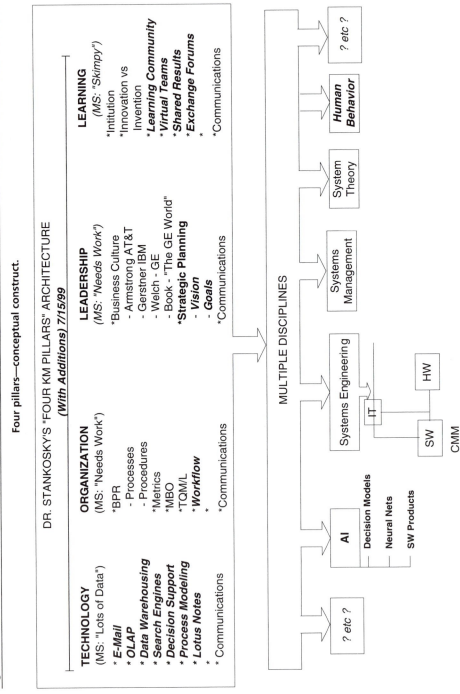

DR. STANKOSKY'S "FOUR KM PILLARS" ARCHITECTURE
(With Additions) 7/15/99

TECHNOLOGY
(MS: "Lots of Data")

* *E-Mail*
* *OLAP*
* *Data Warehousing*
* Search Engines
* *Decision Support*
* *Process Modeling*
* *Lotus Notes*
*
* Communications

ORGANIZATION
(MS: "Needs Work")

*BPR
  - Processes
  - Procedures
*Metrics
*MBO
*TQM/L
*Workflow
*
*Communications

LEADERSHIP
(MS: "Needs Work")

*Business Culture
  - Armstrong AT&T
  - Gerstner IBM
  - Welch - GE
  - Book - "The GE World"
*Strategic Planning
  - Vision
  - Goals
*Communications

LEARNING
(MS: "Skimpy")

*Intitution
*Innovation vs
 Invention
* *Learning Community*
* *Virtual Teams*
* *Shared Results*
* *Exchange Forums*
*
*Communications

MULTIPLE DISCIPLINES

AI

Decision Models
Neural Nets
SW Products

Systems Engineering

IT

SW   HW

CMM

Systems Management

System Theory

Human Behavior

? etc ?

? etc ?

Figure 2-2

Knowledge management architecture in harmony. (Calabrese Directed Research, 1999.)

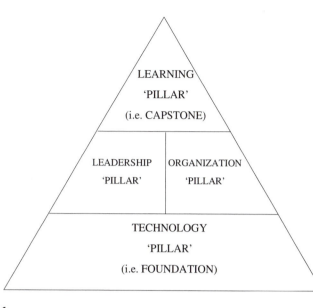

Table 2-1

Pillar Weighting Scores					
Pillar ¶#/Article	T Technology	O Organization	L_D Leadership	L_E Learning	Comments
1.1 Microsoft	10	—	—	—	Multiple products
1.2 IBM, etc.	10	—	—	—	Seven companies/ products
1.3 KPMG	7	2	1	—	Building KM system
1.4 Small Companies	10	—	—	—	Products oriented
2.1 KMC	4	2	2	2	KM consortium
2.2 Hallmark	2	1	3	4	Best-practice example
3.1 CIA, etc.	—	3	4	3	Intelligence community
4.1 ERM	9	1	—	—	Thirty-seven companies
5.1 K&IP	4	6	—	—	Aurgin systems
6.1 SAIC	2	2	3	3	KM session briefings
TOTAL	58	17	13	12	

CIA, Central Intelligence Agency; KM, knowledge management.
From Calabrese, FA, 2000.

Figure 2-3

Knowledge management architecture real world. (Calabrese Directed Research, 1999.)

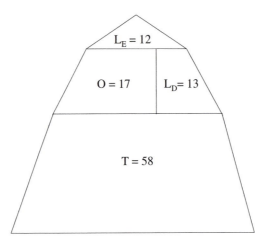

"balanced" four-pillars framework/architecture believed to be necessary for effectively managing an enterprise's knowledge assets. Interestingly the materials available from national intelligence community sources placed emphasis on all pillars except Technology.

Follow-Up Research

Calabrese's initial research was subsequently extended, and led to a postulated KMA/EE (KM architecture of enterprise engineering) (Baldanza and Stankosky, 1999), depicted in Figure 2-4. This depiction stresses the *role* for each pillar as opposed to the defining KSEs in Calabrese's research (Figure 2-5). A further iteration of the KMA/EE portrayed the pillars as spheres and stressed the *balanced interconnectivity between pillars* as shown in Figure 2-6 reflecting Stankosky's analogy to continuously juggling four balls (Baldanza and Stankosky, 1999). The use of spheres led to an excellent postassessment profiling "compass" icon to emphasize the dominant pillars/elements/spheres within the KM system/environment/initiatives/programs of a given enterprise (Figures 2-7 and 2-8) (Baldanza, Calabrese, and Stankosky, 1999).

Expanded Literature Reviews

The initial KM framework research was very preliminary. The quantity of literature on the subject of KM had just begun an explosive growth phase, much of it quite contemporary (i.e., within the last 5 years). A study at the time reflected that the number of new KM articles registered in one of several databases has "more than doubled each year over the last decade" (Despres and Chauvel, 1999, p. 2) (Figure 2-9).

Disciplines

To a large extent, advocates and practitioners attribute or identify "good KM practices" with all the twentieth-century disciplines that have been documented in such

Figure 2-4

Knowledge management pillars to enterprise learning. (From Stankosky, Calabrese, Baldanza, 1999.)

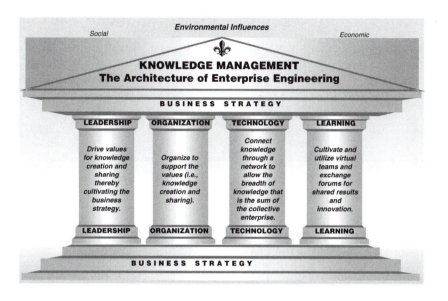

Figure 2-5

Knowledge management pillars to enterprise learning. (Stankosky and Calabrese, 1999.)

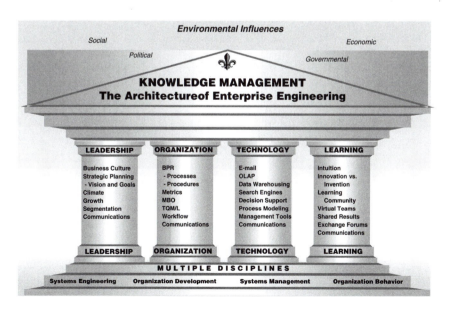

Figure 2-6

KMA/EE balanced interconnectivity relationship.

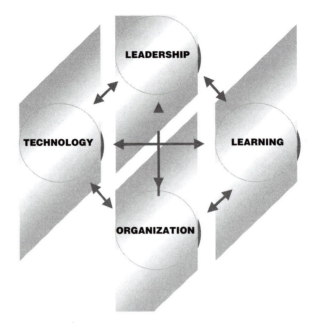

Figure 2-7

Knowledge management architecture of enterprise engineering alignment: strong technology focus.

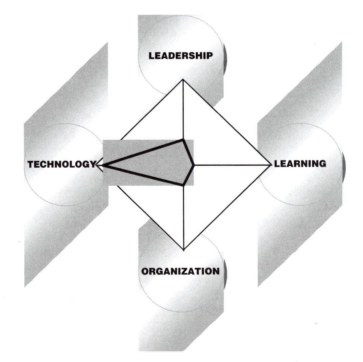

Figure 2-8

Knowledge management architecture of enterprise engineering alignment: strong leadership/organization focus.

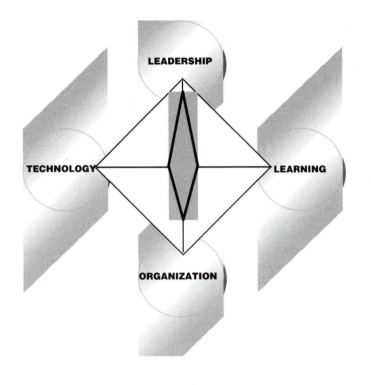

Figure 2-9

New knowledge management articles per year in ABI/INFORM database. (From Depres and Chauvel, 1999.)

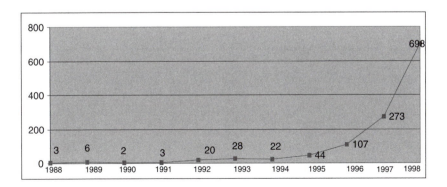

fields as analytic management, systems engineering, artificial intelligence, decision-support systems, transformational leadership, learning organizations, and interpersonal dynamics, to mention a few. Skeptics, on the other hand, claim that KM is just another version of BPR (business process reengineering); TQM (total quality management); CMI (continuous management improvement); change management; integrated product teams, and on and on ad infinitum. Many enterprises believe that knowledge is delivered through the technology of computerized data warehouses and search engines over local area networks, Wide Area Networks (WANs), Virtual Private Networks (VPNs), Internets and Intranets, on a demand basis; at the desktop, laptop, Blackberry or cellular telephone; to the office, home, or in transit; and while rushing to the next key decision meeting by land, air, or video conferencing.

In GW's first dissertation in KM (Calabrese, 2000), Calabrese extended his limited initial literature search (1999) to tabulate an extended listing of the disciplines and KSEs better defining each of the four pillars as shown in Table 2-2. Concurrently, the literature was searched for competing "models" to the GW four-pillar construct as a means of recognizing existing versions, if they existed, to allow collaboration with other researchers or practitioners and to add to the general body of knowledge on this subject. In addition, the more comprehensive literature search reflected a change in the perceived recognition and existence of the four pillars as reflected in Table 2-3. The review and findings were drawn from multiple publications in academia, case studies, general publications, and Web searches. The emphasis on technology had been dramatically reduced to the lowest ranking in the ensuing year since the initial review. This reflected a much larger literature sample and the proliferation of new publications with a broader view of KM.

The most important observations from this expanded literature review are that our postulated four pillars and KSEs exist, they are in use, and they are growing as key influences in shaping both the real world and academic environments of KM. A corresponding indicator is that the "simultaneous review" conducted for the presence of alternate models did not identify any recognizable alternates. There were many references and descriptions of processes used in identifying types and sources of knowledge and the mechanics of capturing and disseminating knowledge. However, with the exception of references to the "learning organization" (Senge, 1990), which has been extended to form the learning pillar, no other "model" was discernible as being comparable to the framework postulated by GW (Stankosky et al., 1999). More explicitly, no other "model" surfaced that was structured to take a disciplined systems approach to the integration of a defined framework encompassing all facets of an enterprise-wide KM program.

Extended Research Efforts

The early research referenced in this chapter and the continuing literature reviews revealed some indicators in the quest to identify the existence and significance of the four key elements (KEs) (pillars), which form the basis for a successful knowledge collaboration environment in the GW model. However, it was clear that more explicit research findings were needed to derive an acceptable level of closure on the question of whether the four-pillar framework constituted a viable construct for designing and implementing an effective enterprise-wide KM system. Hence, the effort moved to surveying respondents. The overall purposes of this additional research were as follows:

1. **Beliefs:** To determine respondent's beliefs when confronted with "a forced choice" between two statements describing different KEs (pillars).

Table 2-2

Disciplines per Pillar/Representative Key Subelements	
Pillars and Disciplines	**Representative Key Subelements Defining Each Pillar**
Technology/tools— Disciplines: Computer science Computational linguistics Operations research Electrical engineering Mathematics/statistics Logic	Data warehousing Database management SW Multimedia repositories Groupware Decision support system Expert systems Corporate Intranet Speech understanding Business modeling systems Intelligent agents Neural networks, etc.
Organization/culture— Disciplines: Psychology Operations research Organizational development Philosophy Sociolinguistics	Process workflows Operating procedures for knowledge sharing Business process reengineering Management by objectives Total quality management Metric standards Hierarchic, centralized or decentralized Matrix-type organization Open/sharing Closed/power based Internal partnering vs. competing-type culture
Leadership/management— Disciplines: Operations research Management science Psychology Philosophy Logic Linguistics Management information systems Behavioral profiling	Strategic planning Vision sharing Specific and general goals and objectives Executive commitment KM programs tied to metrics Formal KM roles in existence Tangible rewards for use of KM Knowledge sharing
Learning enterprise— Disciplines: Cognitive psychology Organizational development Systems engineering Management philosophy Personal mastery Mental models Shared vision Team learning	Tacit and explicit knowledge Management support for continuous learning Capturing, organizing and disseminating knowledge Virtual teams Exchange forums Communities of practice Innovation encouraged/recognized/rewarded
KM, knowledge management; SW, software.	

Table 2-3

Average Scores and Rank Order of Pillars								
Category	Academic		Cases		General		Total	
KE	Avg.	Rank	Avg.	Rank	Avg.	Rank	Avg.	Rank
T	1.4	4	4.2	1	2.6	4	2.7	4
O	4.2	2	3.7[a]	3	3.6	1	3.8[a]	1
L_D	3.2	3	4.0	2	3.4	2	3.5	3
L_E	4.4	1	3.7[a]	3	3.4	2	3.8[a]	1

[a]Tie.
Avg., average; KE, key element; L_D, leadership; L_E, learning; O, organization; T, technology.

2. **Practices:** To verify the level of use and/or value placed on the four pillars as defined by their representative KSEs in the actual day-to-day activities of various enterprises.
3. **Preferences:** To obtain each respondent's preferred rank ordering of importance for the four pillars.
4. **Add-Ins:** To seek augmentation of pillars and/or KSEs if those suggested did not cover existing practices or those more familiar to the respondents.

Survey Instrument Design

The instrument created for this phase of the research was a questionnaire designed in three parts for capturing content data. Part I sought to derive the respondents' belief's of the relative importance between the pillars. The instrument was patterned after the type of questionnaire used in personality-type profiling such as the Meyers-Briggs survey or behavior-typing instruments. The format and structure was taken from the Delta paradigm developed by Dr. Howard Eisner (1989). There were 48 paired (i.e., two statements) questions requiring the respondent to select one of the two statements. Although not conspicuously apparent to the respondent he or she would be choosing between pillars, or at least choosing the one he or she could identify with the best, which would then reflect his or her belief on the relative importance of one pillar over the other.

Part II sought to correlate which pillar, in practice, had the highest use and value in the workplace. There were four categories, one for each pillar with eight representative KSEs for each, and space for respondents to add up to two additional KSEs. Respondents could indicate value or use of KSEs from most (5) to least (1), or either "does not exist" (DNE) or "do not know" (DK). The listed KSEs served to further define/describe the identified pillar and to evaluate which pillar domain was perceived by the respondent to be in greatest use in their day-to-day experiences.

Part III simply listed the four pillars and invited the respondent to add up to two other pillars if they chose and then to record their rank ordering (no ties) as 1 (most important) through 4, 5, or 6 (least important). The respondent had now stated his or her preference for relative importance of each of the pillars. By this point in the data capture phase the respondents would have become reasonably well informed of the description, if not actual definition, of the make up of each pillar. Thus, there should be a level of understanding that would make the respondent comfortable to add pillars perceived to be missing or confidently rank order the importance of the pillars proposed by the study.

From the research perspective, there would now be three semi-independent determinations from which to assess the response, relative weightings, and/or acceptance of the four-pillars model as a feasible construct for creating effective, enterprise-wide KM systems and programs.

Statistical Procedures

The statistical procedures used for this phase of the research are shown in Table 2-4.

Methodology Summary

The research was clearly exploratory in nature and qualitative because it sought to help build a body of knowledge in the initial stages of establishing a basic framework for the whole subject of enterprise-wide KM programs. Hence, some techniques were incorporated into the survey process in an attempt to create checks and balances and multiple means of validating the efficacy of the results.

1. Construct of questionnaire: The questionnaire itself was a semi-independent "self-checking" instrument. Each of its three parts sought an answer to the same basic questions: Do the postulated "four pillars of KM" exist? How are they valued? How are they used? Are there other pillars or KSEs in use or identifiable?

Table 2-4

Statistics Used in Analysis	
Statistic	**Description**
N	Total number of data within the area of description
Range	Difference between the largest and smallest numbers in the set
Min and Max	Minimum (min) and maximum (max) numbers within a set
Mean	Sum of responses divided by the number
Standard deviation	Measure of how values are spread around a mean (clustered or widely dispersed)
Variance	Sample standard deviation divided by the square root of the sample size
Comparison of means analysis	Measures the degree to which two variables are related and similar or different
ANOVA	Analysis of variance used to compare the means of group relationships
t test	Used to test if the means of paired elements differ
Factor analysis	Measures the alpha value of multiple factors to determine relative strength(s) (i.e., >0.80)
ANOVA, analysis of variance.	

2. "Expert group" baseline: The widespread confusion over what constitutes KM and the lack of generally accepted hard ground rules/architecture/framework(s) led to the creation of a built-in "baseline standard." A subgroup of 28 individuals (12%) from the respondent population, were placed into an "Expert Group" because they either carried knowledge officer/director KM titles or were known to be conversant with the lexicon of terms surrounding the basis of this research. Thus, the methodology was rounded out to use this expert baseline to help calibrate the returns from the general respondent populations.

Profile of Survey Respondents

The questionnaire instrument used to collect survey data for this exploratory research was distributed to approximately 600 individuals. A major portion of the 240 responses came from individuals in the greater Washington, DC, metropolitan area, generally including Northern Virginia, the District of Columbia, and Southern Maryland. Approximately 80% of the respondents were employed by professional services/technology-based enterprises and comparable government entities. The remaining 20% represented areas from health plan administrative, legal, property management, local government, university research, and public educational fields, to name a few. The overall sense is one of a respondent with better than average educational levels, business experience, and sophistication.

Visually, the profiling data show that the largest representation of total respondents are in the executive/management positions; 51% represent large companies and correlating workforce numbers; 66% are in services, with an 18% government representation; 30% of the firms have a KM program; and 15% have a chief knowledge officer (Figures 2-10 through 2-15).

Figure 2-10

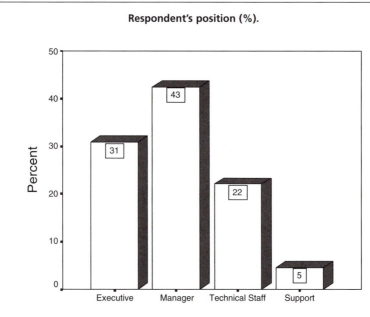

Respondent's position (%).

Figure 2-11

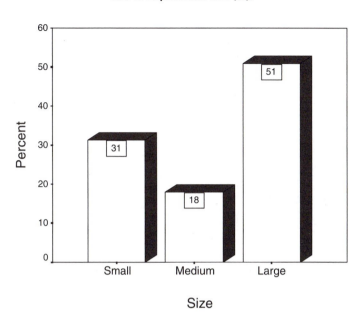

Size of respondents firm (%).

Figure 2-12

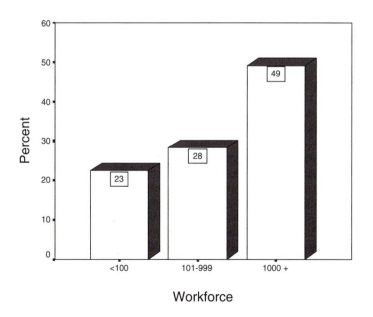

Respondent's workforce levels (number of employees).

Figure 2-13

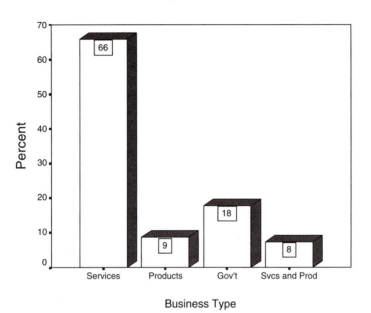

Respondent's type of business (%).

Figure 2-14

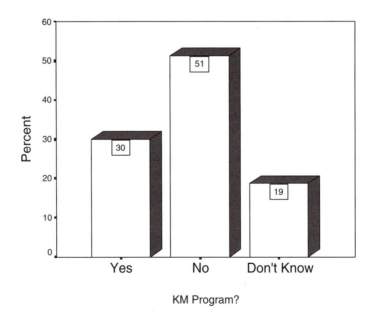

Does the firm have a knowledge management program?

Figure 2-15

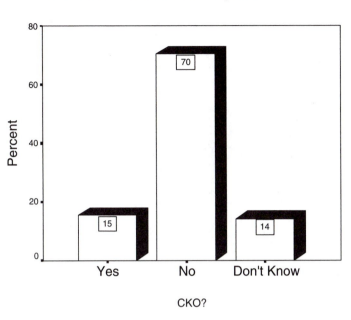

Does the firm have a chief knowledge officer? (%).

Analyses of Respondents Beliefs

The existence of Stankosky's (1999) four-pillars (KEs) framework was a fundamental assumption of this research study. The four KEs of the framework were embedded in 96 line items in part I of the research survey. Using the forced-choice technique described, the respondents identified items that when summarized, would reflect their beliefs about the most important elements of KM-type activities in their enterprises. It was anticipated that the respondents would view these elements (pillars) to be of equal importance.

Each time the respondents made a choice between the paired-items, they were choosing one of the four pillars of the proposed KM framework. The responses were tabulated and a sum of the scores for each element was calculated, resulting in a raw score for each category for the 240 respondents. Those raw sums were divided by 24 (the maximum total possible raw score for each pillar) to yield a ratio variable score for each element for each respondent that was set to a maximum value of 1. Figure 2-16 captures the distribution of the four KEs. Statistical comparison of the means and standard deviations for each KE pillar supports the visual data reflecting the total respondents' beliefs that although the leadership and learning pillars are equal, the four pillars are not equal especially in the case of the organizational element.

Validation of the Proposed Knowledge Management Framework

Because of the extreme qualitative nature of the belief findings, and given the non-equal findings for the four pillars, the research undertook an additional statistical

Figure 2-16

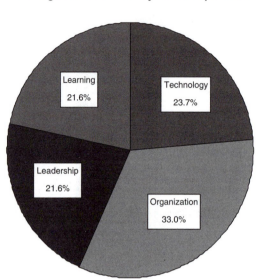

Percentage distribution of key elements per belief.

Table 2-5

Alpha Communalities: Strength of Key Elements	
Key Elements	**Extraction**
Tech Pillar	0.999
Org Pillar	0.994
Leader Pillar	0.998
Learning Pillar	0.996

analysis to determine relative strength of each of the four KEs. A factor analysis technique was used to help determine if the "alpha commonalities" of the KEs (pillars) were greater than 0.80 (SPSS 8.0 Applications Guide, 1998). If so, that would indicate that while not all four pillars were equal, they were all strong factors in the KM concept being surveyed. Factor analysis results are shown in Table 2-5. All four pillars show alpha factor measurements at the 0.99 levels, well above the required 0.80 measurement criteria.

Analysis of Nonexpert versus Expert Group Beliefs

As previously indicated, the research methodology created a checks-and-balance mechanism in the event the random sample portion of the respondents (88%) might have collectively misunderstood the concept(s) or terminology of the four-pillar framework. It had been anticipated that there would be a difference in the response profiles of the expert (baseline) and nonexpert groups. An additional analysis was undertaken

Figure 2-17

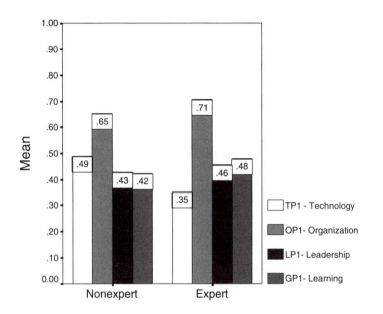

Comparison of means of nonexpert versus expert groups.

through comparison of the statistical mean profiles as replicated in Figure 2-17. The results of this analysis statistically validate that there are no significant differences between the beliefs of the two groups at the 95% confidence level for the organization, leadership and learning pillars. On the other hand, the experts placed a much smaller value than the nonexperts on the importance of technology as KE of KM programs, which is intuitively consistent with a greater understanding by the experts of the inter-connectivity of elements other than technology required for a successful KM program.

Analysis of Industry versus Government Findings

With 18% of the respondents based in government organizations, it was statistically viable to explore the beliefs findings on an industry-versus-government basis. The analysis demonstrated that there are no significant differences in the findings between the industry and government respondents, as shown in Figure 2-18.

Analysis of Respondent Findings on Beliefs and Practices

In addition to the findings on beliefs (part I of the questionnaire), the research also sought to measure actual practices in the respondents' firms through part II of the survey as reflected by a sample portion of the instrument at Figure 2-19. The use or value perceived by the respondent for each KSE was graded on a scale of 5 (most) to 1 (least). The categories of DNE and DK were captured, but not given any numeric value. Those two factors will be addressed later.

PART II: KEY SUBELEMENTS: If you choose, you can add (and evaluate) up to two subelements in each category below (i.e. items 9 and 10).

Figure 2-18

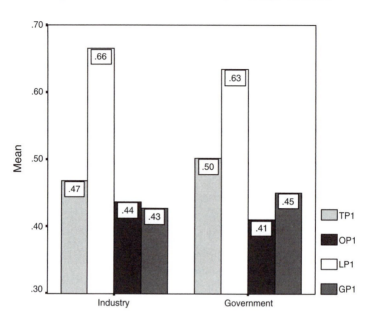

Comparison of beliefs means—industry versus government.

Figure 2-19

Key subelements valuation—technology pillar.

	5	4	3	2	1	DNE	DK
1. Data Warehouses							
2. Data Base Management SW (Oracle, Informix, etc)							
3. Multimedia Repositories							
4. GroupWare (Lotus Notes; Autonomy; e-mail; etc.)							
5. Decision Support Systems (Executive Information; Expert Systems)							
6. Corporate IntraNet							
7. Business Modeling Systems							
8. Intelligent Agents							
9.							
10.							

TECHNOLOGY/TOOLS: Please indicate which type of technology support tools/processes exist in your enterprise pertaining to KM programs/systems, and your sense of MOST (5) used, LEAST (1) used, Doesn't Exist (DNE), or Don't Know (DK).

The research had anticipated that the scoring for use/value of the pillars in actual practice would result in the same relative relationships as had emerged in beliefs. That is, that the respondent's beliefs about the relative importance of the four pillars would be consistent with the way he or she perceived the use/value of the pillars in the day-to-day KM practices in his or her enterprises. Anticipated findings were not borne out by the statistical analysis reflected on a side-by-side ranking in Table 2-6.

Analysis of the Gap between Beliefs and Practice

The comparison of rankings shows a clear gap between the respondents' beliefs of the relative importance between pillars and what they experience in the actual practices of KM activities in their enterprises. Two comparative checks and balances were undertaken before proceeding further. One compared the industry-versus-government findings, the other compared the experts versus nonexpert baseline. Both outcomes reflect no differences between the groups on this point, as reflected in Figures 2-20 and 2-21.

Exploration of the Causes for the Gap

The fact that both the industry/government segments and the nonexpert/expert groups delivered similar results does not explain the basis for the gap. Consequently, the study turned to a more in-depth exploration for the underlying causes.

As part of the questionnaire refinement process, the category DNE was added to the DK measure for responding to the KSEs portion in part II of the questionnaire. The revision became significant because a KSE might not be perceived to exist in the respondent's environment when, in fact, it is readily obtainable if it is identified properly (i.e., data warehousing, decision support models, etc.) as part of an effective KM program.

It appeared from a visual perusal of the respondents survey instruments that there were a very significant number of DNE and an appreciable number of DK entries for KSEs in each of the four KE sections for the practice area. *The "gap involves the difference in rankings of KEs between beliefs and practices.* Because all 48 questions determining the beliefs rankings were answered, it seemed logical to explore the impact of such a large number of DNE/DK (i.e., nonscored) entries in the ratings for KSEs, which in turn would impact the pillar rankings emerging from the practice area.

Table 2-6

Ranking of Key Elements by Beliefs and Practice		
Key Element	Belief Ranking	Practice Ranking
Technology	2	2
Organization	1	3
Leadership	3	4
Learning	4	1

Figure 2-20

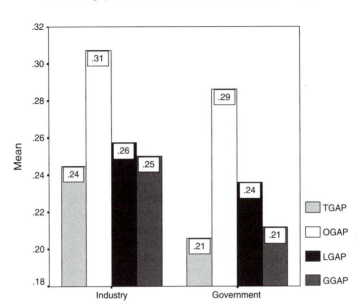

Means of gap variables of industry versus government.

Figure 2-21

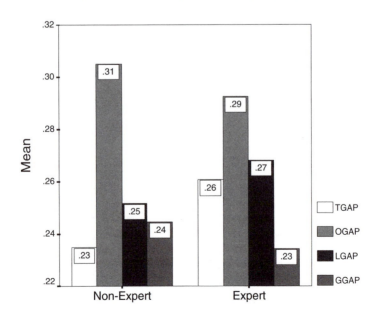

Gap variables of nonexpert versus expert groups.

Figure 2-22

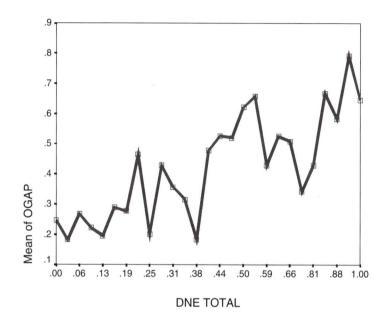

As "does not exist" total increases, organization gap increases significantly.

DNE TOTAL

The relative increasing impact of the number of DNE and DK entries in the practice findings for the organization and leadership pillars is reflected in Figures 2-22, 2-23 and 2-24. Because there is a ready audit trail to the respondent sources, those enterprises with the most significant gaps could be alerted in a real world assessment engagement to the need for more thorough communications throughout the enterprise on the existence and use of key subelements.

Respondents Preferences Rankings of Key Elements

Part III of the survey instrument simply asked respondents to rank order the pillars. There would be the four proposed or up to six if the respondent added pillars. The rankings were to reflect 1 (most important) to 4 or 6 (least important). Since the add-in inputs were inconsequential, the research only compiled the consolidated ranking order against the four pillars proposed by the study. Those results are displayed below:

#1 Leadership   **#2 Learning**   **#3 Organization**   **#4 Technology**
Conclusions
Findings

The preference ranking appears to best echo a popular credo often voiced during this research:

> People want their leaders to set the tone, and create the management practices and organizational structures and policies that will form a culture receptive to knowledge sharing and facilitated through technology tools and networks to achieve a learning-enabled enterprise (Calabrese, 2000).

Figure 2-23

As "does not exist" total increases, leadership gap increases significantly.

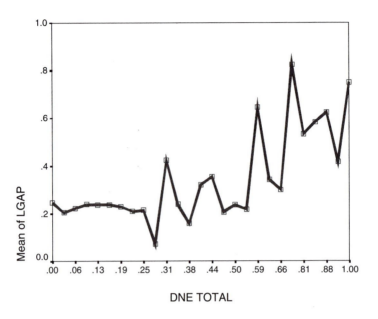

DNE TOTAL

Figure 2-24

As "don't know" total increases, organization gap increases significantly.

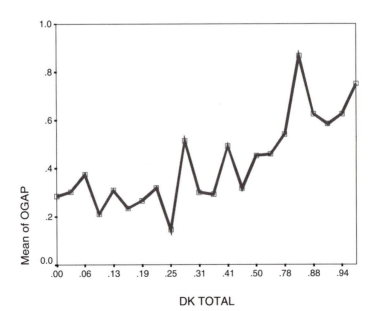

DK TOTAL

Perceived Research Achievements

- Validated existence of the four pillars in contemporary literature and survey returns.
- Identified multiple, recognized disciplines supporting each of the four pillars.
- Expanded inventory of KSEs to help define each pillar.
- Created a survey instrument adaptable as an in-depth assessment tool.
- Documented a framework that can provide a blueprint for a disciplined systems approach to designing and establishing integrated, enterprise-wide KM systems, programs, and initiatives.

The Classroom Crucible: Moving to the Practice End

Doctoral research and theory notwithstanding, the fall of 2000 saw a large influx of students in pursuit of GW's graduate certificate, master's, and doctoral degrees. Those enrolled for the certificate program were primarily driven to acquiring a basic understanding of the KM movement and a reference framework for discussing KM and putting it into context in a functional organizational sense. The emphasis was heavily slanted to the latter, not the former need. Dr. Murray had anticipated the situation and engaged me in a collaboration to create some clear and easily applied guidelines for people to use in analyzing a need and designing solution(s) to perceived gaps and opportunities and/or risks in identifying and properly using people's knowledge in their enterprise's day-to-day operations. We cobbled together our "eight easy-steps" artifact through a combination of original work and some applicable processes and techniques in systems and process mapping. The remainder of this chapter presents that artifact in the form of lecture graphics with minimal textual guidance. It concludes with a representative listing of the various organizational areas for students to use the artifact in analyzing and designing a KM solution—all within a 12- or 15-week semester course. We had now clearly reached the other end of our continuum by assembling a toolkit titled:

"Applying the Principles of Knowledge Management to Improve Business Performance in Eight Easy Steps!"

The following lecture visuals and narrative linkages created by Dr. Murray and Dr. Calabrese in the fall of 2000 describe a journey along path 1 (Figure 2-25) (Murray & Calabrese, 2000). The destination, as noted, is the creation of a project plan for a specific KM initiative, preferably within the student's/practitioner's organizational unit or overall enterprise. All materials are copyrighted to the authors or the specific references noted where publicly available materials have been used or adapted within the eight steps.

We begin by stating the purpose of this exercise as follows:

- Locate your knowledge-critical functions
- Apply KM principles to increase performance and reduce vulnerabilities

This usually leads to the reasonable question: Where do I start?
Responses include the following:

- Look at the work your organization needs to perform.
- Identify critical work processes in which knowledge is not properly applied or is at risk.

Figure 2-25

George Washington University's knowledge management dual tracks practice and theory.

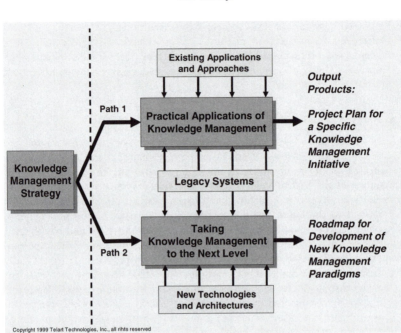

- Create an environment that will influence knowledge-sharing behaviors and work habits.

These responses are followed by questions such as, "Is there a specific format or method for documenting the work, processes, and so forth?" We suggest use of Alter's work-centered analysis (WCA) format as depicted in Figure 2-26.

An example of a completed WCA is shown in Figure 2-27 to aid the student/practitioner in applying this approach to his or her target organization. The viewpoint should be from the top level of the enterprise before focusing on a specific organizational unit.

Once the enterprise-level analysis has been completed, it will be necessary to develop a process model of the "as is" environment for the specific organizational unit, function, or procedure to be considered and analyzed. Normally the best place to start is with the enterprise-level business processes from the WCA in step 1. At this stage, it is best to limit the process model to three levels as shown in the example seen in Figure 2-28.

A second example of a process model is represented as step 2 in Figure 2-29. This is the model that will be evolved in steps 3 and 4 in the approach.

For the process diagrammed in Step 2, identify in Step 3 (Figure 2-30) what appear to be the critical in the following areas:

1. Knowledge gaps: The needed knowledge is simply not available; "holes" in your corporate knowledge base.

Figure 2-26

Work-centered analysis.

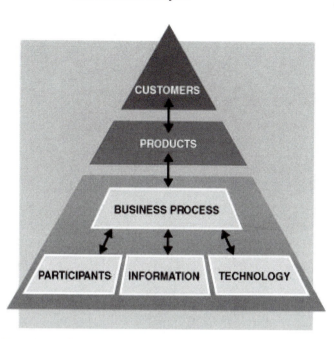

¹http://www.prenhall.com/alter/about/wca.html

Figure 2-27

An enterprise-level work-centered analysis perspective for Amazon.com.

Amazon.com Provides a New Way to Shop for Books

CUSTOMER
- Person who purchases books
- Wholesalers that supply the books
- Amazon.com's shipping department

PRODUCT
- Information about books that might be purchased
- Information describing each book order
- Books that are eventually delivered

BUSINESS PROCESS

Major steps:
- Purchaser logs on to www.amazon.com
- Purchaser identifies desired book or gives search criteria
- Purchaser looks at book-related information and decides what to order
- Purchaser enters order
- Amazon.com orders book from wholesaler
- Wholesaler sends book to Amazon.com
- Shipping department packages order and sends it to the purchaser

Rationale:
- Instead of forcing book buyers to go to typical bookstores, permit them to use online access from home or from work.

PARTICIPANTS
- People interested in purchasing books
- Order fulfillment department of wholesaler
- Shipping department of Amazon.com

INFORMATION
- Orders for books
- Price and other information about each book

TECHNOLOGY
- Personal computer used by purchaser
- Computers and networks used by Amazon.com for order processing

Figure 2-28

Example of Three Level Process Flow.

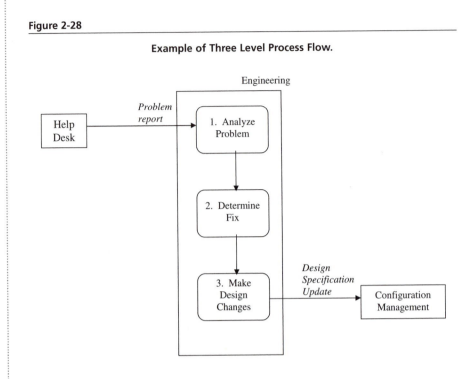

Figure 2-29

Broad process model for specialty cuisine restaurant.

STEP 2 - DEVELOP PROCESS MODELS[1]

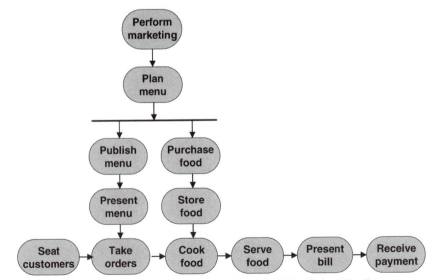

[1]Adapted from Steven Alter, *Information Systems: A Management Perspective*, Addison Wesley, 1999, p. 40

Figure 2-30

Knowledge gaps, opportunities, and risks.

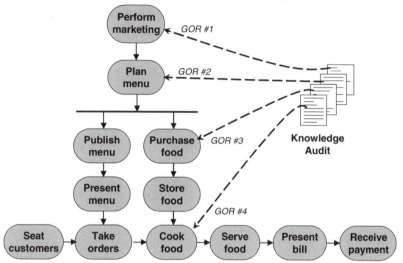

STEP 3 - IDENTIFY KNOWLEDGE-CRITICAL GAPS, OPPORTUNITIES AND RISKS[1]

[1]Based on Knowledge Survey developed by Knowledge Research Institute, Inc, Arlington, TX.

2. Knowledge opportunities: Existing knowledge assets or resources that are not being used, exploited, or leveraged; practices that, if implemented, would enhance knowledge elements across the four pillars.
3. Knowledge risks: Existing *critical* knowledge assets that are currently being used and, if they were to suddenly disappear, your business process would be severely affected; entrenched practices (habits) that inhibit or create imbalances in the four pillars.

In step 4 (Figure 2-31), prioritize the gaps, opportunities, and risks (GORs) identified in step 3. Use any reasonable rating system consistent with the nature of the organizational environment. For this restaurant example, customer satisfaction and profitability were given the highest weightings. The intent is to derive the most critical GOR node(s) to minimize the amount of effort required to initiate a successful "pilot" and then incrementally attack the remaining GORs as positive results build greater support for the full effort.

Preparing for step 5, we ask and answer the question: how do I apply KM strategically?

- Orchestrating the change
- Working within corporate culture rather than against it
- Understanding the role corporate culture plays in catalyzing or paralyzing performance improvement
- Balancing the four strategic spheres of KM
- Leadership

Figure 2-31

Prioritization of gaps, opportunities, and risks.

STEP 4 - PRIORITIZE AND ESTABLISH GOALS[1]

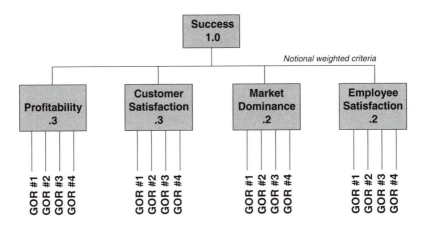

[1]Thomas L. Saaty, *The Analytic Hierarchy Process*, McGraw-Hill, 1980.

- Organization
- Technology
- Learning

Step 5 involves formulating the strategy to carry the knowledge transformation to successful acceptance and institutionalization. Some key considerations are suggested in Figure 2-32. A copy of the enterprise's strategic vision, goals, and objectives is key to this and the ensuing critical aspects of steps 6 through 8. The KM goals and objectives determined here should be in alignment with the enterprise's goals and objectives.

Steps 5, 6, and 7 are at the critical core of positioning the "tactical" process/function selected in steps 2 through 4 as an enterprise-wide KM system solution(s). In preparing to develop the KM requirements in step 6, consider some of the example events wherein proper use of knowledge can make a difference:

- Interpretations
- Selections
- Estimations
- Categorizations
- Judgments
- Procedures
- Algorithms
- Simulations
- Conclusions

Figure 2-32

Formulate knowledge management strategy, goals and objectives.

STEP 5 - FORMULATE STRATEGY[1]

- **Choose Strategic Focus**
  - **Replication vs. Communities of Practice (Distributed Braintrust)**
  - **Practical Applications vs. Investment in Future**
- **Ensure Alignment with Overall Corporate Strategy**
- **Address Corporate Culture Impacts and Responses**
- **Formulate Program Scope and Budget**
  - **Clear Definition of Boundaries and Constraints**
- **Develop Program Plan**
  - **Creates Vision of the New Environment**
  - **Defines Series of "Small Steps" KM Initiatives**

[1]See Hansen, et al., "What's Your Strategy for Managing Knowledge?," Harvard Business Review, March-April 1999.

- Problem resolutions
- Decisions
- Innovations
- Trend indicators
- Actions

The breath and complexity of evolving the knowledge system requirements required to complete step 6 are summarized in Table 2-7.

In the full guidelines documentation, this summary table expands to a seven-page work booklet to assist in the compilation of critical data, information, knowledge, interrelationships, decision paths, decision makers, criticality level, and business functions, operations, products, services, and results involved and affected by any proposed KM solution(s).

Step 6 characterized the requirements of the knowledge that must be managed. Step 7 requires the determination for managing this knowledge at each stage of the knowledge life cycle (Figure 2-33). The representative questions to be answered in planning the approach to managing this knowledge, step 7 (Figure 2-34) are as follows:

1. How will you capture, generate, or otherwise acquire the knowledge?
2. How will you codify or otherwise retain the acquired knowledge?
3. How will you validate and maintain the integrity and veracity of the knowledge?

Table 2-7

Knowledge System Requirements		
Characteristics	**Type**	**Form**
Describe the knowledge you want to manage What is it? Where is it? Who owns it? Who needs it? How will it be used?	Tacit Implicit Explicit	Knowledge Information Data
Agent	**Management Level**	**Pillar Supported**
Individual Organizational Automated	Strategic Tactical Operational	Leadership Organization Technology Learning

Figure 2-33

Knowledge life cycle.

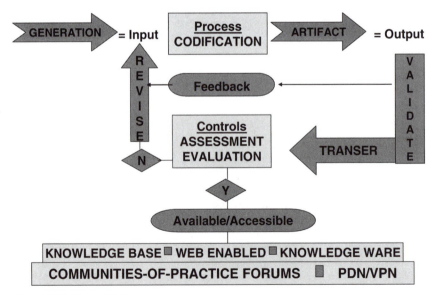

KNOWLEDGE LIFE CYCLE – SYSTEM DIAGRAM

Figure 2-34

Develop the knowledge management approach (Murray and Calabrese, 2000).

STEP 7 – DEVELOP KNOWLEDGE MANAGEMENT APPROACH[5]

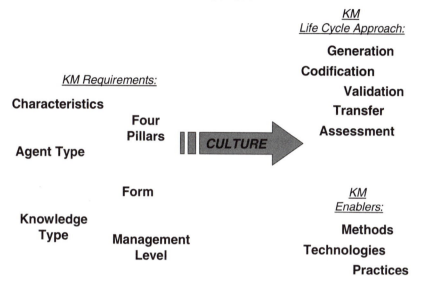

4. How will you enable the transfer of the knowledge? How will you balance **access** versus intellectual property **protection?**
5. How will you determine how well the knowledge is being applied? What mechanisms will you put in place to continually assess and refine the knowledge?
6. What enablers will you use to carry out the above approaches?
7. What are needed changes to the business process?
8. Which are the best tools and technologies that support the methods?
9. What fits and integrates into the organization and culture?
10. Are there any remaining issues that need to be addressed?

As we move toward the final crucial step of developing the implementation plan to get enterprise approval for the KM initiatives, we do a thorough review of steps 2 through 7, as portrayed by Figure 2-35.

The suggested seven key portions of a systems plan for getting senior management approval for the selected KM initiative are reflected in Figure 2-36, followed by a representative timeline and key milestone schedule (Figure 2-37). A key question that can be anticipated from executive management is "How do I measure success?" Some representative quantitative and qualitative responses are as follows:

- Improved quality
- Improved productivity
- Reduced rework
- Faster innovation
- Increased economic performance

Figure 2-35

Bridging steps 2 through 7.

MOVING TOWARD A KM IMPLEMENTATION

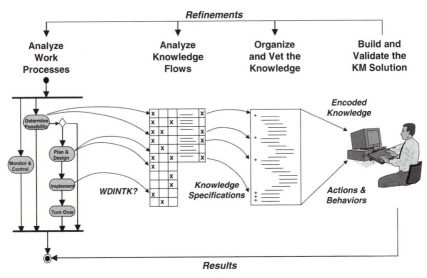

WDINTK = What Do I Need To Know? (Murray, 2000)

Figure 2-36

Key aspects of a knowledge management initiative system plan.

STEP 8 – DEVELOP AND SELL PLAN OF ACTION TO SENIOR MANAGEMENT

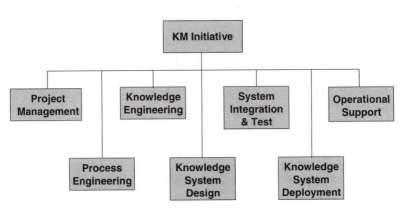

[1]Methodology documented in *A Guide To the Project Management Body of Knowledge*, PMI, 1996.

Figure 2-37

Step 8: Example timeline and key milestones.

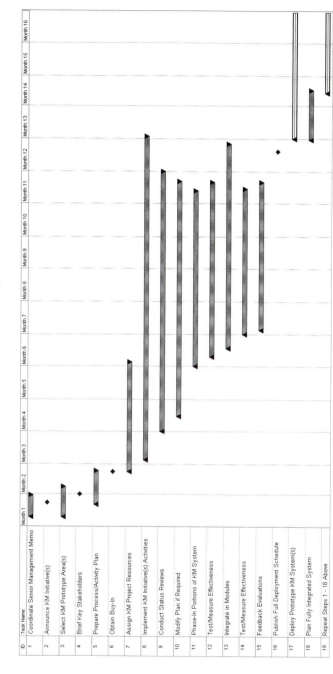

ID	Task Name	Month 1	Month 2	Month 3	Month 4	Month 5	Month 6	Month 7	Month 8	Month 9	Month 10	Month 11	Month 12	Month 13	Month 14	Month 15	Month 16
1	Coordinate Senior Management Memo																
2	Announce KM Initiative(s)																
3	Select KM Prototype Area(s)																
4	Brief Key Stakeholders																
5	Prepare Process/Activity Plan																
6	Obtain Buy-In																
7	Assign KM Project Resources																
8	Implement KM Initiative(s) Activities																
9	Conduct Status Reviews																
10	Modify Plan if Required																
11	Phase-In Portions of KM System																
12	Test/Measure Effectiveness																
13	Integrate in Modules																
14	Test/Measure Effectiveness																
15	Feedback Evaluations																
16	Publish Full Deployment Schedule																
17	Deploy Prototype KM System(s)																
18	Plan Fully Integrated System																
19	Repeat Steps 1 - 18 Above																

- Positive changes in culture and work habits
- Better product and process integration

Utility of Eight-Step Approach

Over the course of the last 4 years, approximately 100 students have used the eight-step approach to describe, analyze, and recommend solution(s) to knowledge gaps, opportunities and/or risks they've identified in their business enterprises, community organizations and personal circumstances. Private for-profit and non-profit; government, federal and local; associations local, national, and international; and academic environments have all been represented.

The applications range over many functional, process, and procedural areas: Business development, marketing, and sales is heavily represented. Recruiting, performance reviews, salary systems are favorites in the context of the Human Resources function for many enterprises. Procurement and acquisition decisions from personal buys to major agency/corporate commitments appear in many papers. Knowledge swapping, transfer, coordination and collaboration inter and intra organizational and/or at the enterprise/major agency levels have received a sizable share of the inventory generated.

We believe that this rudimentary tool, artifact, and methodology or "model" has proven its utility in the academic environment for which it was initially created, and allows reasonably diligent individuals to better grasp and utilize both ends of our theory to practice continuum. We know that some of the solutions have actually been implemented, but do not have adequate feedback to comment on the relative success or continuity factors of these efforts. We hope to compile a fully researched and analyzed document for future publication.

Closing Thoughts

Much that was written just 5 years ago may now seem obvious and of more limited applicable value. Yet, despite the exponential explosion in publications that began about that time, there have been few, if any, breakthroughs in new concepts, practices, or discoveries. The KM label is still used, abused, and misinterpreted by most enterprises and agencies that stand to benefit from enlightened application of an enterprise-wide balanced framework of systems, processes, practices, communities, and tools to identify, capture, and create multimedia knowledge artifacts/nuggets for dissemination to the right people at the right time to enhance competitive operational decisions consistent with the enterprise/organization's business/mission goals, objectives and results.

Five years later, we have moderated the way we infuse the attributes of KM into dialogues with both believers and the still sizable population of naysayers. Today, we speak to managing the enterprise's intellectual assets; to establishing an environment of trust, and encouraging collaboration and knowledge sharing; to focusing on knowledge that is accurate, relevant to the enterprises' business decision processes, and provided to the right decision maker in a timely manner and appropriate form/media. Dr. Stankosky often applies a straightforward litmus test in his question, "Main event or side show?" Today's response remains a bit ambiguous, but the trend continues toward the center ring and the main event!

> If we only knew what we know, viz., in the use of certain words and concepts that are so subtle in application, we would be astonished at the treasures contained in our knowledge. (Immanuel Kant, Vienna Logic.)

Developing a Foundation for a Successful Knowledge Management System

Charles H. Bixler, D.Sc.

> Knowledge is information that changes something or somebody—either by becoming grounds for actions, or by making an individual (or an institution) capable of different or more effective action. (Peter F. Drucker, 1988.)

The Concept of Knowledge Management

Knowledge is information that has value: It is relevant, current, and applicable to meeting performance goals. As Peter Drucker stated, the key to unlocking the value of information and knowledge is "action," that is, it must be dynamic. The active and dynamic implementation and management of knowledge are critical to enabling organizational performance enhancements, problem solving, decision making, and teaching (Liebowitz, 1999). Knowledge management (KM) defines the processes required to effectively manage knowledge. KM is the systematic, explicit, and deliberate building, renewal, and application of knowledge to maximize an enterprise's knowledge-related effectiveness and returns from its knowledge assets (Wiig, 1997). KM applies systematic approaches to find, understand, and use knowledge to create value (O'Dell, 1996). The processes and terminology associated with KM often sound abstract, only hype, or simply new "management verbiage"; however, it is concrete, practical, and profoundly important (Leonard, 1995). The understanding of KM is particularly vital to technical enterprises, both new and established. Knowledge and KM are rapidly evolving as the starting point for action in all businesses, and over the past 10 years, this understanding has surfaced as a major focus for its role in the enterprise value process. To renew and sustain a competitive edge in today's business environment, an enterprise must capture and use all the knowledge and skills of its employees. Knowledge and information are now the most important resources that a firm can muster. Today's managers depend on a wide array of knowledge to take action, solve problems, enhance performance, and simply "get things done" in technical enterprises. The new information-based service economy places a premium on knowledge due to the explosive and accelerating pace of new information and subsequent knowledge. This knowledge explosion requires explicit attention to developing the knowledge stocks of managers, professionals, and workers so that they can cope and compete successfully (Eccles and Nohria, 1992).

Two primary streams of concern have surfaced: (a) the ability to generate, increase, and exploit knowledge and (b) solving the problem of measuring knowledge and its value to a firm (Roos et al., 1998, v.). There are many drivers for the need of KM in today's technical enterprises; however, the four major drivers are as follows:

1. The primary driver is the **information technology (IT) progress** that has recently evolved and revolutionized the way information is processed and stored. It has had dramatic influence on the development and growth of technical capabilities and new products and processes; it is within this development context that the requirement for effective KM is critical.

2. **Communication technology, transportation, and the new global economy** have increased cognizance of KM as a core competence. This, coupled with recent advances in IT, such as local area networks and the Internet, has dramatically enhanced organizational interest in KM.

3. Clients' **level of sophistication and expectations** have significantly increased. There is much lower tolerance for inferior products and services as a result of the competitive environment and availability of professional goods and services. Clients expect planned cost, schedule, and performance parameters to be completely met.

4. The **need to innovate technology and processes** has increased dramatically over the past decade. It is overwhelmingly evident that innovation is essential for growth and business survival.

Most current technology-based conceptualizations of KM have been primarily based on heuristics (embedded in procedure manuals, mathematic models, or programmed logic) that capture the preferred solutions to the given repertoire of an organization's problems. Some current ad hoc solutions in the form of hardware and software offer solutions that are expected to enable a productive KM system. These solutions generally offer a means for capturing knowledge of "best practices" and known proven processes and methodologies that are devised by experts and placed in information databases. Although these systems are a good starting point and may be adequate for stable and predictable organizational environments, they are based primarily on rules and procedures embedded in technology and fall short in meeting the knowledge needs of the current dynamically changing business enterprise environment (Malhorta, 1998). The key to effective KM implementation is its ability to solve the enterprise's problems; that is, providing the right knowledge, "just in time and just enough," to successfully meet the needs of the employees or "knowledge workers." KM, as the basis for enterprise integration, formalizes and distributes experience, knowledge, and expertise that create new capabilities, solves problems, enables superior performance, encourages innovation, and enhances customer value (Liebowitz, 1999).

The Value of Knowledge Management and a Knowledge Management System

KM is rapidly being introduced to technical organizations and is becoming a key element of successful enterprises. It has a strong potential to become foundational in solving an enterprise's problems, enhancing innovation, and providing a basis for integrating technology, organization, leadership, and learning. Currently, there is a critical need for formal and well-organized KM development within technical enterprises. The primary success drivers for the creation of growth and improved technologic and process capabilities for a firm are (a) continuous improvement of existing products/services and (b) development of new innovative products/services.

The new business environment demands foresight, conversion, innovation, and adaptation in contrast to the traditional emphasis on optimization. It is an environment in which organizational business theories must be continuously reexamined for their alignment and validity. Current business literature indicates that in view of today's globally competitive environment with its rapid technology insertion, technical enterprises must maintain a focus on their firm's core business, while at the same time repositioning for the future if markets become saturated with limited potential. The enterprise must also understand that the client's problems and needs are paramount and are the primary driver of continuous improvements and innovation. Clients now demand products and services to be better, faster, and more affordable. As technology grows rapidly, the enterprise should exercise care in the insertion of technology and stay within the limits of the firm's financial and technical capability to control the inherent risks.

Technical enterprises need the right people/processes/technology at the right time and the right place to sustain competitiveness. As a result, the new business enterprise environment is characterized by continuous redefinition of organizational goals, purposes, and the tried and trusted "ways in which things have always been done" (Malhorta, 1998). New knowledge always begins with the individual (Nonaka, 1998). It is the individual employee or "knowledge worker" at all levels within a firm that enables the ability to transform technology rapidly into solving problems and enhancing performance for new products, services, and processes. A new KM system must provide the dynamics for effectively solving problems, enabling innovation, and providing the environment for continuous process and product improvement.

The new business environment of technical enterprises imposes the need for two essential elements in KM:

1. *Knowledge growth and maturity:* Development of a well-disciplined "systematic and systemic" knowledge maturity system for employees that is continuous, well disciplined, relevant, value-added, and measurable. It must solve "today's" problems.
2. *Knowledge innovation:* Provide an environment with the physical and procedural methods of generating and introducing challenging ideas and innovation to existing knowledge bases. Introduce ways to stimulate continuous improvement within the enterprise.

The new business environment demands knowledge growth and maturity that is relevant, applicable, and value-added. In short, it must be able to solve enterprise-wide problems to be effective and valuable. Knowledge creation should be the foundation of a company's human resource strategy. It is critical that knowledge be interpreted, deciphered, analyzed, and applied in terms of relevance to the knowledge worker. Additionally, an enterprise must provide an environment that enables knowledge workers to better deal with problem solving in terms of the uncertain and unpredictable future. With more proactive and continuous involvement of human imagination and creativity, technical firms can achieve greater levels of growth, the ability to develop innovative solutions, and enhance overall success in measurable performance/productivity.

Successful adoption of a KM system will require thoughtful, incremental redirection of skills and knowledge bases. The management of knowledge is a skill, like financial acumen, and managers who understand and develop the skill will dominate competitively (Leonard, 1995). KM demands the ability to move knowledge in all directions throughout an organization (Leonard, 1995). Fast perception of, and reaction to, changes is essential. The ability to recognize trends and forecast the future is becoming a necessity for continued enterprise survival. In today's environment, it is critical to be a first mover or a product/service leader (vice follower) (Roos et al., 1998).

The need for KM and a knowledge growth system is critical in order to transform information and knowledge into a valuable enterprise asset. A KM System and framework, based on enterprise KM maturity, must be developed and measured over time in terms of: knowledge acquisition, knowledge access, knowledge distribution, shared knowledge, and applied knowledge. The framework must provide a deliberate, organized, and measured system that is translated into robust action, resulting in enhanced enterprise performance. The KM architecture and foundation must center on the ability to solve enterprise problems and enhance an enterprise's environment to stimulate innovation. A KM system must be developed with the understanding that there will be measurable improved enterprise performance. Additionally, for a successful KM system to be introduced to an enterprise, the initial requirements and conditions for its establishment must be determined.

The need is to identify the value of KM to a technical enterprise in terms of its ability to solve enterprise-wide problems and enhance innovation. The identification and validation of a specific set of problems that KM could resolve will provide the basis for developing a KM framework of architecture for technical enterprises. This framework will provide the foundation for creating key process areas based on enterprise problems to support an organized KM framework. The framework's purpose will be to ultimately measure performance enhancements resulting from an enterprise's KM System. The goal of the framework is to inspire technical firms to systematically develop intellectual capital and have an action-based corporate-wide knowledge growth continuum as depicted in Figure 3-1.

The Emerging Need for Knowledge Management

> Ideas are everywhere, but knowledge is rare. (Thomas Sowell)

To implement a successful KM framework within an enterprise and specifically to implement a value-added KM System, it is necessary to understand and consider the following concepts:

1. KM is increasingly important because of the shift from predictable enterprise paradigms to one governed by discontinuous and often unpredictable change. A well-constructed KM system will help solve and alleviate the problems associated with this discontinuous and unpredictable change.
2. KM is not merely collecting information from various domain experts and creating databases supported by organizational Intranets. It must be dynamic and problem solving in nature.
3. KM is essential for organizational strategic survival: Problem solving, knowledge creation, and innovation are core competencies of any successful organization.
4. KM is not a separate function characterized by a separate KM department or a specific and isolated KM process. KM must be embedded into all the enterprise's business processes.

Figure 3-1

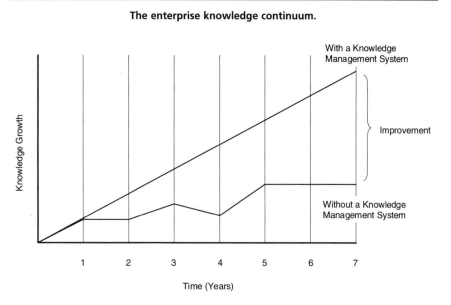

The enterprise knowledge continuum.

5. Latest advances in information and communication technology can facilitate processes, such as channeling, gathering, or dissemination of information; however, the final burden is on the managers and knowledge workers to translate this information into actionable knowledge that enhances performance. This requires creation of a foundational enterprise-wide KM system.

6. Having the best leading-edge technologies and information systems does not necessarily ensure the creativity and innovation that is necessary for organizational competence. Effective utilization of knowledge, information, and technology in terms of action and successful implementation is requisite. A KM system supported by a KM framework is required to encourage (or mandate) effective use and collaboration of knowledge and intellectual capital.

The KM enterprise framework and architecture address the critical issues of KM as it relates to organizational adoption, competence, and survival in the face of an increasingly discontinuous business environment change. The KM enterprise framework and architecture will embody organizational knowledge processes that seek the synergistic combination of data and information-processing capacity of ITs and the creative and innovative capacity of the knowledge workers. It must be a measured system and provide the basis of "prediction of performance" for enterprise leadership and prospective clients; understanding that the maturity of an enterprise's knowledge system and processes helps predict its ability to meet performance goals.

As Yogi Berra once stated, "If you don't know where you're going, you could wind up somewhere else." KM is essential for enterprises to determine "where they are going," and for organizational survival, given that knowledge creation is the core competence of any organization. This knowledge may relate to new products or services, to new product/service definitions, to new organization/industry definitions, or to new channels of distributions. Regardless of how the knowledge relates, the bottom line is

Figure 3-2

Knowledge management in relation to information system architecture and business process reengineering.

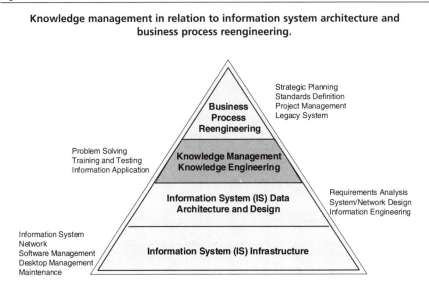

that it enables problem solving of critical enterprise issues. KM is essential to today's enterprise growth and evolution. IT has had an extreme impact on today's technical business environment. KM provides the means in terms of organizational control to capture the IT benefits and produces major business process reengineering (BPR) events. Figure 3-2 depicts a potential "fit" of KM within the enterprise.

The need for KM translates throughout the entire enterprise. KM it is not a separate function characterized by a separate KM department or a KM process, but must be embedded into all of the enterprise's business processes. Not only is KM crucial to achieving a permanent competitive advantage, but also must be an efficient knowledge-intensive core process, established to meet the demands of improved enterprise performance.

People are an essential element to KM success. Latest advances in information technology can facilitate the processes, such as channeling, gathering, or dissemination of information; however, the final burden is on the humans to translate this information into actionable knowledge depending on an acute understanding of their business context. This actionable knowledge brings value to an enterprise in its ability to enhance performance, solve problems, and stimulate innovation.

KM is a key requirement to future successful enterprises and is rapidly being recognized by technical firms to be of major strategic importance.

Knowledge Management System Value to Solving Enterprise Problems

In building and sustaining a practical and value-added KM system, identification of enterprise problems are required to form the foundation of a value-added KM system. The KM system must provide knowledge distribution for *problem solving* and measurable improved performance. The ability to distribute knowledge effectively to the knowledge workers is required to solve problems and thus enhance performance throughout the entire organization.

Statistical research and evaluation were conducted to determine a specific set of problem areas in which a KM system could provide the optimum benefit for problem resolution. Additionally, to develop the foundation for an effective KM system, requirements for establishing a KM system and identifying the benefits that managers expect from investing in a KM system, were identified to determine an acceptable and value-added KM architecture.

Table 3-1, which is based on statistical results from GW (Bixler and Stankosky, 2000), provides priority analysis results in three categories. These data provide a prioritized focus for managers establishing a KM system. Additionally, the data provide a well-defined, problem-based foundation for key process areas for the development of a KM framework or architecture. It is recommended that an enterprise focus on Category 1 problems for resolution by a new or existing KM System.

Initial Requirements to Support a Knowledge Management System

In building and sustaining a viable, practical, and value-added KM system, technical tools and organizational/leadership attitudes are essential. The system must provide tools to employees in technical organizations who need to optimize the control, management, and improvement of their product and service areas. As a minimum, the potential tools and processes of the KM System must provide the following four enhancements to the enterprise:

1. *Provide knowledge distribution for problem solving and improved performance.* Distribute knowledge effectively to the knowledge workers who need it to solve problems and enhance performance throughout the entire organization.
2. *Enhance innovation.* Enable the communication and enterprise "sharing" for the creation of new knowledge and innovation to support the development of new product/processes.
3. *Provide opportunities for continuous improvement.* Produce the methods and enterprise culture for product/process continuous improvement and quality.
4. *Provide the knowledge database for legacy enterprise knowledge.* Protect and archive critical knowledge for future use and prevent the loss of this critical information. (i.e., knowledge worker attrition and turnover).

KM tools provide a tangible foundation to solidify and enhance the enterprise's ability to sustain a competitive edge in today's dynamic business environment. Tools are the enablers for a viable KM system and KM enterprise framework and architecture.

Additionally, the following are potential organizational requirements for successful KM system implementation:

- Enterprise leadership involvement, support, and advocating of KM
- An enterprise-wide climate of openness and thinking "outside the box"
- Continuous education of employees on the value of KM and how to effectively use it
- Enterprise dedication of resources to manage knowledge as to relevance, accuracy and value to the enterprise—ability to eliminate old, outdated, incorrect, or unnecessary information and knowledge
- From the top down, develop and promote employee sharing and collaboration
- Deploy KM advocates and champions throughout the enterprise

Table 3-1

Set of Problems for a Knowledge Management System Priority Analysis		
Ranking	**Specific Problem**	**Problem Area**
Category 1: Highest area of KMS value		
1	Proposal writing (past performance, resumes, technical inputs)	Business development
2	Identification of best practices in business practices and processes	Project management
3	Generating an environment that stimulates innovation	Managing innovation
4	Product and process planning and design	Project management
5	Identifying/understanding the market potential for existing products/s	Business development
6	Product or process management	Project management
7	Improving current products/services through innovation	Managing innovation
8	Product and process construction or "build"	Project management
9	Identifying enterprise strengths and weaknesses from a competitive	Business development
10	Management decision making	Enterprise management
11	Identifying and managing project risk	Project management
12	Identifying and understanding competition	Business development
13	Planning and deployment of resources	Project management
Category 2: Moderate area of KMS value		
14	Quality management	Project management
15	Strategic planning	Gen business processes
16	Identifying specific business development opportunities	Business development
17	Employee training	Employee Management
18	Diagnosing and correcting internal business inefficiencies and proble	Gen business processes
19	Monitoring project cost, schedule, and performance	Project management
20	Client satisfaction assessment	Client management

Table 3-1

Set of Problems for a Knowledge Management System Priority Analysis (cont'd)		
Ranking	**Specific Problem**	**Problem Area**
21	Identifying enterprise internal strengths and weaknesses	Gen business processes
22	Client interaction and communications	Client management
23	Identifying management and leadership problems	Enterprise management
24	Enterprise financial management	Gen business processes
Category 3: Lowest area of KMS value		
25	Staffing and recruiting	Employee management
26	Employee performance assessment	Employee management
27	Employee retention	Employee management
28	Employee morale and motivation	Employee management
KMS, knowledge management system.		

Enterprise Task Areas Requiring a KM System and Associated Tools

The following is a preliminary sample list of task areas that KM tools and process would support within the technical enterprise:

- Planning and deployment of resources
- Scheduling and rescheduling
- Product and process design
- Decision making, simulating problems, rationalizing options
- Optimizing existing products and services through improvements
- Diagnosing problems for client
- Diagnosing internal production and business processes
- Interpreting data and information

Potential Tools to Deploy in an Enterprise KM System

The following areas were identified through the literature search as the primary functional systems required in an effective KM system:

1. *Enterprise collaboration system*
   - Primary system to develop a community of collaborative knowledge workers. Requires IT infrastructure and responsive communication system.

- Primary purpose is to connect the enterprise's knowledge workers to promote an environment of innovation and continuous improvement.

2. *Knowledge database* (best practices, internal processes, general practice)
   - Internal system (Intranet, group decision support systems) designed to provide easily accessible data and knowledge to the knowledge workers.
   - External system (Internet, conferences) to access knowledge workers to data and knowledge external to the enterprise.
3. *Performance tracking system*
   - Computer-based performance tracking system for cost, schedule, and performance of business
4. *Client interface system*
   - Client Web site interface
   - Client relations and management systems
5. *Business development knowledge and information system*
   - Computer-based systems to track current business development initiatives, competition, emerging contracts
6. *Knowledge worker value data system and internal business processes KM system*
   - Basic KM system for the enterprise knowledge workers

Current Information Technology Solutions to Support the Knowledge Management System

The following is a summary of current tools available to support a KM system within an enterprise (Cochran and Blagg, 1997, p. 99):

1. Internet
2. Intranet, e-mail, group calendar/scheduler and electronic messaging systems
3. Electronic performance support systems
4. Knowledge inventory system
5. Artificial intelligence
6. Computer-based training
7. Web-based training
8. Interactive electronic support manuals
9. Electronic meeting systems and groupware to support enterprise collaboration (asynchronous)
10. Group document handling systems
11. Desktop video and real-time data conferencing (synchronous)
12. Group decision support systems
13. Knowledge-based computer-aided design tools for developing new products

In addition to these traditional technologies, some enterprises are using new and more advanced software designed to meet the demands for tools that specifically address KM systems (Sena, 1999).

Establishing the Enterprise Knowledge Management and Knowledge Management System

Statistical research and evaluation were conducted to determine a set of conditions and requirements for establishing a successful KM System. Table 3-2, which is based on statistical results from GW (Bixler and Stankosky, 2000), provides priority analysis results in three categories. The table identifies and prioritizes the necessary initial

Table 3-2

Requirements and Conditions for a Knowledge Management System Priority Analysis	
Ranking	**Initial Requirements and Conditions for a Successful KMS**
Category 1: Very Highly Necessary for Developing a KMS	
1	Organizational buy-in and support of Knowledge Management
2	Leadership involvement, support, and advocating of KM
3	Allocating resources to manage enterprise knowledge as to relevance and value
4	Effective and efficient methodology of distributing knowledge to employees
5	Developing an enterprise repository and database of knowledge to support a KMS
Category 2: Highly Necessary for Developing a KMS	
6	Gathering/formalizing existing internal enterprise knowledge for present/future use
7	KM advocates and champions within the enterprise
8	Developing and promoting employee sharing and collaboration
9	Gathering and formalizing existing external knowledge for present and future use
10	Identifying enterprise core competencies and necessary knowledge domains
11	Climate of openness and thinking "outside the box"
12	Continuous education of employees
13	Improvements in IT infrastructure to support the KMS
Category 3: Necessary for Developing a KMS	
14	Rewards system based on employee KMS participation and support

requirements and conditions for a successful enterprise KM System. It is recommended that an enterprise would focus on Category 1 initial requirements and conditions for initiating a new KM System. Category 2 should also be considered and implemented as needed and as applicable.

Benefits and Expectations Associated with a Knowledge Management System

Economic pressures such as growth and profit—the yardsticks of our economic system—force institutions to be increasingly competitive (Probst and Bettina, 1997). Competitive pressures in the current technic environment have forced firms to increase growth, conquer new markets, and remain on the leading edge of technology. The current technical business environment is characterized by a strong focus on quantitative growth. To facilitate corporate growth and "better change," the enterprise must be guided by a balanced set of performance measures (Price Waterhouse Change Integration Team, 1995). Effective KM and KM enterprise framework and architecture measurement will be essential to provide a basis for a value-added KM system that promotes growth, enhances enterprise performance, and stimulates innovation.

Designing and implementing KM and a KM enterprise framework and architecture can be a complex task due to the potential for unforeseen consequences. What is measured, how it is measured, and the importance (or value) placed on the metric will determine what gets done, how it is accomplished, and just as important, what gets ignored in the KM system. The basis for an enterprise's KM system should be founded on its ability to resolve enterprise problems. This ability must be measurable. Traditional management and measurement techniques that focus on only financial performance can be misleading and counterproductive in a development environment (Ellis, 1997) when applied to KM. Appropriate metric design is critical to the success of any KM system development and subsequent improvement effort, because it will serve to reinforce a set of standards, behaviors, and KM system outcomes. To support enterprise performance growth leading to the ability to sustain growth and competitiveness, enterprises need methods to assess their progress in all areas relating to performance. KM is an essential element required for sustaining and improving performance. The associated KM metrics must be identified to enable the enterprise to continuously evaluate and improve its KM systems. An effective KM enterprise framework and architecture will systematically provide the basis for these measures. To develop a value-added KM system based on KM enterprise framework and architecture, the framework must be supported by metrics that covers the array of dimensions that measure performance and growth in the new business environment. The metrics must be manageable in terms of efficient collection, interpretation, presentation, and overall value-added.

Designing a Knowledge Management System and Knowledge Management Enterprise Framework Metrics

In designing a set of KM system and KM enterprise framework and architecture metrics, first, a clear definition of the desired behavior is required. Behaviors will define the knowledge culture of the enterprise and impact the level of risk people are willing to take in their jobs, the degree to which they will collaborate across functional groups within the organization, and ultimately the degree of KM support employees will bring to the development process. With desired KM goals (based on solving enterprise problems) and behavior (based on levels of collaboration) completely described, individual metrics must be designed with the four attributes described previously in mind. Each metric should be tested at least mentally for relevance, completeness, timeliness, and imposition, and then the method by which the metric is actually gathered and applied should be adjusted appropriately.

Additionally, distinctions must be made among process metrics, engineering performance metrics, and management performance metrics. Where processes are concerned, once again the criterion is desired behavior. The primary interest is in measures that indicate the state of the process and the results that it produces. Processes have various attributes called "state variables," analogous to the state variables of a physical system. It is possible to predict how that system will behave if we know the parameters of the system and the state variables at any given time. Processes, such as product development, have an analogous set of state variables. If they can be established, they will serve as process metrics, to be tracked for the purpose of understanding and controlling the process (Ellis, 1997).

Knowledge worker performance metrics concern such properties as expertise, quality, and quantity of work, judgment, teamwork, and "robustness" of the knowledge worker. Engineers with robustness have the ability to stay on track and do what makes sense regardless of the influences that tend to distract them, managerial or otherwise. Again, these measures reflect desirable behaviors found in the best knowledge workers (Ellis, 1997).

Managerial performance must be measured in other ways. In particular, the quality of decisions that managers make is a key measure of their performance. Other measures of managerial performance include their leadership skills, their process expertise and how well they apply it, their ability to manage change, their business judgment, and their use of corporate assets. Again, each of these qualities relates to desired and expected managerial behavior.

Evaluating managers' performance by the results they achieve is a natural tendency. Results are usually measured by the performance factors: financial targets, schedules, market share, growth, profitability, and so on. However, these measures reflect management quality only to the degree that the manager has control over current results. In many situations, current results are only loosely related to recent actions of the manager. Measuring decision quality, however, is more difficult than measuring results. Measuring results often becomes a simple matter of reading the bottom line and comparing it with expectations.

Effective KM systems and KM enterprise framework and architecture performance measures should encompass a structured focus on project efficiencies, performance, and ultimate client satisfaction. The following is a list of potential KM impacts and aspects. These impacts form the foundation for a KM system and KM enterprise framework and architecture measurement system.

- Impact on cost and schedule performance
- Impact on the enterprise's strategic direction
- Impact on product/service quality
- Impact on client satisfaction (repeat business)
- Impact on corporate culture
- Impact on employee morale (employer turnover)
- Impact on product/service reliability and maintainability
- Impact on product/service ease of use (user friendly)
- Impact on product/service comprehensiveness and completeness
- Impact on time and effort required to develop product/service (efficiencies)
- Impact on product/service compatibility and interoperability
- Impact on user and management attitudes on KM
- Ability for the enterprise to identify and assimilate new technologies
- Impact on existing product/service innovation and improvement
- Impact on organizational processes
- Integration of related technologies across the organization
- Enhancement of employee working knowledge, skills, and talents
- Identification of problems in products, services, and processes
- Impact on the ability to create a legacy database of knowledge, in particular working knowledge

In driving enterprise change through a KM system and KM enterprise framework and architecture, well thought out expectations and measures are essential to developing an effective system. Measurement must be evaluated and reevaluated to lay the foundation for enterprise continuous performance improvement. Only a variety and well-organized set of measures will tell the whole story.

Benefits of Enterprise Knowledge Management and Knowledge Management System

Statistical research and evaluation were conducted to determine a specific set of benefits that manager's would expect from a KM system. Based on statistical results from GW (Bixler and Stankosky, 2000), the following Table 3-3 provides the specific priority analysis results in the three categories. Table 3-3 provides a foundation for the desired measurable benefits and outcomes of an enterprise KM System. It is recommended that an enterprise would focus on Category 1 benefits when assessing the effectiveness of a new or existing KM System. Category 2 and 3 should be considered on a case-by-case basis.

Conclusion

The concept of KM has evolved over the last 10 years, and there has been an explosion of interest over the last 4 years in the form of literature, consortiums, and some enterprise applications. This discussion provides the primary requirements for developing and identifying the basis for a valid and useful foundation to provide a springboard for establishing a viable and realistic approach to successfully deploying a KM system within an enterprise. KM will enable the formalizing and integrating of experience, knowledge, and expertise to create new capabilities, solve problems, enable superior performance, encourage innovation, and enhance customer value.

Table 3-3

Knowledge Management System Benefit Expectation Priority Analysis	
Ranking	**Expected Benefits from a KMS**
Category 1: High Value Benefit Expectation of KMS	
1	Formalized knowledge transfer system established (Best practices, lessons learned)
2	Enhanced transfer of knowledge from one employee to another
3	Improved ability to sustain a competitive advantage
4	Improved overall enterprise performance
5	Means to Identify industry best practices
6	Better methods for enterprise-wide problem solving
Category 2: Some Value Benefit Expectation of a KMS	
7	Enhance business development and the creation of enterprise opportunities
8	Enhance the development of business strategies
9	Enhanced enterprise innovation and creativity
10	Better on-the-job training of employees
11	Enhanced and streamlined internal administrative processes
Category 3: Nominal Value Benefit Expectation of KMS	
12	Enhanced client relations–better client interaction
13	Development of an entrepreneurial culture for enterprise growth and success
14	Stimulation and motivation of employees

KM is still a business process and requires project management and ongoing support—it is not magic. In the words of T. Davenport, "KM is expensive—but so is stupidity!"

KM's potential is extraordinary and vital to the future of successful enterprises. KM may well lead to a new global renaissance, vaulting not only enterprises, but also the world's society, into a new revitalized era of improved performance, innovation, and overall improved quality of life.

An Empiric Study of Organizational Culture Types and their Relationship with the Success of a Knowledge Management System and the Flow of Knowledge in the U.S. Government and Nonprofit Sectors

Juan Román-Velázquez, D.Sc.

Introduction

In the 1980s, 1990s and continuing into the twenty-first century, there has been a realization of the need to address the changing role of employees within the enterprise. Now, things happen faster than ever, distances are shrinking, networks are expanding exponentially, interdependencies are growing, uncertainty dominates business activities, and complexity overwhelms our lives (Bennet and Bennet, 2001). Public, private, and nonprofit enterprises must survive and thrive in this environment. The adoption of knowledge management (KM) in the U.S. government and nonprofit sectors is rapidly growing. KM provides the capability to engineer the enterprise structure, functions, and processes necessary for the enterprise to survive and prosper. KM leverages the existing human capital/intellectual assets to help generate, capture, organize, and share knowledge that is relevant to the mission of the enterprise. Furthermore, the implementation of a KM system (KMS) enables the effective application of management best practices and information technology tools to deliver the best available knowledge to the right person, at just the right time, to solve a problem, make a decision, capture expertise, and so forth, while performing their work. The KMS can comprise formal systems, processes, management directives, and others that, when combined, help generate, capture, organize, and share available knowledge that is relevant to the mission of the enterprise. Therefore, the successful implementation of a KMS can increase effectiveness, efficiency, and innovation. However, the adoption of KM technologies and tools is only a small part of the solution when considering the desired outcome of the enterprise. A successful KMS involves more than just implementing a new technology that can be acquired in a "box"; it requires understanding and integrating its human aspects and the culture in which it operates. Therefore, this chapter presents results of our research of KM in the U.S. government and nonprofit sectors (Roman, 2004; Roman, Ribière, and Stankosky, 2004).

The research characterized the sectors' culture using taxonomy of four culture types that identified their composition and dominant culture type. In addition, it validated a model used to determine the main approach used by employees for the flow of knowledge (Roman, 2004; Ribière, 2001). Furthermore, the associated KMS success level was assessed through the evaluation of eight critical success factors. These areas were compared and contrasted at different hierarchic levels of the enterprise, namely the organization and the work unit. The analyses allow understanding of the effects the enterprise culture has in the implementation of a KMS. As a result, chief knowledge officers (CKOs), knowledge managers, and others can benefit by gaining greater insight into the likelihood of success when implementing a KM effort within the government and nonprofit sectors, while integrating the human aspect to leverage the enterprise intellectual assets in the most efficient and effective way. Furthermore, in the next chapter (Chapter 5), Dr. V. Ribière identifies critical cultural components for building a knowledge-center culture.

Knowledge Management in the Government and Nonprofit Sectors

The adoption of KM programs and systems in the U.S. government and nonprofit sectors is rapidly growing. As affirmed by Bixler, Moore, and other experts in the field, KM is thriving and delivering value to those organizations embracing it (Bixler, 2001; Moore, 2001). In the current environment, there is a critical need for the government to effectively integrate KMS efforts with the aim of transcending boundaries to disseminate essential knowledge throughout many departments, agencies, local governments, and others entities, including nonprofit institutions. Similar to the private sector, KM is transforming the way government operates its business transactions, the relationship among government organization and citizens, and the value placed on human capital. The U.S. Navy, General Services Administration (GSA), Government Accounting Office, Federal Aviation Administration, National Aeronautics, and Atmospheric Administration, and many others have recognized the need for formal KM in their organization and are reaping the benefits of their efforts (Eisenhart, 2001; Liebowitz, 2002, 2004). Furthermore, many nonprofit institutions, such as the American Association of Retired People and several colleges and universities (e.g., Jackson State University, MI; Cuyahoga Community College, OH), are applying KM to their operations (Graham, 2001; Eugene, 2001). Although the key reasons for undertaking KM initiatives may differ, the practice of KM in the public, nonprofit, and private sectors is similar when observed at the highest level.

The federal government named its first CKO in the summer of 1999 at the GSA (Remez, 2001). Since that time, other CKOs, knowledge architects, and knowledge managers have emerged at every level. Opportunities to apply KM and realize its impact are comprehensive. For the most part, the knowledge that civil servants hold is meant to be shared with colleagues and, ultimately, the public. This knowledge becomes useful only when it is dispersed to citizens and agencies at the federal, state, and local levels and government partners in the private sector (Chiem, 2001). A thriving KM management program requires the active participation of all workers in the enterprise. These employees must contribute, as well as seek information and processes that will help them to accomplish the mission of the organization and work unit. When trying to encourage the sharing of knowledge in the public sector, most practitioners recommended linking it to performance rather than payment for contributions. The performance link demonstrates to workers that participating in the organization's KMS is a necessary part of their jobs. In addition, managers should view sharing knowledge as a way of transforming employees into better workers. However, genuine recognition in the form of tokens of appreciation, such as letters of achievement, awards ceremonies, or small gifts, gives employees a sense that their contributions matter and are noticed by supervisors and upper management. Nevertheless, public servants want to know that KM initiatives will yield concrete results, such as cost savings, productivity gains, or decreased workloads—instead of appeals of social responsibility and knowledge sharing because is good for the organization (Chiem, 2001).

In 1996, President Clinton created the Federal Chief Information Officer (CIO) Council to serve as a focal point where CIOs and their deputies from 28 federal agencies could interact and coordinate on information technology (IT) challenges that cross government boundaries. Although the federal government has no single, overarching KM strategy, in January 2000, the CIOs' council, under the auspices of the Committee on Enterprise, Interoperability, and Emerging Information Technology, established the Knowledge Management Working Group. The KM Working Group brings together guidance on the content, process, and technology needed to ensure the federal community makes full use of its collective knowledge, experience, and abilities by leveraging their most important resource—the knowledge employees have (*Federal Chief Information Officers' Council Knowledge Management Working Group Charter 2001*). In addition, the group shares KM efforts among the different agencies and addresses the issues related to culture, processes, and technology.

Organizational Culture

Many authors have speculated that the study of organizational culture achieved prominence in the late 1970s and 1980s, primarily driven by falling performance levels of big business in United States and Europe and by the Japanese management methods and practices that were gaining popularity (Pettigrew, 2000). The literature on organizational culture indicates that most successful companies (those with sustained profitability and above-normal financial returns) have a major distinguishing feature that is their most important competitive advantage—their organizational culture (Cameron and Quinn, 1999). Cameron and Quinn indicate that an organization's culture is sometimes created by its founder (e.g., Walt Disney). It may emerge over time, as the organization faces challenges and obstacles (e.g., Coca-Cola) or may be developed consciously by the management team, such as the case of General Electric and its former chief executive officer (CEO), Jack Welch. Eisner emphasizes that the vision and culture of an organization sets the tone for much of what occurs within the organization, influencing most strategic activities (Eisner, 2000).

Kotter and Heskett, after conducting four cultural studies, concluded that the culture of the company has a powerful effect on the performance and long-term effectiveness of the organization. They summarize the power of culture as, "We encounter organizational cultures all the time . . . when the cultures are our own, they often go unnoticed—until we try to implement a new strategy or program which is incompatible with their central norms and values. Then we observe, first hand, the power of culture . . ." (Kotter and Heskett, 1992). They also point out that, although we usually talk about organizational culture in the singular form, all enterprises have multiple cultures associated with different functional groupings or geographic locations. Moreover, Harrison affirms that although most organizations have a dominant culture type, they can also manifest characteristics of more than one type (Harrison, 1979).

Goffee and Jones (1998) assert that the culture of an organization is perhaps the most powerful force for the cohesion in the modern organization, and unless you are very near the top of the organization, its overarching values, beliefs, and behavioral norms are pretty much out of your hands. When a new employee starts working for a company, he or she joins its culture because it is something that is deeply embedded in the fabric of an organization and is not easily changed. The concept of culture, in a very broad and holistic sense, represents the qualities of any human group that are transmitted from one generation to the next (Kotter and Heskett, 1992). For a culture to develop, however, the group of people must have shared a significant number of experiences that have allowed them to develop a common view of the world around them. It is important to recognize that organizational culture is an enduring set of values, beliefs, and assumptions that characterize organizations and their members, and thus should not be confused with organizational climate, which refers to more temporary attitudes, feelings, and perceptions of individuals that can change quickly and dramatically (Cameron and Quinn, 1999).

There are many definitions of organizational culture: some are based on an anthropologic foundation and others are based on a sociologic foundation. In addition, the definitions vary in terms of the required depth or levels that need to be unfurled to uncover the organization's true culture. Schein (1992) defines culture as

> A pattern of shared basic assumptions that the group learned as it solved its problems of external adaptation and internal integration, that has worked well enough to be considered valid and, therefore, to be taught to new members as the correct way to perceive, think, and feel in relation to those problems (page 12).

In simpler terms, organizational culture is the "taken-for-granted basic assumptions held by the members of a group or organization" (Schein, 1992). However, Schein argues that there are three basic levels to which the culture is visible to the observer. The first level is identified as *artifacts*, which include the visible behavior of the group, organizational structures, and processes. This level is easy to observe and difficult to decipher. The second culture level is the *espoused values*, which become strategies, goals, and philosophies serving as a source of identity and core mission to the group. The third and final level is the *basic underlying assumptions*. That is, unconscious, taken-for-granted beliefs, perceptions, thoughts, and feelings that are the deeper level of culture and source of values and actions. Schein associates this level with the "essence of culture." He argues that the concept of organizational culture is hard to define, analyze, measure, and manage. However, efforts to understand it are worthwhile because much of the complex and mysterious problems in organizations suddenly becomes clear when we understand the culture.

Cameron and Quinn (1999) use the following definition of organizational culture:

> Organizational culture refers to the taken-for-granted values, underlying assumptions, expectations, collective memories, and definitions present in an organization. It represents how things are around here. It reflects the prevailing ideology that people carry inside their heads. It conveys a sense of identity to employees, provides unwritten rules and, often, unspoken guidelines for how to get along in the organization, and enhances the stability of the social system that they experience (page 14).

These definitions clearly indicate that cultural analysis helps us to understand the interaction of different teams with different cultures, especially when they must work together in meaningful ways to achieve a common objective or goal. Moreover, for an enterprise to achieve the necessary level of adjustment to attain its optimum performance, it requires the understanding and awareness of the different culture composition (culture types) operating within its boundaries that comprise its overall enterprise culture. This awareness is of paramount importance when designing and implementing effective processes, tools, and technologies across the different culture types. In addition, a cultural analysis is necessary to grasp how implementing KM efforts influence the enterprise and at the same time, are influenced by the enterprise. The implementation of a KMS at the enterprise-wide level crosses many different cultures, and the interaction of these different culture types impinge on the KMS implementation, acceptance, and its overall success. If the KMS implementation encounters high organizational friction, undermined by the different cultures interactions, it will not be successful.

McDermott, Carlin, and Womack (1999) revealed that no matter how strong is the commitment and approach to KM, the organizational culture is stronger. To break down this barrier, they recommend the creation of a KM strategy that fits the culture and is linked to core culture values (McDermott and O'Dell, 2000). A survey conducted by Knowledge Management Review (published by Melcrum Publishing Limited with editorial offices in London and Chicago, www.km-review.com) to gauge the key concerns of KM practitioners revealed that 38% considered "encouraging cultural adoption of KM" as the biggest challenge and 28% considered "encouraging people to share" the next highest challenge (Knowledge Management Review, 2001). However, because sharing knowledge is part of the organization's cultural adoption of KM, the combination of the two comprise 66% of the respondents. *InformationWeek* conducted a survey of 250 IT executives from the top 500 companies. The executives were asked about the difficulties they experienced in bringing about change in their company's culture to encourage knowledge sharing and collaboration. Sixty percent of respondents replied that was very difficult or somewhat difficult (Ricadela, 2001).

Based on the above arguments from organizational scholars and KM practitioners, we can conclude that a good understanding of the enterprise culture and its composition throughout different hierarchic levels of the enterprise is an essential step for the successful implementation of KM efforts.

Enterprise Levels and Culture Analysis

In our context, the enterprise is defined as a complex system divided into two levels—organization level and work unit level. The organization level represents the entire set of employees, structure, and processes that, when analyzed in its entirety, provides an overall depiction of the institution, its shared values, interests, and purpose. Conversely, the work unit level represents a subgroup of the larger organization. It is the smallest organized grouping of employees, such as a formal business unit or a project team, where employees interact very frequently and on a regular basis with each other to accomplish their work. When both of these levels are analyzed, they provide a detailed picture of the overall enterprise culture composition.

Numerous discussions are available in the scholarly and business literature that define the theoretic foundation of organizational culture and the controversies that surround the precise definition of culture, how to measure culture, and the key dimensions that should characterize it (Ribière, 2001; Schein, 1992; Yeung, Brockbank, and Ulrich, 1991; Quinn and Spreizer, 1991; Cameron and Quinn, 1999; Park, 2001). Although the concept of organizational culture emerged prominently in the late 1970s and 1980s, disagreements remain on the best methodology to use to assess culture (Ashkanasy, Broadfoot, and Falkus, 2000). Nonetheless, Lundberg (1990) acknowledges that surfacing organizational culture is a process that is potentially enhancing, because culture awareness becomes another source of information upon which everyday decisions, actions, and activities are based.

There are three main strategies available for to study organizational culture: (a) the holistic or qualitative approach in which the investigator becomes immersed in the culture and engages in in-depth participant observation; (b) the metaphoric or language approach in which the investigator uses language patterns in documents, reports, stories, and conversation to uncover cultural patterns, and; (c) the quantitative approach in which the investigator uses a questionnaire to assess particular dimensions of culture. The lack of consensus on the best approach to analysis is based primarily on the debate revolving qualitative versus quantitative research. Meek (1988) states that organizational culture is an "all-encompassing" concept that needs to be broken into manageable proportions for study. However, the appropriate means of assessment depends on the cultural level to be examined (Rousseau, 1990; Ott, 1989).

The holistic or qualitative point of view, advocated by Evered and Louis (1981), Schein (1992), and others, encourages the investigator to use in-depth, open-ended interviewing, observation, and long-term ethnographic investigations. They claim that qualitative methods for organizational culture assessment provide the opportunity to maximize the value of heurism, flexibility, adaptiveness, depth, and realism. Therefore, the primary purpose of this approach is to gain a rich and detailed understanding of the cultural complexity from the insider's point of view. Sackmann (2001) identifies several other strength and weaknesses of the qualitative approach. A key strength is the development of grounded theory in regard to the cultural issues under investigation; other strengths are its adaptability and flexibility. As insights are gained, they can be used to adjust sampling techniques, data collection methods, and research questions. On the other hand, the results gained from qualitative research are limited to specific cases under investigation. Direct comparison cannot be made between the results from other studies unless the research is specifically designed in that manner. Furthermore, results cannot be generalized to other settings and links to organization's performance are rarely explored. One significant weakness to the qualitative method is the time needed for data collection and analysis, which makes the research more costly and time consuming.

Tucker et al. (1990), after completing ten survey studies of more than 1,200 employees in ten different organizations and ethnographic observations and detailed interviews with 50 leaders and managers of private and public organizations, concluded that organizational culture can be accurately assessed by a quantitative approach, providing meaningful and useful results that can be used as an aid for managerial decision making and planning. Based on their extensive research, the authors indicate "scrutability of organizational culture, in the final analysis, is an empiric question of a rather large scope." Furthermore, they argue that, although it is clear that two different groups or organizations do not posses the same culture, using a qualitative approach holds little significance for the possibility of identifying key dimensions of culture that can be generalized and have salient features across most or all of them. Ashkanasy et al. (2000) affirm that because behavior and attitudes are determined not by objective reality, but by the perception of reality, it is clearly appropriate to use quantitative methods to measure culture based on perceptions rather than on reality.

Cameron and Quinn (1999) emphasize that the qualitative approach must be used to conduct culture comparisons among many different organizations, because it becomes almost impossible when the qualitative method is needed for each one of them. Ott (1989) states that there are many important theoretic questions that cannot be addressed until culture can be measured with a reliable, easily administered instrument, which allows the systematic observation of organizational culture. In contrast to the qualitative approach, the quantitative method provides an opportunity to maximize the importance of precision, systematization, repeatability, comparability, convenience, large-scale assessments, and unobtrusiveness (Tucker, McCoy, and Evans, 1990). Other advantages include allowing comparative studies, helping the evaluation and initiation of culture change efforts, and providing data that can be analyzed through multivariate statistical techniques (Ashkanasy, Broadfoot, and Falkus, 2000). Therefore, it is evident that questionnaires can play an important role in the quantitative analysis of organizational culture.

The key requirements for an accurate and well-designed questionnaire are found in the literature (Ashkanasy et al., 2000; Tucker, McCoy, and Evans, 1990) and are summarized as the ability to (a) meet appropriate psychometric standards of internal consistency, reliability, and content validity; (b) demonstrate discriminant validity with respect to plausible independent culture dimensions; (c) demonstrate convergent validity; and (d) assist managers in predicting certain features of organizational behavior. Several organizational culture instruments found in the business and academic literature were evaluated against these requirements (Payne, 2001; Ashkanasy et al., 2000; Goffee and Jones, 1998; Cameron and Quinn, 1999). The organizational culture assessment instrument (OCAI), which is based on the theoretic competing value framework (CVF), was selected as our research instrument because it meets the above requirements and was the most adequate for our study.

The Competing Value Framework and the Organizational Culture Assessment Instrument

The CVF framework emerged from a series of empiric studies on the notion of organizational effectiveness. It was derived by Quinn from 39 indicators of organizational effectiveness, where two major dimensions emerge that are organized into four main clusters (O'Neill and Quinn, 1993; Cameron and Quinn, 1999). The framework is shown in Figure 4-1.

The vertical dimension of the framework differentiates effectiveness criteria that emphasize flexibility, discretion, and dynamism from criteria that emphasize stability, order, and control. The horizontal dimension differentiates effectiveness criteria that emphasize an internal orientation, integration, and unity from criteria that emphasize an external orientation, differentiation, and rivalry. When considering both dimen-

Figure 4-1

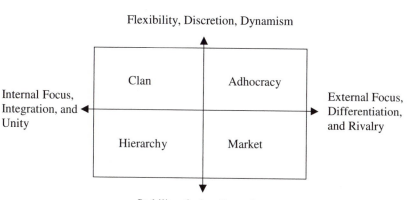

The competing value framework. (From Cameron and Quinn, 1999.)

sions together, they form four clusters or quadrants with each one represents a distinct set of organizational culture types (*clan, adhocacy, market, and hierarchy*). Cameron and Quinn (1999) described them as:

"**The clan culture:** A very friendly place to work where people share a lot of themselves. It is like an extended family. The leaders, or the heads of the organization, are considered to be mentors and perhaps parent figures. The organization is held together by loyalty or tradition. Commitment is high. The organization emphasizes the long-term benefits of human resources development and attaches great importance to cohesion and morale. Success is defined in terms of sensitivity to customers and concern for people. The organization places a premium on teamwork, participation, and consensus (page 58)."

"**The adhocracy culture:** A dynamic, entrepreneurial, and creative place to work. People stick their necks out and take risks. The leaders are considered innovators and risk takers. The glue that holds the organization together is commitment to experimentation and innovation. The emphasis is on being on the leading edge. The organization's long-term emphasis is on growth and acquiring new resources. Success means gaining unique and new products or services. Being a product or service leader is important. The organization encourages individual initiative and freedom (page 58)."

"**The market culture:** A results-oriented organization whose major concern is with getting the job done. People are competitive and goal oriented. The leaders are hard drivers, producers, and competitors. They are tough and demanding. The glue that holds the organization together is an emphasis on winning. Reputation and success are common concerns. The long-term focus is on competitive action and achievement of measurable goals and targets . . . (page 58)"

"**The hierarchy culture:** A very formalized and structured place to work. Procedures govern what people do. The leaders pride themselves on being good coordinators and organizers who are efficiency-minded. Maintaining a smooth-running organization is most critical. Formal rules and policies hold the organization together. The long-term concern is on stability and performance with efficient, smooth operations. Success is defined in terms of dependable delivery, smooth scheduling, and low cost. The management of employees is concerned with secure employment and predictability (page 58)."

This framework has been found to have a high degree of congruence with well-known and well-accepted categoric schemes that recognized the way people think, their values and assumptions, beliefs, and the ways they process information. In addition, the CVF provides a simple way to model the complexity of organizational culture that practitioners can use in the diagnosis and intervention of organizations (Quinn and Spritzer, 1991). Yeung et al. (1991) state that selection of Quinn's typology for their study was based on its "theoretical soundness in integrating cultures to other organizational components and its operationalization through a psychometrically sound instrument."

The OCAI was developed using the competing values framework. The instrument assesses organizational culture using 16 indicator variables grouped into four cultural constructs as identified in Table 4-1.

Each culture type is related to a set of core values, beliefs, and assumptions that represent the differences within the organization. The OCAI is classified as a "typing survey" by Ashkanasy et al.'s (2000) classification of quantitative surveys. The main objective of this class is to yield discrete sets of organizational culture types that are accompanied by descriptions of behaviors and values associated with each culture type. This style of questionnaire allows us to understand the different culture types within an enterprise and to compare them on the basis of their membership to a type category. Furthermore, the OCAI can also be used as an "effectiveness profiling instrument" that relates culture to organizational outcomes through an effectiveness trait

Table 4-1

Culture Types and Associated Core Values	
Culture Type	**Core Values**
Clan	Trust Respect for people Honest communication Cohesive relationships
Adhocracy	Innovation and change New ideas Visionary thinking Trying new concepts
Market	Producing results Getting the job done Goal attainment Outcome excellence
Hierarchy	Order Stability and continuity Analysis and control Predictable outcomes

approach. It provides different scores for each of the four dimensions, allowing for the generation of the organization culture profile and the identification of the dominant culture type. In addition, the OCAI was validated based on rigorous academic research demonstrating the four dimensions of the CVF. Lastly, OCAI beliefs and values address Schein's second level "exposed values" of organizational culture. These core values and beliefs are also found in the KM literature, and are important organizational traits for KM efforts in the government and nonprofit sectors.

According to Cameron and Quinn (1999), "This list is not comprehensive, of course, but it has proven in past research to provide an adequate picture of the type of cultures that exists in an organization. Therefore, by having organization members respond to questions about these dimensions, the underlying organizational culture can be uncovered", (p. 137). Furthermore, organizations tend to develop a dominant organizational culture over time as they adapt and respond to challenges and changes in the environment. Having a diagnostic instrument such as the OCAI to identify the organizational culture composition can be an especially useful tool in the effective management of the enterprise. Furthermore, by mapping the dominant culture type and the complementary culture types that are also present as well, we have a deeper understanding of the cultural composition.

The OCAI has been used in many large-scale studies and found to be useful and accurate with all coefficient alpha reliability estimates (Chronbach, 1951) ranging from 0.73 to 0.93 (Roman, 2004; Quinn, 2001; Quinn and Spreitzer, 1991; O'Neill and Quinn, 1993; Hooijberg and Petrock, 1993; Yeung, Brockbank, and Ulrich 1991; Cameron and Quinn, 1999). Furthermore, the OCAI validity was demonstrated in the research conducted by Quinn and Spreitzer (1991) where convergent validity and discriminate validity were tested using a multitrait—multimethod analysis that provided solid support for both types of validities (Quinn and Spreitzer, 1991). Therefore, the reliability and validity of the OCAI tool found in the above studies provided confidence that the OCAI measures are what they claim to measure—the key dimensions of the organizational culture that produce a significant impact on organizational and individual behavior.

Knowledge Management Strategic Approach to Knowledge Flow

Two main strategies or approaches emerge in the literature when considering the flow of knowledge throughout an enterprise. Different authors identify them differently; however, the purpose and essence are the same. For example, Denning (2000) categorizes the two approaches as the "connecting and collecting dimensions"; Weidner (2000) names them "connect and collect," and Hansen, Nohria, and Tierney (1999) describe them as "codification" and "personalization." These two approaches represent the complex knowledge utilization throughout the enterprise. At the core of these conceptualizations is the notion that organizations are comprised of knowledge-producing and knowledge-exchanging subsystems (Schulz, 2001). Therefore, the acquisition and sharing of knowledge are primary mechanisms in knowledge-based organizations.

We used the knowledge flow taxonomy developed by Hansen et al. (1999). The "codification" approach is generally defined as the formalization of tacit knowledge that is typically difficult to express or explain by developing processes that acquire it, or by developing mechanisms that allow this knowledge to become explicit, and then become documented. The codification strategy is based on a people-to-document approach, and it uses information systems to carefully codify knowledge and store it in a location that can be accessed and reused by everyone in the enterprise. An example of the codification approach can include an electronic document system that supports the life cycle (codifies, stores, disseminates and reuses) of the knowledge objects. The knowledge object can be key pieces of a document, an analysis, or something similar.

On the other hand, the "personalization" approach is the sharing of tacit knowledge by direct contact from person-to-person; therefore, allowing the flow of knowledge that probably could not be codified. It is focused on dialog among individuals, teams, and groups of employees in formal and informal settings. The personalization approach can help them achieve deeper insight by engaging in an open dialog. The knowledge is kept close to whoever developed it, and it uses information systems to help communicate that knowledge, but not for storing it. An example of the personalization approach can consist of a network of people within their enterprise resulting in a network of colleagues. Using information systems, such as an expert locator or directory of expertise, people can benefit from their experiences. Electronic document systems are also used, but their purpose is finding documents to help users get up to speed in a particular subject matter, and identifying who has done previous work on the topic in order to approach them directly. Many organizations have found that both codification and personalization approaches are needed for an effective KM effort. However, the emphasis of one approach over the other or a balanced approach depends on the enterprise overall strategy. The correct balance can be influenced by the way the enterprise serves its clients or stake holders, the economics of its business (e.g., for-profit, nonprofit, government), and the human capital it possesses.

A validated model was used to determine the dominant strategic approach (*codification* or *personalization*) that people predominantly use to facilitate the flow of knowledge throughout the enterprise. The determination was made on the basis of the assessment of employee's practices, technologies, and tools that are predominantly use for the acquisition and dissemination of knowledge throughout the enterprise. The model was foundationally based on a tool developed by Ribière (2001); however, it was modified for this research based on an extensive literature review (Hoyt, 2001; Kemp et al., 2001; Shand, 1998; Marwick, 2001; McKellar and Haimila, 2002). It was validated using confirmatory factor analysis (CFA) using path analysis with latent variables. The PROC CALIS procedure on version 8e of the SAS system was used. The SAS 8e system is developed by the SAS Institute Inc. (www.sas.com) with headquarters in Cary, North Carolina, U.S. These analyses use the maximum likelihood method of parameter estimation and were performed using the raw questionnaire data with the covariance option. Prior to CFA, descriptive statistics were calculated for each of the 20 theoretic indicator variables to evaluate the veracity of the data. Four operational variables (one-on-one conversations, peer interaction, Intranet/Internet and telephone call/teleconference) were eliminated from the analysis due to their deviation from normality with a Skewness and Kurtosis above ±2.0. Figure 4-2 shows the validated model with the corresponding factor loading for each of the operational variables using organization level data (Roman, 2004; Roman, Ribière, and Stankosky, 2004). All factor loadings were significant at $p < 0.001$.

The model was also tested using the work unit data set without any additional modifications. Values of all indices were similar to the indices for the organization data, which provides an independent sample for double cross-validation and demonstrating a good model fit (Roman 2004).

Figure 4-2

Validated measurement model of codification and personalization factors using organization level data. (From Roman 2004; Roman, Ribière, and Stankosky 2004.)

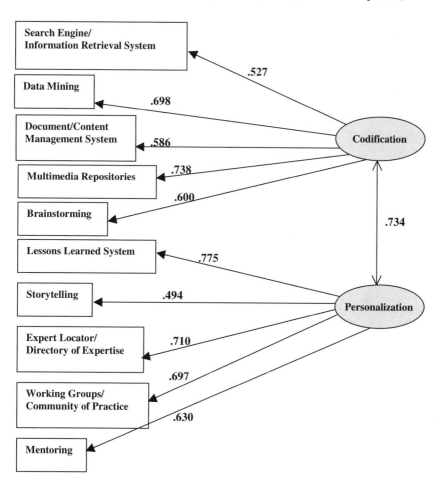

Knowledge Management Critical Success Factors

According to Berkman (2001), KM has fallen victim to a mixture of bad implementation practices and software vendors eager to turn a complex process into a pure technology play. However, more enterprises are now starting to realize that "KM deployment is not an overnight installation but a complex shift in business strategy and process, one that requires thorough planning and must involve end users" (Dyer and McDonough, 2001, p. 15).

In KM efforts, just like for any other business efforts, reasonable results in a few areas ensure successful performance. They are areas where things must go right for the endeavor to flourish. These areas are defined as critical success factors. Critical success factors are useful for structuring environmental analysis in the enterprise, because there is an important connection between environmental analysis and the factors leading to organizational success (Digman, 1990). The analysis and evaluation of success factors provides important insight through identification of the core areas that are critical in KM implementations. Therefore, KM efforts need to evaluate these core areas to gauge the potential for KMS success. The findings from leading KM practitioners, researchers, and recent studies are the major sources that can be used to identify the critical success factors for KM. However, there is a diverse perspective within the KM field regarding the identification of these factors (Jennez and Olman, 2004; Alazmi and Zairi, 2003; Chait, 2000; Choi, 2000; Kemp et al., 2001; Stankosky and Baldanza, 2001; Baldanza and Stankosky, 1999). All these factors are targeted at generating an environment that provides the enterprise with a sustainable competitive advantage through which it can leverage its knowledge resources. Moreover, they provide the opportunity and set the tone where KM functions and systems can flourish.

After conducting an empiric study of factors affecting successful implementation of KM, using 217 responses from different sectors, Choi concluded that top management leadership, fewer organizational constraints, and information systems infrastructure were the top three critical success factors for KM to succeed (Choi 2000). Kemp et al. (2001) presented a collection of success factors based on the experience of implementing KM at the Software Productivity Consortium. They identified clear goals, strong sponsorship, realistic expectations, an interactive approach, a system approach, a flexible framework, an evolutionary process, integrated measurement, a capability model, and technical maturity as critical factors for their program success and key to any KM implementation effort. Another collection of success factors are identified by Chait (2000), derived from the experiences assessing, planning, pilot testing, and implementing a successful KM system for the Arthur D. Little consulting firm. Chait identified three factors and four domains that are key in the successful implementation of any KMS: ensuring vision and alignment, managing four domains, and creating an effective plan. The four domains included content, culture, process, and infrastructure. He stressed that information technology supporting the KMS is only one element in a broad effort to maximize the potential of the knowledge resources.

Furthermore, Stankosky and Baldanza postulated four key elements or critical success factors for KM implementation–leadership, organization, technology, and learning (Baldanza and Stankosky, 1999; Stankosky and Baldanza, 2001). Each of these factors is present in an interrelated harmony and providing the foundational building blocks for the long-term success of the KMS. These factors were validated by Calabrese (2000), and later by Bixler (2000), and determined to be essential for the foundation of KMS architecture. However, the overall goal, as Stankosky and Baldanza (2001) detail, ". . . is not to have a perfect alignment among these elements as it is to develop a construct suitable to the business strategy and to the environmental influences that impact strategy on a day-to-day basis (page 273)."

Table 4-2 adapted from Alazmi and Zairi (2003) compiles a summary of the diverse perspectives of some of the leading authors in the field regarding critical success factors for KM implementation (Chait, 2000; Stankosky and Baldanza, 2001; Kemp et al., 2001; Alazmi and Zairi, 2003; Jennex and Olman, 2004). An evaluation of the literature on the subject revealed that many authors tend to provide a comprehensive list of factors, whereas others suggest factors based on the researcher's background. Additionally, some critical success factors identified in Table 4-2 are best used in a qualitative research, where the researcher can formulate in-depth questions that

Table 4-2

Critical Success Factors for Knowledge Management	
Authors	**Critical Success Factors**
Bassi (1999)	1. People learn (how, what) 2. People implement (how) 3. Sharing
Chait (2000)	1. Ensuring vision and alignment 2. Managing four domains: content, culture, process, and infrastructure 3. Creating an effective plan
Choi (2000)	1. Employee training 2. Employee involvement 3. Teamwork 4. Employee empowerment 5. Top-management leadership and commitment 6. Organization constraints 7. Information systems infrastructure 8. Egalitarian climate, benchmarking 9. Knowledge structure
Davenport, De Long, and Beers (1998)	1. Link to economic performance or industry value 2. Technical and organizational infrastructure 3. Standard, flexible knowledge structure 4. Knowledge-friendly culture 5. Clear purpose and language 6. Change in motivational practices 7. Multiple channels for knowledge transfer 8. Senior management support
Davenport and Prusak (1998)	1. Technology (network) 2. Knowledge creation and dissemination 3. Knowledge sharing 4. Electronic repositories of knowledge 5. Training, culture, and leadership 6. Issues of trust 7. Knowledge infrastructure
Finneran (1999)	1. Creation of culture 2. Sharing of information and knowledge 3. Creative knowledge 4. Workers' buy-in (90% of the success of KM is involved with gaining buy-in of knowledge users and encouraging knowledge sharing)
Haxel (2000)	1. Knowledge structured 2. Knowledge organized (goal is to share and apply knowledge faster and more efficiently than your competitors)
Heising (2001)	1. Store experiences from expert 2. Existing e-mail culture (corporate culture) 3. Senior management support 4. IT director business-focused and business process-oriented 5. Integrated among KM processes (creat, store, distribute, apply knowledge) 6. KM task must be combined with daily work task and integrated into daily business processes

Table 4-2

Critical Success Factors for Knowledge Management (cont'd)	
Authors	**Critical Success Factors**
Jennex and Olfman (2004)	1. Integrated Technical Infrastructure including networks, databases/repositories, computers, software, KMS experts 2. Acknowledge strategy that identifies users, sources, processes, storage strategy, knowledge, and links to knowledge for the KMS 3. A common enterprise wide knowledge structure that is clearly articulated and easily understood. 4. Motivation and commitment of users including incentives and training 5. An organizational culture that supports learning and the sharing and use of knowledge 6. Senior management support including allocation of resources, leadership, and providing training 7. Measures are established to assess the impacts of the KMS and the use of knowledge as well as verifying that the right knowledge is being captured 8. There is a clear goal and purpose for the KMS 9. The search, retrieval, and visualization functions of the KMS support easy knowledge use 10. Work processes are designed that incorporate knowledge capture and use 11. Learning organization 12. Security/protection of knowledge
Kemp et al. (2001)	1. Clear goals 2. Strong sponsorship 3. Realistic expectations 4. An interactive approach 5. A system approach 6. A flexible framework 7. An evolutionary process 8. Integrated measurement 9. A capability model 10. Technical maturity
Liebowitz (1999)	1. KM strategy with support from senior leadership 2. Chief knowledge officer 3. Knowledge ontologies and knowledge repositories to serve as organizational/corporate memories in core competencies 4. KM systems and tools (technology) 5. Incentive to motivate employees to share knowledge 6. Supportive culture for KM
Manasco (1999)	1. Knowing community 2. Creating context 3. Overseeing context 4. Supporting infrastructure (proper technology) 5. Enhancing process (creating and sharing knowledge)
Morey (1998)	1. Available (if knowledge exists, available for retrieval) 2. Accurate in retrieval (if available, knowledge retrieved) 3. Effective (knowledge retrieved useful and correct) 4. Accessible (knowledge available during time of need)

Table 4-2

Critical Success Factors for Knowledge Management (cont'd)	
Authors	**Critical Success Factors**
Skyrme (2000)	1. Top management support 2. Clear and explicit links to business strategy 3. Knowledgeable about knowledge 4. Compelling vision and architecture 5. Knowledge leadership and champions 6. Systematic knowledge processes (supported by specialist in information management [librarians] but close partnership between user and providers of information) 7. Well-developed knowledge infrastructure (hard and soft) 8. Appropriate bottom line measures 9. Creation of culture that supports innovation, learning, and knowledge 10. Technical infrastructure that supports knowledge work
Skyrme and Amidon (1999)	1. Strong link to a business imperative 2. Compelling vision and architecture 3. Knowledge leadership 4. Knowledge creating and sharing culture 5. Continuous learning 6. Welled developed technology infrastructure 7. Systematic knowledge processes
Stankosky and Baldanza (2001)	1. Leadership 2. Organization 3. Technology 4. Learning
Streels (2000)	1. Staff must buy into the new model 2. Lines of communication must be kept open 3. Sharing information 4. Writing weekly updates 5. Management supporting
Trussler (1999)	1. Appropriate infrastructure 2. Leadership and strategic (management commitment) 3. Creating motivation to share 4. Find right people and data 5. Culture 6. Technology (network) 7. Available to collaborators (transferring) 8. Training and learning
Wiig (1996)	1. Knowledge assets—to be applied or exploited—must be nurtured, preserved, and used to the largest extent possible by both individuals and organizations. 2. Knowledge-related processes—to create, build, compile, organize, transform, transfer, pool, apply, and safeguard knowledge—must be carefully and explicitly managed in all affected areas

IT, information technology; KM, knowledge management; KMS, knowledge management system.

provide the needed assessment for the given success factor. Others are more practically implemented in questionnaires, where respondents can assess their appropriate level.

After careful analysis and applicability toward our research objectives in the government and nonprofit sectors, we decided to use the critical success factors for KM implementation identified by Davenport, DeLong, and Beers (1998). They address the practical realities of KM projects, are considered comprehensive in their scope, and are the most applicable for our research objectives. These critical success factors were derived from a study based on 31 KM projects in 24 companies and were found to be the major factors that contributed to their success. According to Davenport et al. (1998), "Success and failure are ambiguous terms . . . but we identify eight key characteristics that we judged successful." These factors are not the only ones that have been linked to KM success. Nevertheless, they are commonly found in the literature, or they are part of other authors' lists of critical success factors. In addition, the Davenport et al. (1998) success factors can be easily implemented in a quantitative survey format as key operational variables, providing the best way to evaluate the potential for success of different KMS efforts within the government and nonprofit sectors as well as at the organization and work unit levels within the enterprise. However, to minimize the introduction of reliability and validity issues with the success measurements, we restrained from "cherry-picking" from a long list of critical success factors found in the literature in order to develop our own. This approach would have unduly introduced issues relating to a new set of factors.

Research Methodology

A carefully crafted research questionnaire addressing the key areas under study (culture type, aggregated success score, codification, and personalization) was distributed as hard copy and also made accessible through an interactive Web-based environment, using Survey Solutions XP software, which was located on the George Washington University (GW) Interactive Multimedia Applications Group's server. The government sector was defined as all federal government agencies, departments, administrations, and state and local governments. The nonprofit sector included colleges, universities, and other nonacademic entities such as national/international professional societies and associations, research and development institutions, and public policy institutes. The targeted participants were executives, managers, technical staff, support staff, and employees in these sectors.

A total of 1,800 e-mail messages and 200 hard-copy questionnaire in a preaddressed and stamped envelope were distributed. Participation in the survey was on a voluntary basis. A total of 346 subjects participated in the research during the data collection period. Only five subjects were considered unacceptable for use and were excluded from the analysis. As a result, a sample size of 341 was used as the body of data collected and analyzed. Table 4-3 and Figure 4-3 show the questionnaire responses by category and the functional roles and responsibilities of the respondents. After the data was collected, it was analyzed using SPSS 10.0 and the SAS System version 8e statistical analysis software packages. [SPSS 10.0 is a product of SPSS Inc. (www.spss.com) with headquarters in Chicago, Illinois, U.S. and SAS 8e is a product of SAS Institute Inc. (www.sas.com) with headquarters in Cary, North Carolina, U.S.] The research study used inferential statistical analysis, using the data collected to make estimates about the much larger government and nonprofit population. Using $N = 341$ as the responses collected and a 95% confidence level, the confidence interval was

Table 4-3

Questionnaire Responses by Category		
Category	Respondents	%
Federal departments	104	30.5
Federal agencies	137	40.2
FFRDC	9	2.6
Federal administrations	20	5.9
Federal commissions	2	0.6
State government	6	1.8
Local government	0	0
Universities/colleges	23	6.7
Nonprofit institutions	26	7.6
Other	14	4.1
Total	341	100.0
FFRDC, Federally funded research and development centers.		

Figure 4-3

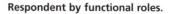

Respondent by functional roles.

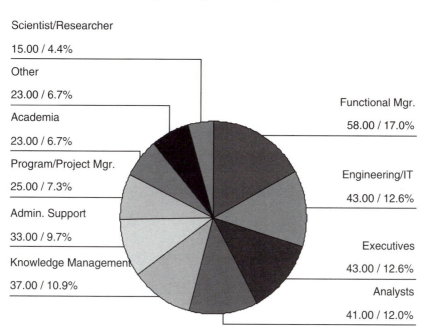

Scientist/Researcher

15.00 / 4.4%

Other

23.00 / 6.7%

Academia

23.00 / 6.7%

Program/Project Mgr.

25.00 / 7.3%

Admin. Support

33.00 / 9.7%

Knowledge Management

37.00 / 10.9%

Functional Mgr.

58.00 / 17.0%

Engineering/IT

43.00 / 12.6%

Executives

43.00 / 12.6%

Analysts

41.00 / 12.0%

calculated to be ±5.31 (Babbie, 1998; Sekaran, 1992). This implies that for any given statistic in the research, we are 95% confident that it falls within ±5.3 of the parameter stated.

The data were collected using a Likert 7-point scale for the dependable variable and a nominal scale for the classification variable. Therefore, to understand the data analysis, it is important to consider three perspectives that were used in this study. First, the absolute rating, where 1 is "very minimum extent" and 7 is "very great extent." Because the midpoint is 4.0, mean scores below 4.0 are considered low scores. Second, the change in the rating of an item—that is, how each item mean score differs between the organization level and the work unit level. A test of group difference was performed to calculate the probability that the difference between the two levels occurred by chance. Last, is the item ranking—that is, how the rating of an item at the organization level compares with the rating of the same item in the work unit.

Two types of tests were used during the study. The first type was the "test of group difference," performed to determine whether two sample populations differ with respect to their mean scores on the dependent variable. The second type test was the "test of association" in which a single sample population of respondents was evaluated to determine whether there is a relationship between two or more variables within the population. We considered the research hypothesis as acceptable only if the null hypothesis is unacceptable (rejected) because of its associated low probability. A significant level of less than 5% ($p < 0.05$) was used to test the null hypothesis for rejection.

In addition, during the data analysis, we considered the bias effect that could be introduced from responses provided by managers versus employees and responses corresponding to different levels of the enterprise when assessing the overall success factor score of the KMS. A factorial design allowed us to divide the sample population into two groups with each group having two levels (Hatcher and Stepanski, 1994). The first group under consideration, "knowledge worker," comprised responses provided by managers and employees. The second group, "enterprise level," consisted of answers given regarding the two enterprise levels under study—the organization and work unit. By evaluating the data in terms of these groups, we controlled for group effects, thus, assessing significant differences that may introduce bias. This statistical test uses the general linear model-univariate procedure (PROC GLM) to test for significant effects using version 8e of the SAS Systems. After considering all the relevant statistics calculated from the sample population, we concluded that the main effect was very weak and the groups had no significant interaction between them; therefore, the overall bias effect was negligible (Roman, 2004).

Research Findings

The research findings revealed that KM is being widely accepted and implemented throughout the government and nonprofit sectors. Most (78%) of the enterprises that implemented KMS efforts had them supporting organization and work unit levels. Of the 341 responses collected, only 18% reported no KMS efforts in place within the enterprise. Furthermore, respondents were asked to evaluate the extent to which KM was critical to the success of the enterprise. For the government sector, 79% at the organization level and 81% at the work unit level reported scores between "great extent" and "very great extent." A similar behavior emerged from the nonprofit sector. This indicated a significant awareness and understanding of the critical role that KM has within the enterprise. Also, the study evaluated the capability of replacing an employee, in the event he or she were to leave their position, with another employee who had the knowledge required to fulfill the same responsibilities. Results identified that the greatest problem exists at the work units level, with 54% of work units in the government, as well as 59% in the nonprofit sectors, lacking this critical capacity. The organization level is also deficient, with 45% and 54% in the government and nonprofit sectors, respectively. Their status regarding human capital reveals an increased threat to their effective operation in the event of a significant personnel loss or retirement.

We discovered notable similarities and differences between the organization and work unit values. Table 4-4 presents the mean, ranking, and standard deviation (SD) for each of them.

The values *getting the job done*, *goal attainment*, and *outcome excellence* were ranked first, second, and fourth for the organization and work unit levels, respectively. In addition, they had the same or very similar mean scores, indicating they transcend organization and work unit boundaries throughout the enterprise. These findings also demonstrate that the organization and work unit levels are focused on accomplishing the work and meeting the established goals in an excellent manner. However, *order* was ranked fifth at the organization level, but was given significantly less importance, ranking almost last by the employees at the work unit. Moreover, *trust* was ranked eighth at the work unit, but considerably lower at the organization level, where it ranked fourteenth. Overall, it indicates that, although employees have

Table 4-4

Similarities and Differences of Organization and Work Unit Values						
Core Values and Beliefs	Organization			Work Unit		
	Ranking	Mean	SD	Ranking	Mean	SD
Getting the job done	1	5.76	1.18	1	5.76	1.25
Goal attainment	2	5.45	1.27	2	5.43	1.28
Predictable outcomes	3	5.10	1.41	6	5.04	1.43
Outcome excellence	4	5.06	1.53	4	5.21	1.48
Order	5	4.91	1.47	15	4.84	1.46
Analysis and control	6	4.89	1.50	12	4.90	1.43
Stability and continuity	7	4.69	1.61	11	4.90	1.47
Respect for people	8	4.63	1.58	3	5.26	1.61
Creative problem-solving	9	4.59	1.44	7	5.02	1.55
Honest communication	10	4.57	1.54	5	5.19	1.58
Direction and goal clarity	11	4.53	1.37	10	4.94	1.51
Trying new concepts	12	4.45	1.37	9	4.94	1.52
Innovation	13	4.40	1.47	13	4.87	1.54
Trust	14	4.31	1.63	8	4.99	1.72
Cohesive relationships	15	4.23	1.47	14	4.86	1.58
Visionary thinking	16	4.15	1.62	16	4.56	1.69

higher *trust*, *respect for people*, and *honest communication* with those they work very closely on a day-to-day basis, there is a significant reduction in these values outside the small-group nucleus. Furthermore, order, stability, and continuity are less appreciated in the dynamic environment present within small groups (project teams or work units).

In terms of the existing culture composition within the government sector, we found that market culture was the dominant culture type at the organization level for federal departments, federal agencies, and federal administrations—achieving the highest mean score. Figures 4-4, 4-5, and 4-6 show their culture profile. In addition,

Figure 4-4

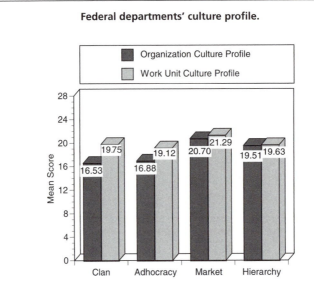

Federal departments' culture profile.

Figure 4-5

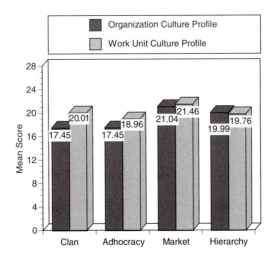

Federal agencies' culture profile.

Figure 4-6

Federal administrations' culture profile.

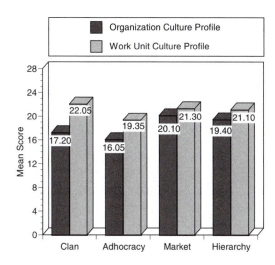

market was the dominant culture type at the work unit levels for both federal departments and federal agencies. The key values of a market culture are *producing results, getting the job done, goal attainment, and outcome excellence*. These research findings could be an indication that those elements within the President's management agenda and the human capital strategy that focus on *greater accountability* and a *culture of results* are actually changing the overall culture of the government sector—hence, a dominant market culture instead of the traditional hierarchy culture (United States. Office of Management and Budget, 2001). Note: the reference is included at the end of the document.

The government faces the pressures of increased accountability, budget limitations, and a shortage of human capital. Furthermore, there is an increased expectation for the government to introduce innovation and operate more efficiently. All these factors are transforming the culture of the government sector. This cultural change is observed as more civil servants are competing with contractors for jobs and winning as part of the government competitive sourcing effort (Peckenpaugh, 2004). An example of this finding is a group of machinists at the U.S. Treasury Department's Bureau of Engraving and Printing. In Mach 2003, the bureau started a job competition in its machine shop in Washington, DC. Almost a year later, the incumbent group of civil servants' machinists won the competition, underbidding Allied Aerospace by $3.2 million. Robert Thomas, one of the machinists, stated, "We bid that contract like we were a private entity. We trimmed it down to what we needed." (Peckenpaugh, 2004). In addition, at the Forest Service 2,187 of 2,474 jobs put up for competition have been retained by civil servants. At the National Institutes of Health, 1,464 civil servant triumphed in two major competitions but the teams had to eliminate 486 jobs to win (Peckenpaugh, 2004).

The nonprofit sector was divided in two categories: universities/colleges, and nonprofit entities that are not directly affiliated with educational institutions. Their existing culture compositions were evaluated as well and are illustrated in Figures 4-7 and 4-8. It was found that universities/colleges had the most congruent culture profile, with less than 8% variation among all four-culture types. Market was the dominant culture for both organization and work unit levels. However, their cultural

Figure 4-7

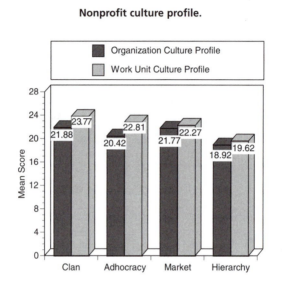

Nonprofit culture profile.

Figure 4-8

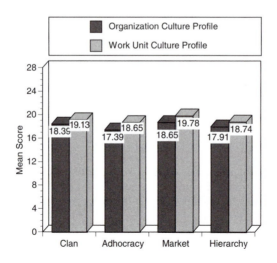

Universities/colleges' culture profile.

strength[1] was the lowest among the government and nonprofit sectors, corresponding to very weak cultures. Hence, the employees had the lowest level of affinity with the core values that are fostered within the enterprise. In contrast, the nonprofit entities category had the highest cultural strength compared with all other categories indicating a high intensity and affinity to the core values that are fostered and practiced by employees. The dominant culture type for the organization and work unit levels was "clan." This culture type attaches high importance to *teamwork*, *participation*, and *consensus* among all employees.

In terms of the technologies, support tools, and processes that respondents mostly use to generate, organize, and share knowledge at the work unit level were *one-on-one conversations, peer interaction, staff/group meetings*, and *brainstorming sessions*. They enabled the flow of knowledge from "one-to-one" or within a small group. However, the preference at the organization level was for: *Intranet/Extranet, phone calls/teleconferencing, search engines/information retrieval system, working group/communities of practice*, and *document management/content management*. Table 4-5 presents the associated descriptive statistics for the organization and work unit levels.

These technologies, processes, and tools enabled the flow of knowledge from "one-to-many" or "many-to-many." From these results, we can arrive at the following conclusion. When establishing a KMS effort, the selection of technologies, tools, and processes to be implemented by key KM decision makers should be based primarily on the knowledge distribution process that is desired (i.e., one-to-one or many-to-many) for the particular enterprise level where it will be deployed.

A more in-depth analysis of the knowledge flow throughout the enterprise using the validated model (Figure 4-2) revealed that *codification* was the dominant approach employed by 60% and 58% of the respondents at the organization and work unit levels respectively. In contrast, *personalization* was the dominant approach utilized by 32% of the respondents at the organization, with a slight increase to 35% at the work unit level. Only a small number, 8% and 7% at the organization and work unit, respectively, use both approaches with the same emphasis.

The success of the enterprise KMS efforts was evaluated by combining the eight critical success factors into an overall composite success score. The data collected and analyzed revealed that 56% of KMS efforts at the organization level and 66% at the work unit level were categorized as having a high success level score (*successful KMS efforts*). Moreover, beyond the top two success indicators (*KMS provides benefits* and the availability of the *IT infrastructure needed*), the organization and work unit differed significantly as shown in Table 4-6.

One key difference between the two enterprise levels is the *people infrastructure* element. Analysis showed that the work unit level had a greater availability of people fostering the generation and capture of knowledge than the organization level. Another key difference between the two levels was *management support* for the KMS. Respondents identified work unit management as more supportive than organization level management. However, the largest success difference between the organization

---

[1] Yeung, Brockbank, and Ulrich (1991) define cultural strength as the degree of intensity that members of an enterprise feel about different aspects of their organizational cultures. In other words, how strong or how weak is the overall organization culture composition, considering the clan, adhocracy, market, and hierarchy cultures. It is calculated by the sum of the mean scores for the four culture types.

Table 4-5

Descriptive Statistics for the Enterprise Technologies, Support Tools, and Processes						
Technologies, Support Tools, and Processes	Organization			Work Unit		
	Ranking	Mean	SD	Ranking	Mean	SD
One-on-one conversations	1	5.87	1.22	1	6.12	1.04
Intranet/Extranet	2	5.78	1.37	4	5.67	1.44
Telephone calls/ teleconferencing	3	5.77	1.28	3	5.68	1.49
Peer interaction	4	5.71	1.23	2	5.96	1.13
Staff meetings/ group meetings	5	5.33	1.52	5	5.52	1.38
Search engine/information retrieval systems	6	4.93	1.68	6	4.87	1.84
Working group/ community of practice	7	4.34	1.81	8	4.32	1.96
Brainstorming sessions	8	4.22	1.79	7	4.73	1.76
Document management/ content management	9	4.21	1.83	10	3.97	1.95
Mentoring/tutoring	10	4.08	1.84	9	4.08	2.00
Workflow and tracking system	11	3.93	1.87	11	3.82	1.99
Web-based training/ e-learning	12	3.89	1.73	15	3.37	1.86
Video conferencing	13	3.76	1.85	18	3.06	1.98
Benchmarking/ best practices	14	3.75	1.75	12	3.74	1.96
Data mining	15	3.54	1.90	14	3.38	1.99
Multimedia repositories	16	3.47	1.90	17	3.09	1.93
Lessons learned systems	17	3.42	1.89	16	3.30	1.95
Storytelling	18	3.29	1.97	13	3.58	2.04
Expert locator/directory of expertise	19	3.12	1.99	20	3.03	2.00
Electronic discussion groups	20	3.09	1.94	19	3.04	1.94

and work unit, as identified by respondents, was the existing *motivation to participate* in the capture and sharing of knowledge. The mean score for this success indicator at the work unit level was much higher than at the organization level. When taking into consideration both success elements (*management support* and *motivation to participate*), we uncovered that first-level management directing work units across the enterprise have done a much better job supporting the KMS efforts than top-level

Table 4-6

Knowledge Management System Success Indicators: Descriptive Statistics						
Success Indicators	**Organization**			**Work Unit**		
	Ranking	**Mean**	**SD**	**Ranking**	**Mean**	**SD**
Provides benefits	1	5.23	1.80	1	5.24	1.80
Information technology infrastructure	2	4.53	1.85	4	4.49	1.90
People infrastructure	3	4.27	1.91	2	4.67	1.81
Management support	4	4.03	2.09	3	4.60	2.15
Clear purpose and aligned with mission	5	3.79	2.15	7	4.16	2.16
Multiple ways to capture and share knowledge	6	3.73	2.06	6	4.26	2.06
Motivation to participate	7	3.69	1.96	5	4.40	1.99
Flexible knowledge taxonomy	8	3.47	1.95	8	3.97	1.99

management and executives. When these findings are considered, the study presents evidence that work units are the most important elements in the context of KM, providing the greatest impact to the overall enterprise.

In conclusion, after we compared and contrasted the key variables under study, we found that KMS efforts implemented in organizations with a dominant hierarchy culture have the lowest likelihood of success compared to all other culture types—clan, adhocracy, and market. Moreover, key enterprise values such as *producing results, getting the job done, goal attainment, and outcome excellence* are changing the overall culture of the government sector—hence, a dominant market culture instead of the traditional hierarchy culture. In addition, we found a positive and significant relationship between the organization and work unit cultural strength and their overall success level. That is, organizations and work units with stronger cultural values have a higher likelihood of implementing successful KMS efforts independently from their dominant culture type in existence. Results also supported that a personalization approach for the flow of knowledge is better suited for organizations that have dominant clan or dominant adhocracy cultures. Conversely, a codification approach is better suited for organizations that have dominant hierarchy or dominant market cultures. Another significant finding was that successful KMS efforts in the government and nonprofit sectors focus their knowledge flow strategy strongly toward codification and use the personalization as a complementary strategy, instead of implementing a balanced approach.

On the basis of the data collected and analyzed, we identified critical findings for KMS efforts in the government and nonprofit sectors. Executives, CKOs, knowledge managers, KM designers and implementers, and many others should take into consideration these factors before recommending any specific strategy, application, or solution.

Key Research Insight: Streamlined organizational structures with strong cultures have higher chance of KM success.

Building a Knowledge-Centered Culture: a Matter of Trust

Vincent M. Ribière, D.Sc.

Introduction

In the previous chapter, Dr. J. Roman introduced and demonstrated the critical role of organizational culture in implementing successful knowledge management (KM) initiatives. Roman's empirical study, conducted in the government and nonprofit sectors, sheds some light on the strategic approaches best suited for a given culture and its likelihood for success. The study presented in this chapter is a different and complementary approach designated to decipher the role and the critical components of organizational culture for a KM initiative's success. The population surveyed for this research is mainly composed of high-tech and consulting companies located in the United States. The level of interpersonal trust in a company is used to assess the likelihood of success of a KM initiative, the level of involvement/participation in communities of practice, and finally, the choice of the primary source of problem-solving information.

As presented in Chapter 4, many instruments have been used to assess and describe organizational culture. Different studies with different research goals used different attributes to represent organizational culture. This abundance of instruments reveals that organizational culture is a soft/fuzzy dimension that remains difficult to decode. To make things more complex, companies have subcultures that inherit some values, beliefs, and artifacts from their parent culture (DeLong and Fahey, 2000; Deal and Kennedy, 1982; Schein, 1992, 1999). This inheritance might be more or less influential depending if the parent culture is strong or weak (Deal and Kennedy, 1982). Furthermore, organizational cultures inherit attributes of national/geographical cultures. For example, Western versus Eastern cultures or high-context versus low-context cultures do not carry the same values and beliefs regarding work and knowledge sharing. The study conducted by Drs. William D. Schulte and Po-Jeng Wang presented in Chapter 6 illustrates the importance of this third cultural dimension. Figure 5-1 illustrates the relationships between these three different levels of culture.

One needs to be aware of the influence of the different levels of culture when trying to understand the overall culture of an organization. Much research has been conducted on the critical role of organizational culture in KM, but few have identified the core components/enablers of a knowledge-centered culture. Of note is the work of Dr.

Figure 5-1

Different levels/layers of culture.

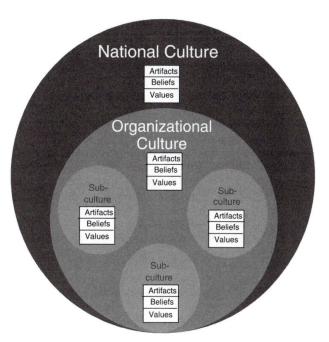

Heejun Park, presented in Chapter 9, as well as the study conducted by Holowetzki (2002). Table 5-1 lists the commonly cited cultural attributes that must be present to nurture a knowledge-centered culture.

Based on an extensive literature review and our consulting experience, we believe that interpersonal trust is the precondition of most factors listed in Table 5-1. Without trust, individuals will not be likely to share and collaborate in knowledge exchanges.

Early in the 1990s, Jack Welsh had already underlined the important role of trust:

> Trust is enormously powerful in a corporation. People won't do their best unless they believe they'll be treated fairly—that there's no cronyism and everybody has a real shot. The only way I know to create that kind of trust is by laying out your values and then walking the talk. You've got to do what you say you'll do, consistently and over time. (Welch, 1993)

The early KM efforts conducted by Buckman laboratories have been crowned with success and once again, trust was mentioned as a critical component:

> It is important to create a climate of continuity and trust so that we may have proactive knowledge sharing across time and space. Organizational culture must change from a state of hoarding knowledge to gain power to one of sharing knowledge to gain power.

> Bob Buckman

Table 5-1

Cultural Attributes Associated with a Knowledge-Centered Culture	
Cultural Attributes	**Author**
Reciprocity, Repute, Altruism, **Trust**	Davenport and Prusak, 1998
Visible support of senior management, clearly defined objectives, meaningful objectives, **high level of trust**, great team leadership, shared rewards	Kinsey Goman, 2002a, 2002b
"8 Cs": Connectivity, Content, Community, Culture (support and vision from top management, shared sense of direction, **trust**, openness, excitement, and a willingness to continually learn from peers are key components of KM culture), Cooperation, Capacity, Commerce, and Capital	Rao, 2002
Collaboration, communication, creativity, empowerment, enthusiasm, **trust**, synergy, sharing, open-mindedness, positive attitude, involvement	Hubert, 2002
Culture, **trust**, strategic intent, organizational design, transparency, learning capacity	Rolland and Gauvel, 2000
High solidarity and high sociability, fair processes and fair outcomes, employees' work recognition	Goffee and Jones, 1998; Smith and McKeen, 2003
Sharing information freely, working closely with others, team-oriented work, **trust**, fairness, enthusiasm for the job	Park, Ribière, and Schulte, 2004
KM, knowledge management.	

> Trust is the one essential lubricant to all social activities. Allowing people to work and live together without generating a constant, wasteful flurry of conflict and negotiations. (Cohen and Prusak, 2001)

Because trust is a critical component of a knowledge-centered culture, and organizational culture is a key component of knowledge management success (Barth, 2000; Knowledge Management Review, 2001; KPMG Consulting, 2000; Microsoft, 1999; Pauleen and Mason, 2002), we decided to conduct a study focusing on this factor and its effects.

Methodology

This study was driven by four research hypotheses:

H_1: Companies with a high interpersonal trust culture are more successful in their KM initiative than are companies with a low interpersonal trust culture.

H_2: There is a positive relationship between the level of interpersonal trust in an organization and the use/participation of communities of practice.

H_3: Employees of organizations with a high level of interpersonal trust culture are more likely to first contact a co-worker when looking for problem-solving information than using internal or external knowledge repositories (knowledge management system [KMS]).

H_4: Employees of organizations with a low level of interpersonal trust culture are more likely to first use an internal or external knowledge repositories (KMS) when looking for problem-solving information rather than contacting a co-worker.

Companies involved in KM were surveyed in order to assess their level of interpersonal trust, the level of success in their KM initiative, their level of involvement/participation in communities of practice, as well as the choice of the primary source of problem-solving information. These different variables are defined more precisely in the following sections.

Trust

As organizational culture, trust is a very broad and complex construct. Diane Ford (2001) summarized the different targets of trust in Table 5-2.

This research assessed the level of interpersonal trust. In addition to the many facets of trust, many tools have been designed to assess its level in organizations.

Table 5-2

Targets of Trust	
Interpersonal trust	"Trust consists of a willingness to increase your vulnerability to another person whose behavior you cannot control, in a situation in which your potential benefit is much less than your potential loss if the other person abuses your vulnerability" (Zand, 1997). (Aulakh, Kotabe, and Sahay, 1996). Also defined as "generalized expectancy that the verbal statements of others can be relied upon" (Rotter, 1967).
Group trust	The willingness of one person to increase his or her vulnerability to the actions of a group of people (Rousseau, Sitkin, Burt, and Camerer, 1998).
Organizational trust	"Organizational trust is a feeling of confidence and support in an employer . . . organizational trust refers to employee faith in corporate goal attainment and organizational leaders, and to the belief that ultimately, organizational action will prove beneficial for employees" (Gilbert and Li-Ping Tang, 1998).
Institutional trust	Institutional trust is a feeling of confidence and security in institutions (e.g., the law, organizations), that the laws, policies, regulations, and so forth are to protect the individual's rights, and will not harm the individual.
Trust in individuals	This is the same as interpersonal trust.
Trust in firms	This is the same as organizational trust.
Trust in institutions	This is the same as institutional trust.
From Ford D. Trust and knowledge management: the seeds of success. Kingston: Queen's KBE Centre for Knowledge-Based Enterprises, 2001.	

Among them is the survey tool designed by Cook and Wall (1980) that has been extended by Wilson (1993). Wilson developed a heuristic conceptualization—in the form of an influence diagram—that can be used by managers in assessing the level of organizational trust. Cummings and Bromiley (1996) designed a survey tool named the *organizational trust inventory* (OTI). Nyhan and Marlowe (1997) developed a 12-item scale to measure an individual's level of trust in his or her supervisor and his or her work organizations as a whole. Ciancutti and Steding (2000) offer an audit questionnaire based on 21 likert type questions as well as six open-ended questions. This questionnaire is designed to detect the overall level of trust and the type of issues in which closure is a concern. Lewis (1999) is more oriented toward how companies build mutual trust and how interpersonal relationships are a critical component. Five interpersonal trust factors defined by De Furia (1996; 1997) were determined to be most relevant to our research: sharing relevant information, reducing controls, allowing mutual influences, clarifying mutual expectations, and meeting expectations. The tool selected, the organizational trust survey (OTS), was developed and validated by De Furia (1996, 1997). Using the OTS, trustworthiness (TW) is based on five behaviors: TW = SI + RC + AI + CE + ME. The variables are defined as follows:

<u>Sharing relevant information (SI)</u> refers to the behaviors whereby one individual transmits information to another person.

<u>Reducing controls (RC)</u> refers to the behaviors affecting the processes, procedures or activities with which one individual (a) establishes the performance criteria or rules for others, (b) monitors the performance of another person, (c) adjusts the conditions under which performance is achieved, or (d) adjusts the consequences of performance (i.e., positive or negative reinforcements).

<u>Allowing for mutual influences (AI)</u> occurs when one person makes a decision that affects both individuals. Mutual influence means that both individuals have approximately equal numbers of occurrences of convincing the other or making the decision for both individuals.

<u>Clarifying mutual expectations (CE)</u> refers to those behaviors wherein one person clarifies what is expected of both parties in the relationship. It involves sharing information about mutual performance expectations.

<u>Meeting expectations (ME)</u> involves any behaviors in which one individual fulfills the behavioral expectations of another person. It is closely related to confidence, reliability, and predictability.

The OTS allows organizations to measure the trust-related behaviors of various categories of people within the organization—upper-level managers, first-line supervisors, and co-workers—in relation to how employees' trust-related expectations are being met. It also measures trust-related behaviors between organizational units and the perceived impacts of organizational policies and values on trust-related behaviors. This tool (questionnaire) is based on 50 questions (ten questions for each of the five factors). Because of the existence of a pretested questionnaire with a small number of variables, necessary because of the somewhat limited size of our data set, the OTS was used for this study.

Knowledge Management Success Factors

Selecting variables to measure a level of "success" is always a difficult and controversial choice. Jennex and Olfman (2004) (Table 5-3) summarized the most common KM success factors cited in the KM literature.

Table 5-3

Knowledge Management Success Factors Summary
1. Integrated technical infrastructure including networks, databases/repositories, computers, software, KMS experts.
2. A knowledge strategy that identifies users, sources, processes, storage strategy, knowledge and links to knowledge for the KMS.
3. A common enterprise wide knowledge structure that is clearly articulated and easily understood.
4. Motivation and commitment of users including incentives and training.
5. An organizational culture that supports learning and the sharing and use of knowledge.
6. Senior management support including allocation of resources, leadership, and providing training.
7. Measures are established to assess the impacts of the KMS and the use of knowledge as well as verifying that the right knowledge is being captured.
8. There is a clear goal and purpose for the KMS.
9. The search, retrieval, and visualization functions of the KMS support easy knowledge use.
10. Work processes are designed that incorporate knowledge capture and use.
11. Learning organization.
12. Security/protection of knowledge.
KMS, knowledge management system. From Jennex ME, Olfman L. *Assessing knowledge management success/effectiveness models.* Paper presented at the 37th Hawaii International Conference on System Sciences, Hilton Waikoloa Village, January 5–8, 2004.

This study adopted four core success factors, which were defined and used by Davenport et al. (1998) in their publication concerning successful knowledge management projects. These factors are as follows:

1. Growth in the **volume** of knowledge available since the KM initiative has been launched (e.g., number of documents available).
2. Growth in the **usage** of knowledge available since the KM initiative has been launched (accesses to repositories, or the number of participants for discussion-oriented projects).
3. The likelihood that the project would **survive** without the support of a particular individual or two, that is, the project is an organizational initiative, not an individual project.
4. Growth in the **resources** (e.g., people, money) attached to KM initiatives.

Success was measured on the basis of two dimensions. Because the main purpose of KM is to facilitate the flow and dissemination of knowledge, an important dimension for success is the fact that employees are involved and participate. Success factors no. 1 and no. 2 were used to measure this dimension of success. The second dimension of success used is based on the "robustness" of the KM initiative. If KM is given the resources, and if there is a clear commitment from senior management to make it happen, robustness is a success factor. Success factors no. 3 and no. 4 were used to measure this second dimension of success. These factors helped us to differentiate highly successful KM projects from less successful projects.

Data Collection and Analysis

Validity and Reliability

As described previously, to measure the level of interpersonal trust in an organization, we used the survey tool designed by DeFuria (1997), which was judged reliable and valid. The measure of the level of KM success was assessed by using the four factors used by Davenport (1998) and previously presented. The combination of these two questionnaires was used for our study.

A pilot study was undertaken to create a more sensitive instrument. Content validity was demonstrated by the review of ten knowledgeable people (academics and professional) highly involved in the field of KM and organizational behavior. Only minor modifications were made to those instruments used in the research reported herein.

A Chronbach alpha value was used to assess the internal consistency of the research instruments. The overall raw alpha score of 0.94 indicates that the scales used to measure trust are reliable. Construct validity was assessed using item-total correlation where the average of each construct was correlated with each item in the same construct. The correlation coefficients for all these constructs were demonstrated to be highly significant.

Data Collection and Analysis

Data were collected through two main mechanisms. An online version and a paper version of the questionnaire were used. Most (98%) of the responses were collected from the online version. The target population was Chief Knowledge Officers (CKOs), managers, and other employees involved in KM initiatives at any level in an organization. A total of 1,050 e-mails, eliciting for participation, were sent out to members of KM groups and associations. A fundamental premise of the research was that targeted organizations must have had experience with KM initiatives. A total of 145 responses were received, representing a response rate of 14%. Of the 145 questionnaires received, only 100 were complete and were representative of organizations involved in KM.

Organizations that participated were predominantly large organizations in the consulting and IT-telecommunications fields and agencies in the federal government. Respondents were mainly service-oriented, offering standardized and customized products/services, and were predominantly located in the United States.

Findings

Research Hypothesis 1

This hypothesis tests the difference between the success factor score (dependent variable) associated with companies with a low and high levels of interpersonal trust (independent variable).

> **H1:** Companies with a high interpersonal trust culture are more successful in their KM initiative than companies with a low interpersonal trust culture.

Table 5-4

Descriptive Statistics of the Two Groups Studied			
	n	$\bar{x}$	SD
High success	69	14.145	3.6125
Low success	17	10.882	6.2027

Table 5-5

Comparison Between Success Scores of Organizations with Low- and High-Trust Culture							
	H_0	H_A	Test	Value	*df*	*p*	Accept H_A?
(1)	$\Phi_{HS} = \Phi_{LS}$	$\Phi_{HS} \approx \Phi_{LS}$	F test for homoskedasticity	1.84	(16,68)	0.0869	No
(2)	$\mu_{HS} = \mu_{LS}$	$\mu_{HS} > m_{LS}$	Independent samples *t* test	3.72	84	0.00275	Yes

The success factor score variable was measured on an interval/ratio scale of values ranging from 4 to 20. The level of trust factor score variable was measured on an interval/ratio scale of values ranging from 25 to 125. A cutoff point of 75 (midpoint score) was used to divide the variable into two sets. Organizations that obtain trust factor scores greater than 75 were categorized as having a *high trust culture* whereas scores less than or equal to 75 were categorized as having a *low trust culture*. An independent-sample one-tailed *t* test was used to analyze the differences of means between the successful and not successful groups. Table 5-4 provides descriptive statistics of the two groups (companies with high and low KM initiative success).

Applying the pooled/standard form of the independent samples *t* test on our two populations (Table 5-5, second row) we obtained a *p* value of 0.00275, which is greater than the preset γ of 0.05. Thus, H_0 is rejected and H_A is accepted (H_1). We can be reasonably certain that companies with a high interpersonal trust culture are more successful in their KM initiative than companies with a low interpersonal trust culture.

Research Hypothesis 2

Hypothesis 2 tests the relationship between the use/participation of communities of practice factor score (dependent variable) and the level of interpersonal trust (independent variable).

H_2: There is a positive relationship between the level of interpersonal trust in an organization and the use/participation of communities of practice.

The use/participation of communities of practice factor score variable was measured on an interval/ratio scale of values ranging from 1 (low) to 5 (high). Figure 5-2 depicts the distribution of respondents. The level of trust factor score variable was measured on an interval/ratio scale of values ranging from 25 to 125 (Figure 5-3). A cutoff point of 75 (midpoint score) was used to divide the variable into two sets.

Figure 5-2

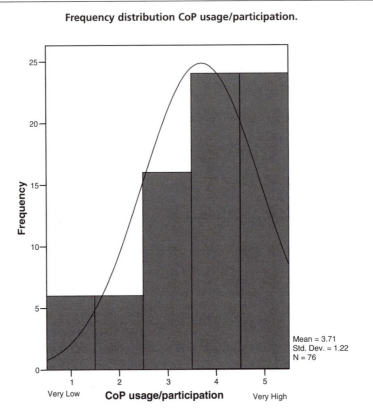

Frequency distribution CoP usage/participation.

Organizations that obtain trust factor scores greater than 75 were categorized as having a *high trust culture* whereas scores less than or equal to 75 were categorized as having a *low trust culture*.

A simple linear regression was used to analyze the relationship between the two variables. Table 5-6 represents the results of this test.

Based on the results, we can be reasonably certain ($p < 0.00005$) that there is a positive relationship between the level of interpersonal trust in an organization and the use/participation of communities of practice.

Research Hypotheses 3 and 4

These hypotheses test the relationship between employee's primary source of problem solving information and the level of interpersonal trust.

H_3: Employees of organizations with a **high** level of interpersonal trust culture are more likely to first contact a co-worker when looking for problem-solving information than using internal or external knowledge repositories (KMS).

H_4: Employees of organizations with a **low** level of interpersonal trust culture are more likely to first use an internal or external knowledge repositories (KMS) when looking for problem-solving information rather than contacting a co-worker.

Figure 5-3

Trust frequency distribution.

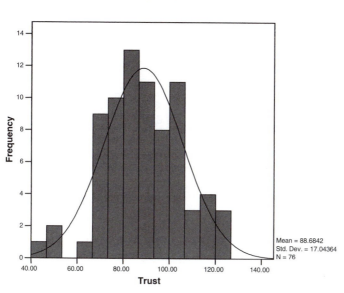

Mean = 88.6842
Std. Dev. = 17.04364
N = 76

Table 5-6

Chi-Square Results					
	n	$\hat{\beta}$	s_β		
	76	0.032	0.007		
H_0	H_A	*Test*	*Value*	d_f	*p*	Accept H_A?
$\beta_1 = 0$	$\beta_1 > 0$	*t* test: simple linear regression	4.38	74	<0.00005	Yes

Respondents were asked the question, "When you look for problem-solving information are you more likely to contact a co-worker or look into a internal or external knowledge repositories (KMS)?" The level of trust factor score variable was measured on an interval/ratio scale of values ranging from 25 to 125. A cutoff point of 75 (mid-point score) was used to divide the variable into two sets. Organizations that obtain trust factor scores greater than 75 were categorized as having a *high trust culture*, whereas scores of 75 or less were categorized as having a *low trust culture*.

A chi-square test test of independence was used to determine if a relationship existed between our two categorical variables (information source [co-worker, KMS] and trust level [high, low]). Table 5-7 presents the results.

These results indicate that there is a statistically significant relationship between the primary source of problem-solving information and the level of interpersonal trust ($p = 0.0437$ and $p < 0.05$, respectively). Research hypotheses 3 and 4 are accepted. As we

Table 5-7

Results of Chi-square test			
Frequency Percent Row Pct Col Pct	Level of Trust		
	Low	High	Total
Primary source of problem solving information KMS	17 17.00 39.53% 58.62%	26 26.00 60.47% 36.62%	43 43.00
Coworker	12 12.00 21.05% 41.38%	45 45.00 78.95% 63.38%	57 57.00
Total	29 29.00	71 71.00	N = 100 100.00

Statistics for Table of Source by Trust			
Statistic	DF	Value	Prob
Chi-Square	1	4.0663	**0.0437**
Likelihood Ratio Chi-Square	1	4.0469	0.0443
Continuity Adj. Chi-Square	1	3.2182	0.0728
Mantel-Haenszel Chi-Square	1	4.0256	0.0448
Phi Coefficient		0.2017	
Contingency Coefficient		0.1977	
Cramer's V		0.2017	

can see on Table 5-7, when the level of interpersonal trust is low, 58.62% of the respondents favor the use of a knowledge repository (KMS; internal or external) as a primary source of problem-solving information rather than contacting a co-worker (41.38%). On the other hand, when the level of interpersonal trust is high, only 36.62% of the respondents favor the use of a knowledge repository (KMS) (internal or external) as a primary source of problem solving information, but 63.38% prefer contacting directly a co-worker.

Conclusion

The findings of this study confirm and reinforce the fact that interpersonal trust is a critical cultural factor that must not be ignored by companies involved in KM or looking to launch a KM initiative. Based on an empirical study involving 100 organizations mainly composed of high tech and consulting companies located in the US, the following hypotheses were statistically validated:

H_1: Companies with a high interpersonal trust culture are more successful in their KM initiative than are companies with a low interpersonal trust culture.

H_2: There is a positive relationship between the level of interpersonal trust in an organization and the use/participation of communities of practice.

H_3: Employees of organizations with a high level of interpersonal trust culture are more likely to first contact a co-worker when looking for problem-solving information than using internal or external knowledge repositories (KMS).

H_4: Employees of organizations with a low level of interpersonal trust culture are more likely to first use an internal or external knowledge repositories (KMS) when looking for problem-solving information rather than contacting a co-worker.

Research hypotheses 2, 3, and 4 reinforce the findings of our previous research (Ribière and Roman-Velazquez, 2005; Ribière and Tuggle, 2005). In this study, it was demonstrated that companies with a high trust culture use/rely more on personalization tools than companies with a low organizational trust culture. These findings can be used as guidance to organizations looking to invest or to deploy KM tools and practices. Companies with a low interpersonal trust culture might want to try to focus on improving their level interpersonal trust. They might not want (at least on short term) to focus their main efforts/resources on a KM personalization strategy (Hansen, et al., 1999), but more on a KM codification strategy where knowledge is codified using a people-to-documents approach (KMS IT-based). On the other hand, companies with a high level of interpersonal trust might want to develop a KM personalization strategy that focuses on developing networks for linking people so that tacit knowledge can be shared and leveraged.

To conclude, interpersonal trust is crucial for establishing a knowledge-centered culture but also it provides other benefits and consequences in its absence (Table 5-8).

Among this list, we can note that high interpersonal trust also stimulates innovation, which is another important dimension of knowledge management.

Table 5-8

Benefits and Consequences of High and Low Interpersonal Trust	
High Interpersonal Trust	**Low Interpersonal Trust**
• Stimulates innovation • Leads to greater emotional stability • Facilitates acceptance and openness of expression • Encourages risk taking	• Values, motives of others are misperceived • Less accurate communication, poor reception • Diminished ability to recognize and accept good ideas • Increased attempt to obtain relevant information (grapevine) • Increased control mechanisms • Self-control replaced by external controls • Delayed implementation of actions and projects • Increased rejection, defensiveness, hostility
From De Furia GL. *A behavioral model of interpersonal trust.* Unpublished Doctoral dissertation, St. John's University, Springfield, LA, 1996.	

The State of Knowledge Management Practice in Taiwan

Po Jeng Wang, D.Sc., and William D. Schulte, Ph.D.

Countries in Asia are embracing the global knowledge-based economy. Taiwan is playing a leadership role in this transition. One of the reasons could be the positive influence of Asian culture on the adoption of knowledge management processes and technologies. National culture is an important dimension of collective human behavior that can be an important source of competitive advantage for the international firm (Takeuchi and Nonaka, 1995).

Culture affects the values and practices of every enterprise at all lower levels and impacts decisions and actions of international managers. Understanding the cross-national differences in knowledge management (KM) can help firms compete and cooperate for sustainable competitive advantage in Asia. The relationship between national culture and KM includes issues that are critical to decision makers in the global knowledge economy (Banerjee and Richter, 2001).

Formalized or codified knowledge that can transfer among individuals is known as explicit knowledge. Tacit knowledge is nonformalized or noncodified. Tacit knowledge is considered to be more important than explicit knowledge (Takeuchi and Nonaka, 1995). This knowledge is embedded in each individual's experiences and is influenced by personal beliefs, perspectives and values. Social culture, described in the literature as national culture, is based on many of those same values. Therefore, knowledge management and national culture are fundamentally linked.

Although much has been written on the relationship between national culture and management in Asia (Davis and Schulte, 1997; Wang, 2004), there is little empirical research published to date on this specific subject. This chapter adds to our understanding of this subject by exploring the relationship between Asian culture and knowledge management practices in Taiwan.

Asian Economy and Chinese Culture

Asian economies have experienced great change and uncertainty and, in cases, had collapsed to some extent (Banerjee and Richter, 2001). Some of those nations recovered more easily than others because of solid economic foundations and technologic strength. (Banerjee and Richter, 2001). For example, China and the "little dragons" of Taiwan, Hong Kong, Korea, and Singapore have been growing rapidly, whereas other countries like Indonesia and the Philippines still struggle (Yoshida, 2001). All Chinese people play an important role in the economic development of these little dragons and Mainland China. They have an important role in the economies of other countries too, such as Indonesia, Malaysia, the Philippines, and Thailand, although they are an ethnic minority there (Hofstede, 1993).

These four little dragons share the influence of Confucius' teaching and a common culture of "hard work, thrift, perseverance, hierarchical ordering of relationships and scholarship" (Hofstede and Bond, 1988; Joynt and Warner, 1996). This common culture incorporates "three main driving forces: prevalent education, a high-quality labor force, and fast regional integration" (Chow and Chow, 1997, p. 21). These small nations of East Asia have successfully improved standards of living over a long term, which makes them a model for other emerging nations. Their successes serve as examples of effective management principles and public policies regarding the industrialized world—successes that have been important in the recent explosive growth of the Chinese economy.

"Knowledge is driving the pace and scope of globalization faster and wider than ever before, and therefore, [Asia's] economic success [depends on its] ability to take full advantage of and contribute to global science and technology advances" (Yoshida, 2001, p. 6) To keep up with such rapid changes in all desirable directions, Asian countries must develop new ways to interpret the significant economic transformations. To gain and retain competitive advantage, they need to use KM in collection, leveraging, and transfer of their knowledge assets within or outside of the country. KM will enrich the capabilities of multi-national enterprises (MNE) that venture into Asian countries and will enable "cultural understanding among peoples around the world" (Chow and Chow, 1997, p. 128).

Taiwan's Profile

Taiwan is a small island located in the western Pacific, just southeast of China. Formally known as the Taiwan, Republic of China (ROC) or as the Republic of China on Taiwan (Copper, 1999; Maguire, 1998), it encompasses an area of 13,814 square miles, which is about the same size as Holland or the combination Massachusetts, Rhode Island, and Connecticut in the United States (Copper, 1999). Its population of about 22 million makes Taiwan the most densely populated country in the world (Copper, 1999). Although it has few natural resources, Taiwan has "achieved an astonishing record of economic growth since 1950" (Maguire, 1998, p. 49). The educational levels in Taiwan are rated very highly (Copper, 1999). In summary, "Taiwan has almost no natural resources and a very unfavorable land-to-population ratio. Its only resource of any importance is its human talent" (Copper, 1999, p. 143).

Economic Achievements

Despite its small population and limited size, Taiwan, as the world's seventeenth largest economy and the fourteenth largest trading nation, is undergoing transition from a high-tech manufacturing economy to a high-tech services economy. In 1991, manufacturing accounted for 41% of Taiwan's gross domestic product (GDP), but it dropped to 31% in 2003. The 1991 figure of 55% for services increased to 67% (special advertising section in a 2003 magazine—unknown source). Even so, Taiwan's GDP ranked as twentieth in the world and twenty-second highest globally in average personal income (McBeath, 1998). Taiwan also ranks as fifteenth in the world in terms of research and development (R & D) expenditures (Yoshida, 2001). Table 6-1 summarizes these findings. Table 6-2 compares Taiwan with China.

Bond and Hofstede (1989) quote Kahn's 1979 suggestion that the common cultural heritage of Confucianism is the reason for Chinese economic success (Bond and Hofstede, 1989, p. 7). "Taiwan has close historical and cultural ties with Mainland China" (Simon and Kau, 1991, p. 71), and shares "the Chinese cultural values that have proven their worth in predicting economic growth" (Bond and Hofstede, 1989, p. 199). "Growing economic links between China, Hong Kong and Taiwan may eventually reshape East Asia" (Engholm, 1994, p. 1).

Taiwanese firms' "[competitive advantages come from building their people management capabilities on a] core cultural value of flexibility, that willingness to act to maximize the benefits derived from altered conditions" (Tsang, 1999, p. 10). This flex-

Table 6-1

Taiwan Economic Statistics	
Category	Rank
Largest economy	17
Largest trading nation	14
Gross domestic product—richest country	20
Research and development expenditures	15
Service industry	60%

Table 6-2

Statistical Comparison of Taiwan's and China's Economies		
	Taiwan	China
Land area (sq. mi.)	13,969[a]	3,706,566[b]
Population	22.42[a]	1.27[b]
Per capita gross national product (US$)	12,876[a]	840[b]
Foreign trade (US$, billion)	230.1[a]	509.8[b]
Foreign exchange reserves (US$, billion)	132.9[b]	233.8[b]
Foreign debt (US$, billion)	34.3[a]	170.1[b]
Global growth competitiveness[a] (X/Y)	7th / 75[c]	39th / 75[c]
Investment climate	5th / 50[d]	21st / 50[d]

[a]From People's Republic of China statistics (http://www.gio.gov.tw/taiwan-website/5-ge/yearbook/chpt06.htm)
[b]From People's Republic of China statistics.
[c]From World Economic Forum.
[d]From Business environment risk intelligence (BERI).

ibility enhances their people-management capabilities and facilitates their international competition with lower cost structures (Tsang, 1999). This value shows in their attitude toward social stature, and they "accept upward mobility as a result of one's talent and capability" (Tsang, 1999, p. 10).

"Manufacturing has long been Taiwan's strong suit, and it still is. The country's workforce is well trained and well educated, which lends itself to [explain why there is] the surge in information-technology companies that are locating there" (Orton, 2001, p. 64). "Taiwan today has the most broadly based computer industry in Asia outside of Japan" (Ernst, 2000, p. 223). It is a world leader in information technology industries behind only the United States and Japan (Yoshida, 2001). Taiwan's other leading industries include the manufacture of precision machinery and specialty chemicals (Yoshida, 2001).

Chinese do business "the Chinese way," according to successful traditional practices, even when they are educated abroad. This system originates in the history of Chinese society, having been guided by the general principle of Confucian virtue (Hofstede, 1993). Chinese business outside of Mainland China has created a collective gross national product (GNP) of $200 to 300 billion (Hofstede, 1993). "There is no denying that it [the Chinese way,] works" (Hofstede, 1993, p. 86).

Taiwan has integrated into the world economy and sought to become better integrated into world organizations, such as the World Trade Organization (WTO) and the United Nations (UN), to enhance its prestige and better defend its economy (Ferdinand, 1996). Taiwan secured membership in the WTO on November 11, 2001 (Lin, 2001). Taiwan plans to join the UN in the future.

Gateway to China and Southeast Asia

Taiwanese, being Chinese, have a network of overseas Chinese (Chinese people who are in countries outside mainland China) in East Asia. This has facilitated access for their business in Southeast Asia and Mainland China. Entry into these two markets provides huge opportunities. Because access to these two markets currently benefits Taiwanese businesses, many foreign multinational corporations (MNCs) want to use Taiwan as a gateway or regional operations center to service the PRC (People's Republic of China) market (Maguire, 1998) in Southeast Asia, which will be the biggest market in the future.

China's huge development and infrastructure needs can provide enormous export and investment opportunities for U.S. companies (Weidenbaum, 2000). Taiwanese (and Chinese communities elsewhere) offer the money and managerial skills that have been essential to the economic success of China, especially in moving toward a modern capitalist economy (Weidenbaum, 2000). Taiwanese companies have been so successful in Mainland China that Taiwan is becoming the interface between China and those foreign businesses that want to manufacture in China but lack the expertise or infrastructure (Norman, 2001). "[Taiwanese businesses] can provide contacts and strategic advice that may greatly facilitate the entrance of Western companies into the PRC" (Weisert, 2001, p. 73). Taiwanese companies accounted for nearly two-thirds of China's IT [Information Technology] exports in 2001 (Norman, 2001).

Taiwan provides China entrepreneurial and business skills enhanced by substantial flows of capital–more than $40 billion to date (Weidenbaum, 2000). Michael Ding, President of International Investment Trust, one of Taiwan's largest fund-management companies, said that this direct link would help companies cut down costs and help them participate in China's growth (Pao, 2001). The Taiwanese businessperson recognizes that China is where the future lies. The businessperson needs the economic resources that Mainland China can offer–cheap land, labor, and a vast potential market (Pao, 2001).

"Taiwan's geographical location makes it a natural springboard for Southeast Asia and for most market destinations in the western Pacific Rim. Most of Southeast Asia is no more than four or five hours by air from Taipei" (Orton, 2001, p. 64). Almost all Asian countries' cultures are influenced by Chinese culture and they are "deeply rooted in Confucianism" (Beschorner, Lang, and Russ, 2001, p. 85). Countries such as Korea, Japan, Vietnam, and Singapore have been influenced by the Chinese culture for thousands of years and by the Confucian values associated with growing economies (Bond, 1989).

Management Implications in Asia Regarding Knowledge Workers

There are several things that managers can do to recognize and support workers' needs for personal growth. They should ensure that communication is open and free, encourage and reward knowledge sharing, encourage better communication between workers, and change their leadership style from bureaucratic to collegial and supportive. Managers should encourage learning from mistakes more so than punishing errors, and they should reward risk-taking and initiative. They should build on extensive social, professional, personal, and community networks that are already in place in Asian culture (Anderson Consulting/EIU Report, 1998, pp. 63–66).

In addition, they should encourage investments in KM, including the following: investment in infrastructure to support, capture, and leverage the knowledge of individuals and teams; allow KM systems to evolve; and, adapt the KM systems to the constantly changing needs of the knowledge worker and content of knowledge work. (The above trends and implications for KM in Asia add to previous discussions regarding the understanding of KM in the international arena. For a more detailed explanation, refer to the report drafted by the Economist Intelligence Unit [EIU] and Anderson Consulting [1998].)

The Asian Challenge

According to a number of sources (EIU, CSPAN news reports), knowledge workers are a growing proportion of workers in Asia. Many technology jobs are being exported to Asia.

> Companies are now realizing that their knowledge workers are the key to growth through innovation and constant adaptability. Successful change lies squarely in the hands of managers–it is their job to foster the high trust and commitment needed to establish and maintain flexibility. Those visionary enough to adapt and evolve will emerge as the growth engines of an Asian recovery (EIU Report, 1998, p. 67).

Taiwan is Now a Knowledge-Based Economy

The technology for manufacturing brought by foreign business to Taiwan has been critical to its economic progress, and Taiwanese business has been excellent in absorbing, adopting, and innovating the foreign technologies (Simon, 1991). This is one way Taiwan increases knowledge resources as a country. Not only does Taiwan "see a technology-dominated future for itself, [but it also pushes] new programs and reforms to ensure its continued success in the global knowledge-based economy" (Yoshida, 2001, p. 5).

In August 2000, the Taiwanese cabinet adopted a plan that identified major issues associated with the global knowledge-based economy for developing new strategies and programs. "The plan represented another step forward for Taiwan in strengthening its science and technology" (Yoshida, 2001, p. 5). The plan continues with its objectives being to develop the following:

- An innovation mechanism to support venture enterprises
- Internet application infrastructure
- Application of information and communication technologies to daily life
- Workforce and training programs
- Customer- and service-oriented government
- Reduced social and economic costs

Additionally, "the government has declared a set of clear goals: developing Taiwan as a 'green [environmentally safe] silicon island,' establishing a technology research and development center, and getting high-tech companies to keep their roots in Taiwan" (Commercial Times, 2001). In fact, "the government will encourage national R & D expenditures to reach 3% of the GDP in 6 years, making Taiwan the ideal Asian base for research, development, and innovation," turning Taiwan into a "green silicon island"(Government Information Office [GIO], Executive Yuan, Taiwan, R.O.C.).

"Challenge 2008" is a Taiwanese government program with funding equivalent to $75 billion intended to increase global competitiveness by introducing professionals, technology, resources, and systems to reinforce the foundations of Taiwan's manufacturing industry so that businesses will be able to maintain their international lead in the highest technology standards, and Taiwan can advance more in core technologies and R & D capabilities.

Several internationally renowned companies have already expressed their interest in setting up R & D centers in Taiwan. According to the Ministry of Economic Affairs (MOEA), many MNCs like Apple, Compaq, Dell, Gateway, Hewlett Packard, IBM, Intel, Microsoft, Motorola, Radio Shack, Solectron, Sony, and Philips are setting up, or are interested in setting up, R & D centers of excellence and they are increasing the purchase of IT products in Taiwan (Asia Times, 2002).

Purpose of the Study

Research on KM in Asia could enhance the understanding of local and regional cultures. Moreover, all stakeholders (i.e., scholars, executives, policy makers, and students) should share cultural information "to reduce the uncertainty and fear of the unknown" in international markets (Davis and Schulte, 1997, p. xxiii). This study explores the state of KM practices in Taiwan compared with those in the United States.

Review of Data Collection Methodology

Questionnaires were distributed through mail and by personal delivery. Both distribution methods were effective. The sample included knowledge workers in businesses, educational institutions, public enterprises, and other organizations.

Survey Response Analysis

Some responses were incomplete and could not be used in this study. The usable response rate was around 41%. The rate of usable surveys from Taiwan is 9.7%, higher than the rate from the United States. Responses are summarized in Table 6-3.

Table 6-3

Survey Responses Summary			
Category	Taiwan	United States	Total
Total surveys sent	700	800	1500
Total surveys returned	409	398	807
Response rate	0.58	0.495	0.538
Total usable response	327	296	623
Rate of usable surveys	0.467	0.37	0.415

Figure 6-1

Percentage of responses by country.

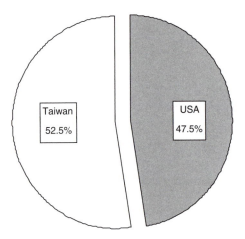

Frequencies of Respondents of Entire Sample

Demographics used in this study to help control for variables other than national culture (country) included size of firm, type of firm, and focus of firm. As shown in Figure 6-1, the percentage of responses from U.S. and Taiwan knowledge workers was not significantly different (47.5% from the United States versus 52.5% from Taiwan).

Percent of Responses by Size

As shown in Figure 6-2, the distribution percentage of the number of responses among different organizational sizes had an interesting U-shaped pattern, with the smallest size organizations (range, 5–500 employees) and the largest size organizations (10,000 employees or more) sharing 62.8% of the total responses. Medium-sized companies of 501 to 1,000, 1,001 to 5,000, and 5,001 to 9,999 employees had response percentages of 12.2%, 15.7%, and 9.3%, respectively.

Figure 6-2

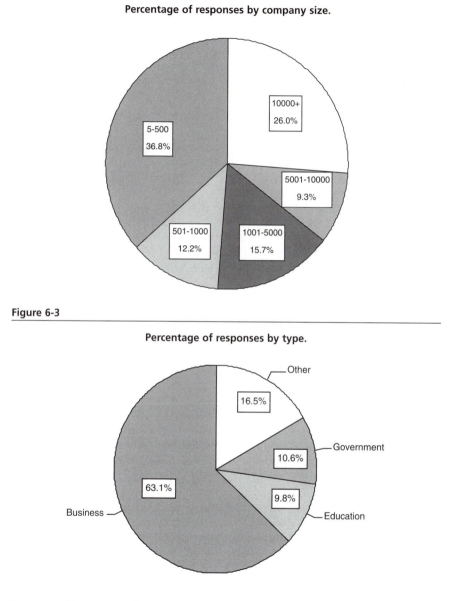

Percentage of responses by company size.

Figure 6-3

Percentage of responses by type.

Percent of Responses by Type

As shown in Figure 6-3, most (63.1%) of the responses were from businesses. The remaining responses were 9.8% for education, 10.6% for government, and 16.5% for others. The "other" category included librarians, political party research center research associates, physicians, nurses, pharmacists, and programmers who chose this category to describe their organizations. Either their organization fit more than one or none of the category options provided.

Figure 6-4

Percentage of responses by focus.

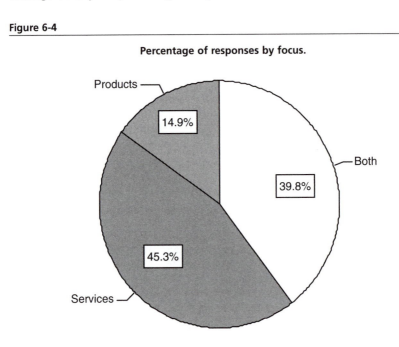

Percent of Responses by Focus

As shown in Figure 6-4, 85.1% of the responses were from service-focused organizations or organizations that focused on products and services. Product-focused organizations made up only 14.9% of the responses.

Frequencies of Knowledge Management Practice Variables

This section summarizes the responses to the items used to measure KM practices in enterprise. The items were measured on a five-point Likert scale ranging from 5 ("strongly agree") to 1 ("strongly disagree"). Table 6-4 provides a summary of the items from the survey regarding KM practices in their enterprise.

Summary of Survey Results

The previous section of this chapter reviewed the data collection methods, response rates, and frequency of variables from all usable responses from the entire sample, including U.S. and Taiwanese knowledge workers. The response rate was very high (over 41%). In addition, the distribution was balanced between U.S. (47.5%) and Taiwan (52.5%) respondents. Most of the responses were from small (36.8%) and very large (26.0%) businesses (63%) that focused on either service (45.3%) or service and products (39.8%).

Implications for U.S. Knowledge Management Vendors, Consultants, and Educators

KM vendors, consultants, and educators from the United States who plan to work in Taiwan need to be aware of the effects of national culture on the following KM practices. These practices measure the state of readiness for KM solutions in Taiwanese organizations. In general, Taiwanese organizations have a higher readiness

Table 6-4

Knowledge Management Practices Variables
KM Practices in my Enterprise
1. The organizational benefits of a knowledge-centric organization are clearly understood by everyone in our organization.
2. KM is a top priority in our organization.
3. Our organization has a clear and strong commitment to KM initiatives from senior management.
4. Our organization has sufficient financial resources to support KM initiatives.
5. Our organizational culture encourages knowledge sharing.
6. People in our organization have the time to share information.
7. Teamwork is a critical component of our organization's culture, structure, and processes.
8. Our organizational strategies, structures, policies, procedures, processes, and reward systems focus on long-term growth.
9. Our organization has evolved from a rigid hierarchical structure to a process-oriented structure.
10. Our organization has invested in effective KM technologies (i.e., Intranet, databases, email, and digital libraries).
11. Our organization has the human resources to support our information technology systems, software, and network.
12. People in our organization are often rewarded for continuous learning or knowledge sharing.
KM, knowledge management.

for KM than those in the United States. This is a factor of the Asian culture. KM practitioners can find this research encouraging for expansion of their products and services into Taiwan. The KM practices that are significantly higher in Taiwan than in the U.S. are listed in descending order in Table 6-5.

This section provides a summary of implications for U.S. KM vendors, consultants, and educators who are expanding their operations into Taiwan. Implications for each of the KM practices for U.S. managers working in Taiwanese organizations are discussed. Bar charts of the relative means for each variable comparing U.S. and Taiwanese respondents are included in the appendix at the end of this chapter.

Our Organization has Invested in Effective Knowledge Management Technologies

There is an old Chinese saying that good beginnings make good endings. It is important when promoting a KM program to make sure the KM technologies are in place and available for the employees to use as soon as is feasible. Managers in Taiwan should focus on investing in effective KM technologies to collect, store, analyze, distribute, and share information to network Taiwanese employees together. Even the simplest technology, e-mail, can enhance the flow of knowledge among workers. Other technologies should include database systems and information retrieval systems for the

Table 6-5

Rank	Rankings of Knowledge Management Practices Affected by National Culture
	KM Practices Implemented More Frequently Taiwan than in the United States.
1	Our organization has invested in effective KM technologies (i.e., Intranet, databases, email, and digital libraries).
2	Our organization has the human resources to support our information technology systems, software, and network.
3	Our organizational culture encourages knowledge sharing.
4	Our organizational strategies, structures, policies, procedures, processes, and reward systems focus on long-term growth.
5	Our organization has a clear and strong commitment to KM initiatives from senior management.
6	Our organization has sufficient financial resources to support KM initiatives.
7	People in our organization are often rewarded for continuous learning or knowledge sharing.
8	Our organization has evolved from a rigid hierarchical structure to a process-oriented structure.
9	People in our organization have the time to share information.
10	The organizational benefits of a knowledge-centric organization are clearly understood by everyone in our organization.
11	KM is a top priority in our organization.
KM, knowledge management.	

knowledge repository, digital library systems, corporate yellow page systems to find who knows what, and Web-based Intranet and Internet KM systems that are available for all employees to use for communication and e-learning. The infrastructure has to be ready and functioning for the users to begin working on it. Hardware and software systems alone cannot make the KM miracle happen, but it is a necessary investment for Taiwanese workers to be productive.

Our Organization has the Human Resources to Support Our Information Technology Systems, Software, and Network

Taiwanese employees are the source of knowledge capital for the business. In recruitment of Taiwanese knowledge workers, the person's personality, experience, and knowledge should fit the job, team, project, and the company systems.

Our Organizational Culture Encourages Knowledge Sharing

Taiwanese knowledge workers tend to share ideas, but only if they are encouraged to communicate. Taiwanese managers should focus on building up the practice of knowledge sharing among employees. By promoting knowledge sharing throughout the organization of the purpose, goals, and mission to be achieved, management embraces the employees with an atmosphere of knowledge sharing. Sharing should become a standard activity, not just a one-time thing or for a short-term project. Once started, sharing in the community will grow and increase productivity of the organization's knowledge workers. Taiwanese management should clearly explain and demonstrate that knowledge sharing will benefit all the employees with improved effectiveness, efficiency, productivity, increased knowledge assets, and profits. Taiwanese, like most Asians, embrace knowledge sharing among their group members if encouraged by management. This philosophy of sharing is part of the Asian culture and mindset.

Our Organizational Strategies, Structures, Policies, Procedures, Processes, and Reward Systems are Focused on Long-Term Growth

Managers should communicate an emphasis on long-term growth focused on learning strategies. Although the learning strategy may seem to be only a small part of the KM system, it is a critical component of the system. All the parts in the system should be balanced and align with the business's long-term growth. Taiwanese knowledge workers have a long-term philosophy toward work and life. It is part of their culture.

Our Organization has a Clear and Strong Commitment to Knowledge Management Initiatives from Senior Management

Management in Taiwan, whether at the top or the bottom, should emphasize the importance of KM and should become committed to it. Convincing leaders to promote KM initiatives will help them lead the whole company toward successful KM.

Our Organization has Sufficient Financial Resources to Support Knowledge Management Initiatives

A sufficient portion of the organization's budget should be allocated to supporting KM initiatives. Taiwanese knowledge workers believe their organizations have sufficient funds to support KM. The funds should be used to set up the hardware and software infrastructures, reward systems, maintenance, and promotion of the KM programs.

People in Our Organization are Often Rewarded for Continuous Learning or Knowledge Sharing

Taiwanese managers should customize their reward systems to motivate the employees through learning and knowledge sharing. Nonfinancial rewards would work well in Taiwanese organizations. Examples of these rewards include promotion and recognition that add to Taiwanese worker self-esteem. The reward system should be realistic with benefits tied to achievable goals and would appeal to the broad base of employees. These systems would gain the attention of Taiwanese workers and encourage them to collaborate, hand in hand, shoulder to shoulder. Nonmonetary rewards for learning and knowledge sharing can be more successful in Taiwan than in U.S. organizations. The sense of team and self-satisfaction is part of the motivation in Taiwanese culture.

Our Organization has Evolved from a Rigid Hierarchical Structure to a Process-Oriented Structure

By focusing on the workflow or processes, Taiwanese managers can reinvent the ways of doing things to increase output for the effort required. Taiwanese workers have stated that their organizations are moving toward a process-oriented structure. Organizations in Taiwan are responding faster to changes in effective organizational structures to support KM than are U.S. firms. International managers should be aware of this trend and support these changes in Taiwanese firms.

People in Our Organization have the Time to Share Information

Traditionally, coffee breaks, cigarette breaks, and water fountain chats were the main source of tacit knowledge exchange in Taiwan, as well as in most cultures. Managers should provide time for Taiwanese workers to share as part of their job. They should formalize a time to share (such as story telling) so the workers do not worry about being reprimanded by supervisors. Sharing should be part of the job. This policy should improve productivity, and Taiwanese workers would respond positively to it as well.

The Organizational Benefits of a Knowledge-Centric Organization are Clearly Understood by Everyone in Our Organization

Managers working in Taiwan should deliver an internal communications campaign to educate workers about how KM is beneficial to both them and the organization. They can promote the guidelines of the knowledge-centered organization using media like posters, brochures, CDs, and multimedia programs.

Knowledge Management is a Priority in Our Organization

The trait *KM is a top priority in our organization* shows that KM is prioritized in Taiwanese organizations. This is a strong enabler. It should be seen as a high priority for all employees to pursue for the benefit of the group. The collectivist mindset of Taiwanese workers provides strong cultural support to overcome the "what's-in-it-for-me" barrier to KM found in many U.S. organizations.

Summary of Implications

The main theme of KM practices is learning and the need to keep developing the workforce manpower and brainpower from the top of the company to the bottom. Therefore, managers who want to do business in Taiwan need to start education programs for employees to increase their knowledge and skills. Top management should show their enthusiasm by developing various kinds of education programs, depending on the needs of different departments. They should choose a KM media that would be most effective. In Taiwan, when the leaders lead, the followers follow. The learning process is developed by input from the employees and the business' education programs. By focusing the education programs on developing a competitive advantage around the core competencies of the business, management can form an environment that will support growth and success.

The KM technology infrastructure is the backbone of any KM program. It must be ready and available for everyone to use at the right time in the right place, and it must provide direction toward the right answer. Not only does it speed up the process of finding solutions, it also enables the workers to digest and integrate what is inside the knowledge base of the organization. Key KM technologies include the database for the repository of essential tacit and explicit knowledge, search engines, and data-mining tools. Sharing knowledge and exchange of information is part of Taiwanese culture and is a strong advantage over U.S. organizations.

With this cultural foundation, a knowledge transfer system can be established easily. With a normally accepted KM system, the implementation of a KM program can improve internal administrative processes, enhance innovation, and enable creativity in Taiwanese organizations. This cultural phenomenon provides strong encouragement for KM technology vendors who may find a receptive client who understands the value of sharing knowledge. It should be easier to sell these KM technologies in Taiwan than in the U.S. because of the differences in national culture. In addition, consultants and educators who want to provide services to Taiwanese organizations may also find less resistance from Taiwanese decision-makers than from those in the United States.

Additional evidence and case studies for these recommendations of international firms and entrepreneurs who are doing business in Taiwan should be investigated to enhance the findings and implications of this study. In conclusion, such work needs to be conducted to fully understand the impact of national culture on KM in many different markets and economies around the world.

Appendix

Means of KM Variables for Taiwan and the U.S.

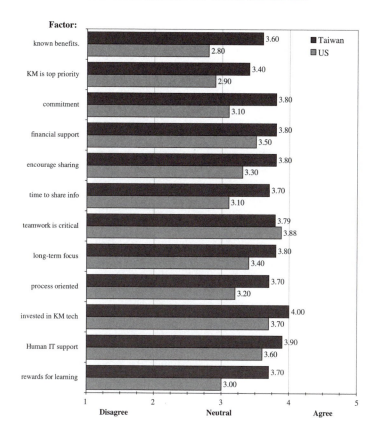

Relationship between Knowledge Management Technologies and Learning Actions of Global Organizations

7

Juan Pablo Giraldo, D.Sc.

Organizations as they grow are continuously facing more complex and dynamic global markets. Traditional approaches to gain competitive advantage and sustain growth are narrow and limited. These strategies usually formulate plans based on linear models that do not address complexity and dynamic workplaces.

This chapter presents findings from my dissertation research. First, it incorporates a validated model that approaches organizations as complex social systems. The main characteristic is that organizational effectiveness is seen as not only a work/performance action, but also a combination of performance and learning actions.

Second, it develops a framework that identifies knowledge management (KM) technologies as a mixture of events that balance technologies, flow of knowledge, context of knowledge, and critical actions that support technology investments.

Sixty-two subjects from 21 organizations participated in this correlational research. Correlations were established between (a) KM technologies and learning actions conducted to adapt an organization to its external and internal environment; (b) KM technologies and learning actions conducted to attain specific goals; (c) KM technologies and learning actions conducted to integrate knowledge and information within an organization; and (d) KM technologies and learning actions conducted to maintain and reinforce organizational culture.

Introduction

This chapter presents a summary of my doctoral dissertation research, which studied the relationship between technologies for knowledge management (KM) and learning actions of global organizations. This research provides a validated framework that aids the decision-making process by providing a clear structure and identifying technology as a mixture of events that balance flow of knowledge, context of knowledge, and critical actions that support technology investments.

This research broadens the perspective of systems engineers and engineer managers by providing an alternative approach to their traditional views. This alternative approach was developed by practitioners in the field of human and organizational development. The main characteristic is that organizational effectiveness is seen as a work/performance action and a combination of performance and learning actions.

This study supports other researchers in refining and modifying their perspectives to maximize knowledge and insight in the evolving field of knowledge and innovation management. This field is still deficient in theories, models, and tools.

Research Framework

Scope of Technologies for Knowledge Management for Global Organizations

Leadership, organization, technology, and learning are the four key pillars that define a framework (Figure 7-1) for KM (Calabrese, 2000). In this section, I will decompose the technology pillar and define the scope of technologies for KM (TKMs). This scope is defined as a mixture of events that balance technologies, flow of knowledge, context of knowledge, and critical actions that support technology investments (Figure 7-2).

Knowledge Management Technologies

The first level of decomposition focuses on KM technologies. For that purpose, it is necessary to identify actions that define the flow of knowledge within an organization,

Figure 7-1

Framework of elements defining enterprise knowledge management. (From Stankosky, Calabrese, Baldanza. 2000).

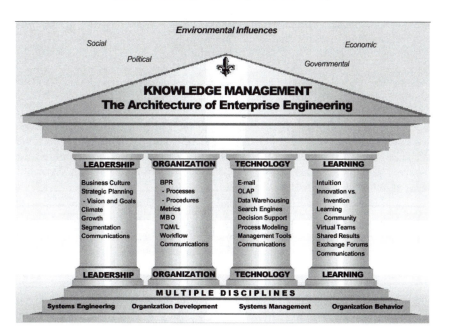

Figure 7-2

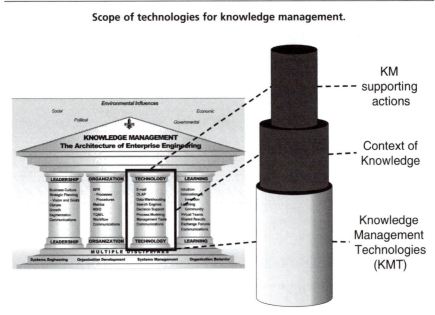

Scope of technologies for knowledge management.

and the flow of knowledge outside the boundaries of an organization. Most of the approaches (Ruggles, 1997; Liebowitz and Wilcox, 1997; Marquardt and Kearsley, 1999) involve the following stages: (a) generation/creation/acquisition, which is summarized as *identification* of knowledge; (b) *validation* of knowledge; (c) *codification* of knowledge; (d) analysis and mining, which is summarized as *storage* of knowledge; and (e) transfer/sharing/dissemination, which is summarized as *retrieving and sharing* knowledge. Figure 7-3 displays the five actions that define the flow of knowledge.

Knowledge flow is supported by six key objectives. Marquardt and Kearsley (1999) presented a list of objectives that define a purpose for the flow of knowledge. They are "knowing what, "knowing how," "knowing where," "knowing when," "knowing who," "knowing why," and the last one expanded to "caring why," also known as "self-motivated creativity" by Quinn et al. (1998). Figure 7-4 depicts these objectives.

The final piece of this level of decomposition is to list technologies for global organizations. Many authors have described the different roles of technology. The following list summarizes the roles:

- Maintaining and keeping track of operational data of global transactions
- Analyzing the global environment
- Supporting the decision-making process of global decisions
- Enhancing collaboration and group decision making among global players

In summary, Figure 7-5 presents the list of 15 KM technologies for global organizations. The technologies are organized around five actions to accomplish six major objectives (knowing what, knowing how, knowing where, knowing when, knowing who, and knowing why).

Figure 7-3

Five actions that define the flow of knowledge.

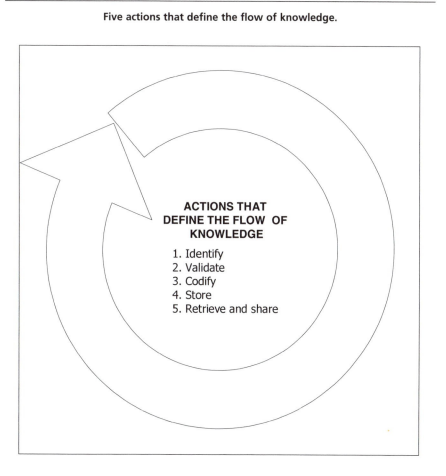

Many authors, like Anand et al. (1998), Matusik and Hill (1998), Cross and Israelit (2000), and Lesser et al. (2000) have introduced two main variables that define the context of knowledge. These two dimensions are (a) communities of practice and (b) organizational settings and define the second level of decomposition for the research model. This model helps practitioners to understand the scope of TKMs.

Communities of practice represent a group of practitioners that share a common interest. Suppliers, partners, clients, and so forth usually define the external communities of practice. Employees, consultants, and so forth define internal communities of practice. Organizational settings define how the flow of knowledge happens within an organization. There are two types of settings—formal and informal. Formal settings are represented by meetings, training sessions, policy briefings, and so forth. Informal settings are characterized by conversations, chats, and coffee hours. Figure 7-6 shows the context of knowledge, which can be defined as dynamic interactions between internal and external communities of practice in formal and informal settings.

Context of Knowledge

Figure 7-4

Variables that define the scope of technologies for knowledge management.

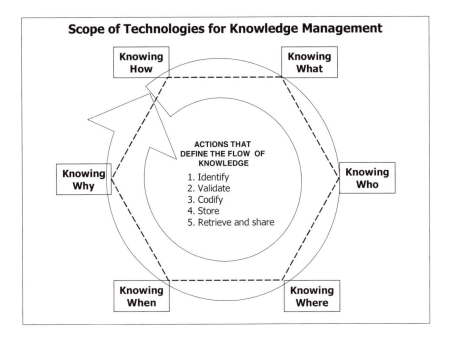

Figure 7-5

Fifteen knowledge management technologies for global organizations.

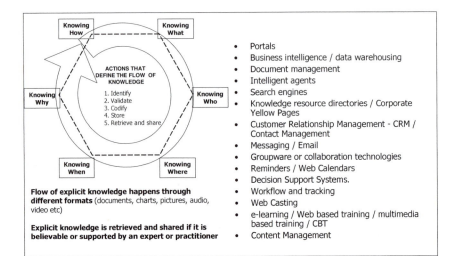

Figure 7-6

Variables that define the context of knowledge.

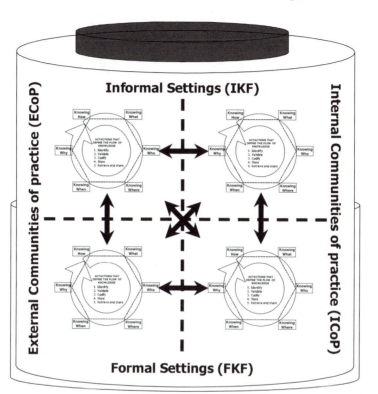

Critical Actions That Support Technology Investments in Global Organizations

More than a decade ago, authors like Bradley (1993) and Clemons (1993) emphasized the need to identify critical actions that support technology investments for global organizations. The following list summarizes the main four topics that have been stressed over the years by many authors:

- KM technologies are linked to corporate strategy.
- TKMs are supported by leaders/champions within the organization.
- Organizations have personnel who are responsible for coaching and mentoring employees on the use of these technologies.
- Organizations provide incentives (recognition, awards, monetary rewards, etc.) to use these technologies.

Global Organizations as Complex and Social Systems

The theory of action by Parsons, which is described in Bluth (1982), presents a list of functions or needs that had to be met if the organizations were to survive and be effective. The most critical is to see and understand organizations as social systems. In Parsonian theory, social action in organizations is "all human behavior motivated and directed by the meanings which the actor discerns in the external world." Croswell (1996) referenced previous research and the relevance to bifurcate organizations into "hard" and "soft" systems images. "Hard" systems thinking image characterizes organizations classically as optimizing through the instrumental, purposeful actions of problem solving and "goal-seeking." The complimentary view of "soft" systems thinking characterizes organizations in the image of learning through communicative, expressive actions to finally characterize organizations as living, human, social systems. According to Parsons, all human behavior in social systems included biologic, psychologic, sociologic, and anthropologic behaviors.

Organizational Learning and Organizations as Dynamic Social Systems

The concept of organizational learning or learning organizations has been evolving for more than two decades (Daft and Weick, 1984; Fiol et al., 1985, Senge, 1990; Schwandt, 1994; Argyris, 1996; Garvin, 1998). Schwandt's (1996) approach provides a counter argument to present strategic management practices that deal *only with performance* change that demands all organizations activities "add value" to their end products, as opposed to *through performance and collective learning.* He focuses on explaining an alternate explanation of change by thinking of organizations as *dynamic social systems* being formed, reformed, and consuming energy in states of punctuated equilibrium, with periodic movements between order and disorder.

Schwandt defines the collective (organization) as an amalgamation of actors, objects, and norms. This is characterized by social phenomena that are more than the sum of individual behaviors and attitudes of the individual actors. The use of the term *dynamic* refers to the social system's patterns of continuous change or growth characterized by complex relationships among actors and between actors and their environment. Schwandt's model is described in detail by two operational systems. The first one is a learning system; the second one is a performing system.

The Learning System

The learning system is represented by four components of subsystems, which interdependently create a system of social action. *The four learning subsystems do not function independently—they are nonlinear and interdependent.* Each subsystem is responsible for carrying out vital functions for the organizational learning system to adapt to its environment. They are (a) environmental interface, (b) action/reflection, (c) dissemination and diffusion, and (d) memory and meaning, which are depicted in Figure 7-7. Each subsystem maintains a critical dependency on each of the other subsystems for process inputs. In other words, the output function of one subsystem becomes an input for each of the other subsystems.

Each of these interdependent relationships among the subsystems is maintained through sets of "interchange media." They form *concrete patterns and invisible networks* that link the learning subsystems. The four interchange media corresponding subsystems are *new information* (product of the environmental interface subsystem), *goal referenced knowledge* (product of the action-reflection subsystem), *structuring* (product of the dissemination and diffusion subsystem), and *sense making* (product of the memory-meaning subsystem). The media are complex patterns made up of organizational variables traditionally used in singular cause-effect relationships. Interdependence of all the learning subsystems is depicted in Figure 7-8.

Figure 7-7

Model of organizational learning. (From Schwandt, 1996.)

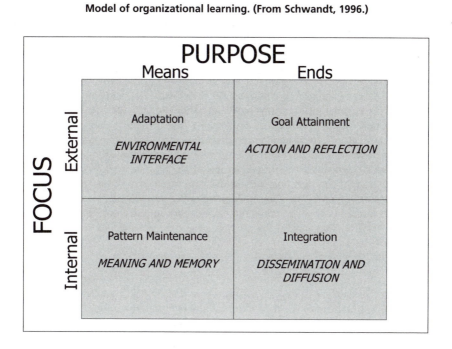

Figure 7-8

Media of interchange for the learning subsystems. (From Schwandt, 1996.)

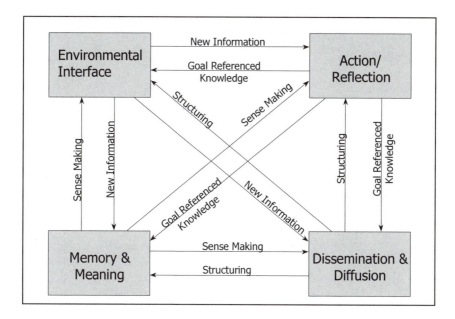

The Performing System

The performing system is represented as well by four components of subsystems. The *four performing subsystems do not function independently—they are nonlinear and interdependent.* The four subsystems are (a) acquisition of resources, (b) production/service, (c) management and control, and (d) reinforcement. They are depicted in Figure 7-9.

This subsystem provides the organizational performance system with the pattern maintenance/latency function. It comprises those elements that contribute to the maintenance and management of tensions regarding the standards, norms, and values that the organization uses to reinforce the organization's performance. Similar to learning systems, each of these interdependent relationships among the subsystems are maintained through sets of "interchange media." The media are complex patterns made up of organizational variables traditionally used in singular cause-effect relationships. Each subsystem in the performing subsystem maintains a critical dependency on each of the other subsystems for process inputs, where the output function of one subsystem becomes an input for each of the other subsystems. Interdependence of all the performing subsystems is depicted in Figure 7-10.

Learning and Performing Actions

The learning and performing subsystems suggest four dependent variables to measure growth/effectiveness of global organizations. They are (a) actions conducted to adapt a global organization to their external and internal environments; (b) actions conducted to attain specific production goals in a global organization; (c) actions conducted to maintain and reinforce organizational culture within a global organization; and (d) actions conducted to integrate knowledge and information within a global organization.

Figure 7-9

The model of organizational performance. (From Johnson, 2000.)

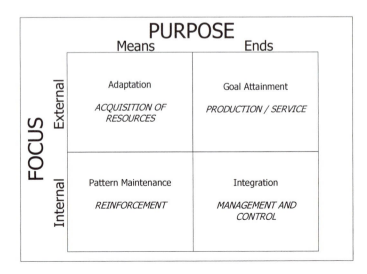

Figure 7-10

Media of interchange for the performing subsystems. (From Johnson, 2000.)

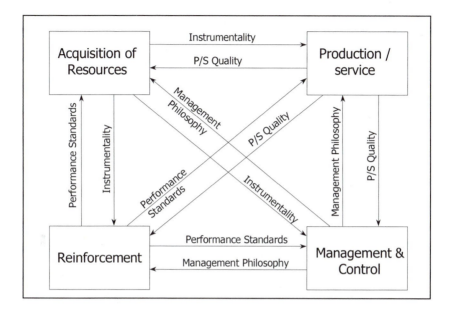

Table 7-1

Attributes and Infrastructures of a Global Organization	
Attributes	**Infrastructures**
• Shared global vision	• Core competencies and expertise
• Measurement	• Shared knowledge and databases
• Local-global balancing	• Human assets, resource allocation
• Information technology	• Project tasking and team assignment
• Understanding global customers	• Performance measurement
• Alliance partners or alliance strategy	• Information and telecommunication

Research Methodology, Questions, and Hypotheses

The type of research conducted in this study was "correlational research." Subjects were selected from a population of global organizations that matched attributes and infrastructures found in the literature review. Table 7-1 summarizes these attributes. The research cycle comprises four phases: (a) selection of global organizations to match attributes from Table 7-1; (b) inviting subjects from selected organizations to participate in the research; (c) completing survey after obtaining informed consent from participants; and (d) data analysis.

Research Instrument

The measuring instrument that was developed for this research was divided into four components—a brief introduction and three sections. The first section captured the organizational profile and the respondent profile. The second section measured the independent variable (KM technologies, flow of knowledge, context of knowledge, and supporting activities for KM technologies). The third section measured the dependent variable (organizational effectiveness through actions toward performance and learning).

Reliability of the Instrument

SPSS 9.0 (SPSS, Inc. Chicago IL) was the statistical software used in this research to compute the reliability of the instrument. A Chronbach alpha (γ) coefficient was computed to provide a model of internal consistency based on the average interitem correlation. Using the data collected and the items selected for the final survey instrument, the reliability of measures based on internal consistency was performed on the six main operational independent variables. The results for the independent variables are as follows: Technologies for Knowledge Management (TKM) $\gamma = 0.86$, external communities of practice (EcoP) $\gamma = 0.93$, internal communities of practice (IcoP) $\gamma = 0.93$, Flow of knowledge in informal settings (IKF) $\gamma = 0.94$ and flow of knowledge in formal settings (FKF) $\gamma = 0.94$. The third section of the instrument was already reliable. Johnson (2000), in his doctoral dissertation, obtained the following alpha coefficients Environmental Interface (AL) $\gamma = 0.78$, Acquisition of Resources (AP) $\gamma = 0.62$, Action Reflection (GL) $\gamma = 0.64$, Production/Service (GP) $\gamma = 0.76$, Dissemination and Diffusion (IL) $\gamma = 0.81$, Management and Control (IP) $\gamma = 0.76$, Meaning and Memory (PML) $\gamma = 0.74$, Reinforcement (PMP) $\gamma = 0.71$.

Research Questions and Operational Hypotheses

Main research questions were divided into the following four questions:

1. Is there any correlation between TKMs, flow of knowledge, context of knowledge, and supporting activities for KM and actions conducted to adapt a global organization to their external and internal environments?
2. Is there any correlation between TKMs, flow of knowledge, context of knowledge, and supporting activities for KM and actions conducted to attain specific production goals in a global organization?
3. Is there any correlation between TKMs, flow of knowledge, context of knowledge, and supporting activities for KM and actions conducted to maintain and reinforce organizational culture within a global organization?
4. Is there any correlation between TKMs, flow of knowledge, context of knowledge, and supporting activities for KM and actions conducted to integrate knowledge and information within a global organization?

To answer the previous four questions, 34 operational hypotheses were derived on the basis of combinations among operational variables. Figure 7-11 depicts the operational scope.

Research Findings

Sixty-two subjects from 21 organizations participated in this correlational research (Figure 7-12). Sixteen operational hypotheses were accepted. In summary, findings

Figure 7-11

Operational hypotheses derived to answer research questions.

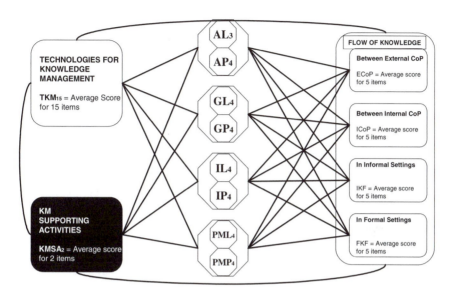

Figure 7-12

Distribution of subjects by organization.

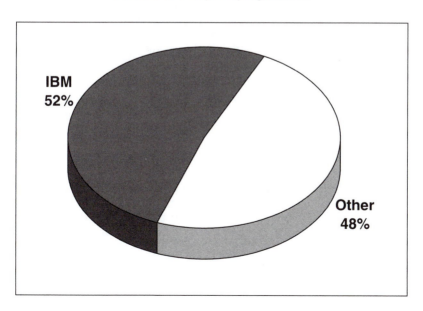

Figure 7-13

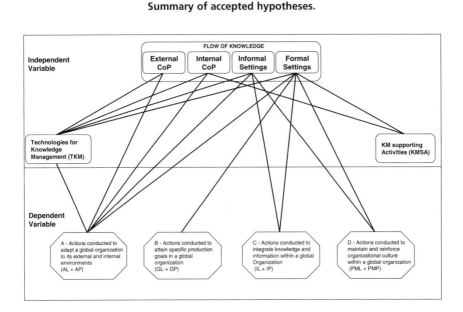

Summary of accepted hypotheses.

indicate that there are correlations (Table 7-2) established between (a) KM technologies and learning actions conducted to adapt an organization to its external and internal environment; (b) KM technologies and learning actions conducted to attain specific goals; (c) KM technologies and learning actions conducted to integrate knowledge and information within an organization; and (d) KM technologies and learning actions conducted to maintain and reinforce organizational culture. Figure 7-13 and Table 7-3 present a summary of the 16 operational hypotheses that were accepted.

Future Research

Low usage of KM technologies in informal settings (IKF) and high correlation with learning and performing actions suggest that future research should strengthen the spectrum of technologies and methodologies for IKF. For instance, developing models and methodologies that combine technologies for informal settings, and performing and learning actions to manage innovation.

Another topic is to study the adoption of social systems approaches in combination with TKMs to foster and manage the development and sustainability of formal and informal communities of practice.

Using the provided instruments to conduct longitudinal studies for global organizations may help determining patterns and relationships between functional roles, positions, and industries.

Many global organizations are embracing the capability maturity model (CMM) and capability maturity model integration (CMMI). A very relevant topic is to study the effect of the presented framework and approach on the optimizing maturity levels.

Table 7-2

Summary of Correlations Between Independent and Dependent Variables

		TKM	ECOP	ICOP	IKF	FKF	ALP	GLP	PMLP	ILP
TKM	Pearson Correlation	1.000	.493[b]	.531[b]	.412[b]	.551[b]	.516[b]	.123	.325[b]	.230
	Sig. (2-tailed)	.	.000	.000	.001	.000	.000	.342	.010	.072
	N	62	62	62	62	62	62	62	62	62
ECOP	Pearson Correlation	.493[b]	1.000	.401[b]	.355[b]	.390[b]	.432[b]	.174	.253[a]	.115
	Sig. (2-tailed)	.000	.	.001	.005	.002	.000	.177	.047	.375
	N	62	62	62	62	62	62	62	62	62
ICOP	Pearson Correlation	.531[b]	.401[b]	1.000	.325[b]	.587[b]	.395[b]	.306[a]	.309[a]	.291[a]
	Sig. (2-tailed)	.000	.001	.	.010	.000	.001	.016	.015	.022
	N	62	62	62	62	62	62	62	62	62
IKF	Pearson Correlation	.412[b]	.355[b]	.325[b]	1.000	.540[b]	.465[b]	.288[a]	.337[b]	.349[b]
	Sig. (2-tailed)	.001	.005	.010	.	.000	.000	.023	.007	.005
	N	62	62	62	62	62	62	62	62	62
FKF	Pearson Correlation	.551[b]	.390[b]	.587[b]	.540[b]	1.000	.531[b]	.433[b]	.468[b]	.388[b]
	Sig. (2-tailed)	.000	.002	.000	.000	.	.000	.000	.000	.002
	N	62	62	62	62	62	62	62	62	62
ALP	Pearson Correlation	.516[b]	.432[b]	.395[b]	.465[b]	.531[b]	1.000	.623[b]	.665[b]	.664[b]
	Sig. (2-tailed)	.000	.000	.001	.000	.000	.	.000	.000	.000
	N	62	62	62	62	62	62	62	62	62
GLP	Pearson Correlation	.123	.174	.306[a]	.288[a]	.433[b]	.623[b]	1.000	.753[b]	.772[b]
	Sig. (2-tailed)	.342	.177	.016	.023	.000	.000	.	.000	.000
	N	62	62	62	62	62	62	62	62	62
PMLP	Pearson Correlation	.325[b]	.253[a]	.309[a]	.337[b]	.468[b]	.665[b]	.753[b]	1.000	.778[b]
	Sig. (2-tailed)	.010	.047	.015	.007	.000	.000	.000	.	.000
	N	62	62	62	62	62	62	62	62	62
ILP	Pearson Correlation	.230	.115	.291[a]	.349[b]	.388[b]	.664[b]	.772[b]	.778[b]	1.000
	Sig. (2-tailed)	.072	.375	.022	.005	.002	.000	.000	.000	.
	N	62	62	62	62	62	62	62	62	62

[a] Correlation is significant at the 0.05 level (2-tailed).
[b] Correlation is significant at the 0.01 level (2-tailed).
ALP, ?; EcoP, external communities of practice; FKF, ?; GLP, ?; ILP, ?; PMLP, ?; Sig, significance.

Table 7-3

	Summary of Accepted Hypotheses
Hypothesis	**Findings**
$H_{a1.1}$	There is a positive correlation between technologies for KM and flow of knowledge between external communities of practice.
$H_{a1.2}$	There is a positive correlation between technologies for KM and flow of knowledge between internal communities of practice.
$H_{a1.3}$	There is a positive correlation between technologies for KM and flow of knowledge in informal settings.
$H_{a1.4}$	There is a positive correlation between technologies for KM and flow of knowledge in formal settings.
$H_{a3.2}$	There is a positive correlation between KM supporting activities and flow of knowledge between internal communities of practice.
$H_{a3.4}$	There is a positive correlation between KM supporting activities and flow of knowledge in formal settings.
H_{a4}	There is a positive correlation between technologies for KM and actions conducted to adapt a global organization to its external and internal environments.
H_{a5}	There is a positive correlation between the flow of knowledge between external communities of practice and actions conducted to adapt a global organization to its external and internal environments.
H_{a6}	There is a positive correlation between the flow of knowledge between internal communities of practice and actions conducted to adapt a global organization to its external and internal environments.
H_{a7}	There is a positive correlation between the flow of knowledge in informal settings and actions conducted to adapt a global organization to its external and internal environments.
H_{a8}	There is a positive correlation between the flow of knowledge in formal settings and actions conducted to adapt a global organization to its external and internal environments.
H_{a14}	There is a positive correlation between the flow of knowledge in formal settings and actions conducted to attain specific goals in a global organization.
H_{a19}	There is a positive correlation between the flow of knowledge in informal settings and actions conducted to integrate knowledge and information within a global organization.
H_{a20}	There is a positive correlation between the flow of knowledge in formal settings and actions conducted to integrate knowledge and information within a global organization.
H_{a25}	There is a positive correlation between the flow of knowledge in informal settings and actions conducted to maintain and reinforce organizational culture within a global organization.
H_{a26}	There is a positive correlation between the flow of knowledge in formal settings and actions conducted to maintain and reinforce organizational culture within a global organization.
KM, knowledge management.	

From Research to Practice: A Practical Point of View

For the last 3 years, I have been applying and promoting the adoption of concepts from this research. In this section, I summarize the most common trends I have seen in the work place.

1. Among all the TKMs, collaboration technologies (TKM$_5$) are the most supported and adopted.
2. Collaboration technologies (TKM$_5$) are widely used in both formal (FKF) and informal (IKF) settings.
3. There is a lack of models and methodologies that guide the use of TKMs for informal settings (IKF).
4. Instant messaging technologies (TKM$_5$) are becoming essential to connect practitioners across organizations, cultures, borders, and time zones.
5. Instant messaging technologies (TKM$_5$) are increasing team cooperation and expertise location (knowing who).
6. Adopters and users of TKMs frequently ignore the need to create incentives and structures that support their deployment. These actions delay the maturity and potential of their teams.
7. Domain-specific knowledge is created when knowledge from subject matter experts (SMEs) is organized through constructs and standards that are familiar to practitioners.
8. Creating and using standards is the most efficient way to identify, validate, codify, and share domain-specific knowledge.
9. There is meaning to practitioners when the knowledge is contextualized (organized around common constructs).
10. Context of knowledge is defined by informal settings (IKF), formal settings (FKF), internal communities of practice (ICoP), and external communities of practice (ECoP). In other words, context of knowledge equals IKF plus FKF plus ICoP plus ECoP.
11. Using graphic standards is one of the most powerful ways to share large volumes of knowledge effectively. Common examples of these graphic standards are information technology architectural artifacts, constructs, models, and so forth.

Key Principle to Remember from this Research

Organizational growth is a mixture of organizational performance and organizational learning. KMTs contribute to organizational growth only if the flow and the context of knowledge are supported.

Leveraging Knowledge Management Technologies to Manage Intellectual Capital

Kevin O'Sullivan, D.Sc.

Introduction

Over the last few years, organizations have invested heavily in knowledge management (KM) initiatives. For most of those organizations, the investment has generally been in the technologic aspects of KM, such as customer relationship management systems, document management systems, and knowledge agents. Although technology is not the only component of KM (it is vital to address the other aspects of KM if a system is to be sustainable in the long run), technology has remained the focus of many KM initiatives.

This chapter discusses the extent to which these technologies are being leveraged to manage intellectual capital. We identify eight main groupings of KM technologies that are examined in the context of the core elements of intellectual capital: human capital, customer capital, and relationship capital. The impact of organizational size on the selection of effective KM technologies is also discussed.

The existence of intellectual capital is being recognized as the foundation of organizational success in the twenty-first century (Wiig, 1997). It has long been recognized that many of the assets of a company—good will, reputation, and patent rights—are intangible. In 1999, Malone and Edvinsson distinguished intellectual capital into two broad categories: *structural capital*, such as business partnerships or customer loyalty and *human capital*, such as employees' key competencies and knowledge. Many variations exist on these broad classifications, such as to separate out those assets protected by law—intellectual property. Intellectual property includes assets such as trademarks, patents, copyrights, and licenses.

Intellectual Capital

The term *intellectual capital* is generally attributed to John Kenneth Galbraith, who coined the term in 1969. Since then, the term has become part of business lexicon. As with any sort of capital, the management of intellectual capital has become essential to many organizations as a source of competitive advantage. Of prime importance to intellectual capital managers is the process of transforming human resources into intellectual assets that can be managed as other assets within the system. Our motivation to manage intellectual capital comes from the inherent value that arises from the process. Identifying a firm's assets, especially its intellectual assets—the proprietary knowledge expressed as a recipe, formula, trade secret, invention, program, or process—has become critical to a company's overall vision and strategic plan, and essential in transactions such as stock offerings or mergers (Sullivan, 2000). In general, those companies that wish to succeed will find it essential to make the best use of their intellectual capital.

Many organizations have established intellectual capital management systems to help them track their intellectual capital. In an information economy environment, intellectual capital becomes a critical metric for determining the economic value of a company. In most companies today, intellectual capital forms the greater part of market value (Ribiere, 2001). This is especially true of service-based organizations, where the use of intellectual capital is essential to the revenue-generating process. With IBM Global Services, the business model is to leverage the intellectual capital of the consultants within the organization, based on superior knowledge of IBM and other product sets.

If intellectual capital is a source of future wealth, embracing an intellectual capital management methodology is essential. By adopting a structured methodology, organizations can measure, and hence manage, intellectual capital. Many methodologies exist and have been implemented successfully, including the Scandia AFS Navigator, a version of the balanced scorecard methodology. The Scandia approach attempts to manage all knowledge that can be converted into value.

For any organization, the definition of intellectual capital and intellectual capital management is essential and to a certain extent, specific to the organization in which the intellectual capital exists. From a broader perspective, one designed to encompass most organizations, intellectual capital management may be defined as the disciplined approach to the identification and productive use of intellectual capital in the creation of economic value in the organization. This includes the management of intellectual assets and artifacts, human capital, and intellectual property. As the definition is broad, it is only useful from a descriptive perspective—in your own organization this definition may be applied, but from the perspective of being useful, the constituent components are to a great extent context specific.

Human Capital

Innovation within an organization originates with the individuals within that organization. By themselves, machines, processes and systems do not innovate, people do. As such, if we consider the factors of human capital, we find that people use knowledge, information, intellectual property, and experience to innovate, leading to the generation of organizational wealth. Environmental factors affecting human capital include the company's values, culture, and philosophy. The reliance on human capital, as opposed to physical capital, to compete in the marketplace, is regarded as a key differentiator of knowledge-intensive firms (Swart, 2003). Bontis (1998) sees the quality of human capital as a source of innovation, and strategic renewal. It includes individual tacit and explicit knowledge (Nelson and Winter, 1982) brought into the organization through its knowledge workers. As part of the human capital management process, it is also important to note that in terms of the supporting innovation, we must also support the individuals that innovate. For example, Capital One has created an integrated Financial Management and Human Resource Management System (HRMS) into a self-service portal, giving employees real-time access to internal procurement, travel, expense, and employee benefit information, accelerating these important internal functions. Another example is DaimlerChrysler, which created a cost-effective method of bringing employees up to speed on its applications. In that case, Web-based training programs reduced the costs of training, overcame employee travel restrictions, and received high end-user marks for usability and effectiveness.

Structural Capital

The objective of structure of any organization is to facilitate that organization in meeting its strategic objectives. From an intellectual capital perspective, that translates into the components that support optimum intellectual performance and therefore, optimum business performance. The term *structural capital* often refers to the hardware, software, databases, organizational structure, patents, trademarks, and everything else of organizational capability that supports employee productivity (Edvinsson and Malone, 1997). Another way to view structural capital is to see it as what remains if one were to remove the knowledge and people from an organization. Another important point about structural capital is that the vast majority of structural capital is explicit; it can and should be owned and managed by the organization. Although this is an apparently obvious statement, it is nonetheless an essential precept in the management of intellectual capital. Because structural capital is explicit, it is the property of the organization. The more intellectual capital that can be transformed into structural capital, the better for the organization—because it is explicit, it is much easier to manage. An example of this "structuralization" is the transformation of product development ideas (human capital) into codified patents that can be legally and physically owned by the firm (Lang, 2001; Williams and Bukowitz, 2001). This process of making the tacit explicit through the use structural capital is one of the main focuses of this chapter, as we investigate the extent to which technology has been implemented to facilitate this transformation.

Two other aspects of intellectual capital include relationship capital and customer capital.

Relationship Capital

Organizations do not operate in a vacuum. On a daily basis, they interoperate with a large number of elements within their environment. Michael Porter discusses this process in detail with his five-forces model. Effectively managing the relationships between these forces enables organizations to add value to its products and services and gain competitive advantage. For example, there is value in an organization having the ability to receive information and knowledge from business partners. The key aspect of relationship capital is that cooperative behavior springs from development of relationship capital between partners. This is critical in transforming the potential value of an alliance into actual economic value. Relationship capital management goes beyond the standard business partner relationship typical of for example, the Microsoft Business Partner Program. These formal business partner programs are not unusual, and are by nature explicit in nature. Relationship capital also encompasses the tacit nature of such relationships, to include the individual relationships between employees of partnered organizations.

Customer Capital

Customer capital represents the relationships that an organization has with consumers of its products. It encompasses processes, tools, and techniques that support the growth of the organizations customer base. An example of this is brand recognition. In 2002, the Coca-Cola brand was worth $69.6 billion, Microsoft $64.1 billion, and IBM $51.2 billion (Baxi, 2002). These are exceptional examples. Customer capital is typically three or four times a company's book value. In many cases, all other factors being equal, a customer selects a supplier because they "like" doing business with that supplier.

Knowledge Management Technologies

There are many ways to group, sort, and organize KM technologies depending upon the situation. From a very high level, however, we can see that all of these technologies currently fit into eight major categories: Internet, Intranet, Extranet, data warehousing, document management/content management, decision-support systems, knowledge agents, and groupware/e-mail. In 2000, KPMG developed this KM technology classification system that codified an approach taken by Nonaka.

To investigate how organizations are leveraging their KM technologies in the management of intellectual capital, we researched 145 organizations of different sizes, geographically dispersed around the globe, and operating in different industry sectors. Of the 145 organizations researched, *all* were found to be managing their intellectual capital in some manner through KM technologies.

An interesting result of this research was the impact that organization size had on the analysis of the utilization of KM technologies in managing intellectual capital. Organizations with more than 10,000 people have success rates for the use of KM technologies that different from those of than smaller organizations. This is significant from the perspective of which technologies are more successful than others.

If we examine large organizations with more than 10,000 people, the rank order of technology success indicates a high degree of success with Intranet, artificial intelligence/knowledge agents, and groupware. Table 8-1 summarizes our finding for organizations in excess of 10,000 people.

The high success rate of artificial intelligence/knowledge agents is of special note. As can be seen from Table 8-2, small to medium organizations, those with less than

Table 8-1

Success of Knowledge Management Technologies in Large Organizations	
Success	**P**
Intranet	0.011
Artificial intelligence/knowledge agents	0.073
Groupware	0.177
Decision support system	0.368
Extranet	0.587
Document management	0.696
Internet	0.846
Data warehousing	0.847

Table 8-2

Success of Knowledge Management Technologies in Small/Medium Organizations	
Success	**P**
Groupware	0.015
Data mining	0.021
Data warehousing	0.081
Extranet	0.089
Artificial intelligence/knowledge agents	0.246
Internet	0.261
Intranet	0.624
Decision support systems	0.839

10,000 people, have different KM technology success rates in managing their intellectual capital. Artificial intelligence/knowledge agents rate much lower as far as success. This can be partially explained by the fact that generally smaller organizations have smaller quantities of data to use in analyzing with knowledge agents, and hence the corresponding utility of such agents is much less with smaller organizations. Price and processing power can further be seen as factors in the reduced rate of success with this technology category. As the area of artificial intelligence/knowledge agents continues to evolve with systems, such as Neugents® from Computer Associates International, this rate of success is expected to grow for smaller organizations.

Small to medium organizations find that groupware, data warehousing, data mining and Extranets are the most successful KM technologies for managing their intellectual capital.

If we drill down into the different aspects of intellectual capital to see which of the technologies are used in managing specific areas of human capital, customer capital, and relationship capital, we find that organizations do not generally differentiate these constituent elements. In other words, organizations tend to lump all intellectual capital together for management with KM technologies. Once again, from an evolutionary perspective, it is expected that this will change. An example of this is customer relations management, where specific aspects of intellectual capital are being managed, and technologies developed specifically for these areas. Innovators in these areas include Seibel, SAP, and IBM.

From the perspective of which general KM technologies are more successful in managing intellectual capital, we find that the technologies can be put in order of success (Table 8-3). This information can be used to predict which technologies will be more successful in organizations (when organizational size is not a factor). Those wishing to select a single tool for managing intellectual capital will find a higher degree of success in using document management than any other technology evaluated. As such, organizations wishing to use KM technologies to manage intellectual capital will have greater success in implementing those technologies incrementally in the order indicated in Table 8-3.

Table 8-3

Rank Order of Success of Knowledge Management Technologies	
Technology Category	**Rank**
Document management	1
Data warehousing	2
Groupware	3
Extranet	4
Decision support system	5
Intranet	6
Internet	7
Artificial intelligence/knowledge agents	8

Conclusion

This chapter has focused on a highly specific area of KM and examines its implementation and success beyond what is generally considered the core of KM. Research and empiric study indicate that KM continues to evolve and change within organizations.

So, what is the impact of this research and discussion? This chapter illustrates the following points:

- KM technologies, as categorized into eight categories, are being used to manage intellectual capital.
- Currently, little distinction is made between the different aspects of intellectual capital, such as: relationship capital, human capital, and customer capital. This may be because the field of intellectual capital management is still in its infancy. As competitive advantage is gained by more specifically managing intellectual capital, the field will develop in sophistication, and the distinction between the different elements of intellectual capital may become more apparent.
- To manage intellectual capital successfully for organizations with less than 10,000 people, document management, data warehousing and groupware are the technologies most associated with success. This may be because document management is more practical in smaller organizations, whereas data warehousing is easier to implement in smaller organizations. Groupware, specifically Lotus Notes® from IBM, has been available to organizations of all sizes for many years; the return on investment for such technology, coupled with the ease with which it can be installed, has made it a popular choice.
- To manage intellectual capital successfully for organizations with more than 10,000 people, Intranet, artificial intelligence/knowledge agents, and groupware are the technologies most associated with success. Intranet is at the top of the list, possibly because of the ease of implementation across large number of employees.
- Of course, every organization is different from internal and external perspectives, with different missions and operating environments and these factors must

be considered as part of the selection criteria when adopting new KM technologies. Research indicates that there is a strong association with success for the technologies indicated when associated with the size of organization.

- As the field of intellectual capital management continues to evolve, it is expected that that the areas of human capital, relationship capital, and customer capital management will continue to evolve and the technologies associated with these disciplines will become more specialized. Currently the technologies associated with success for all of these areas appear to be the same based on organization size. Organizations with less than 10,000 people, for instance, associate document management, data warehousing, and groupware with success for human, customer, and relationship capital management. This may change over time to technologies specific to these disciplines.

Knowledge Management Technology and Organizational Culture

Heejun Park, Ph.D.

Introduction

Many organizations are implementing knowledge management (KM) strategies and infrastructures that are yielding real benefits in terms of knowledge sharing and streamlining processes. Companies are adopting more technologies to maximize the benefit of KM than ever, but there is evidence that they do not take full advantage of them. If a culture of collaboration and knowledge sharing does not exist, those technologies will yield minimal benefit. Before an organization implements technologies for a successful KM implementation, it must address cultural issues. An extensive review of KM research highlights the fact that one of the main barriers to implementation of KM technology is the absence of an organizational culture that promotes knowledge sharing. The same dollar spent on the same system may give a competitive advantage to one company, but only expensive paperweights to another. The key factors for the higher return on the investment in KM technology are the selection of the right technologies for given business contexts and the effective utilization of knowledge using those technologies.

Whereas the acquisition of technology is a rapid process, the development of the social infrastructure that supports knowledge sharing is a much more difficult. Cultural change does not occur in a quickly. Cultural change and technologic support of this change must complement each other so they yield synergism with each other. The impact of the social changes is boosted by technologies that are appropriate for the current organizational culture and reflect the values and distinctions of the new culture. The KM technology market has also evolved, and dozens of products and portal solutions deliver the major functions that KM systems require. There is no single solution as a panacea for the business challenges of the knowledge era. It is important to see beyond the grand promise of a single solution and understand how creative deployment of existing technologies can couple with given business contexts to benefit the organization.

This chapter examines KM technologies from an organizational cultural impact focus. A typology for KM technologies and its usage in ascertaining the ideal organizational structure for each KM technology will be introduced. The cultural issues have a direct impact on technology selection, and thus must be taken into account.

Organizations most successful in KM technology implementation have identified an organizational culture that embodies a mixture of both product and people orientation.

Knowledge Management

To stay ahead in today's highly unstable and competitive business environment, organizations try to develop new products and services with better quality, faster response to market needs, and higher customer satisfaction. It has become increasingly apparent that potential bottlenecks in achieving these goals lie not just in labor or capital management but also in the ability to effectively manage employees' knowledge. Especially as more organizations are defined by working relationships governed by functional interdependencies rather that organizational boundaries, KM is a major challenge for modern organizations.

The rapidly growing importance of knowledge is highlighted by the fact that many organizations now attempt to organize and to make available the relevant collective knowledge of their employees by building an organizational knowledge repository. The reason for the development of knowledge repositories is the recent realization that knowledge comprises the key strategic asset of modern business. However, organizations still have ambiguous ideas on how to discern what they know, what their knowledge is worth, and how to convert that knowledge into useful products and services to maximize earning potential. Many organizations are implementing KM strategies and infrastructures that are giving them a solution to the problems associated with managing their knowledge assets in an efficient and cost-effective manner.

KM is a discipline used to systematically leverage expertise and knowledge to enhance effectiveness, facilitate innovation, and improve efficiency and competency. Systematically means that the discipline does not rely on just water-cooler conversations, but on planned processes, technology, and behaviors. Managing an enterprise's knowledge assets can be more effectively achieved by creating KM programs using a defined framework of key elements. A conceptual framework of "four pillars of knowledge management" by Stankosky shown on Figure 9-1 describes four key elements of KM.

Organizational knowledge could be more effectively created, retained, and shared within an organization by creating KM programs using a defined framework of KM's key elements and subelements (Table 9-1). The value of the four pillars of KM is to leverage the technologies of the era, while at the same time balancing the right alignment of mix of leadership, organization, and learning. The rapid evolution of new processes, models, and business tools make it necessary to capture and cultivate learning, and manage knowledge of all enterprise systems. It is an enterprise-wide endeavor to share knowledge to enhance effectiveness, facilitate innovation, and improve efficiencies and competitiveness.

As noted in Figure 9-2, elements are interconnected and build on each other for successful implementation of KM program. But what constitutes alignment for the organization, its enterprise, or a process is not so much to conduct a perfect alignment among these elements as it is to develop a construct suitable to the business strategy and to the environmental influences that impact that strategy on a day-to-day bias. A balance of these elements must remain flexible in our turbulent and ever-changing environment.

Figure 9-1

Knowledge Management Pillars

Leadership: Leadership develops a business strategy to survive and position themselves for success. Success of a process and/or system must be developed with the business strategy in mind. Leadership establishes and implements the strategy and nourishes the culture and climate the strategy necessitates. It interacts with the environment to position itself for success.

Organization: The organizational structure must support the strategy. The right business processes and performance management system must be strong enough to deal with turbulence yet flexible enough to adapt to change.

Technology: Technology is an enabler—an essential asset for decision support, data warehousing, process modeling, management tools, and overall communications. Technology must support the business strategy, add value, and be measured.

Learning: Positive impact is achieved from lessons learned if they are actualized into improved effectiveness and/or efficiency. It must build from managing information, to building enterprise-wide knowledge, to managing that knowledge, to organizational learning and change. The aim of process/system development is to improve status quo, however, instituting KM may become the only sustainable source of competitive advantage.

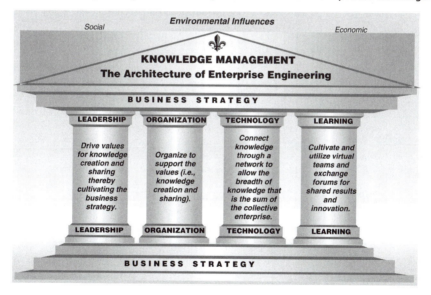

Knowledge Management Technology

The creation, retention, and sharing of knowledge within and among different knowledge communities require the coordinated management and exchange of tacit and explicit knowledge. KM technology provides a seamless pipeline for the flow of explicit and tacit knowledge through four modes of knowledge conversion—socialization, externalization, combination, and internalization—to enable the following:

- Capturing knowledge
- Defining, storing, categorizing, indexing, and linking digital objects corresponding to a knowledge unit

Table 9-1

Key Subelement Inventory	
Key Element	**Key Sub-Elements**
Organization	Process Workflows Operating Procedures for Knowledge Sharing Business Process Reengineering (BPR) Management by Objective (MBO) Total Quality Management (TQM) Metric Standards Organization Structure Organizational Culture
Leadership	Strategic Planning Vision Sharing Specific and General Goals and Objectives Executive Commitment KM Program to Tied Metrics Formal KM Roles on Existence Tangible Rewards for Use of KM Special Recognition for Knowledge Sharing Performance Criteria Including KM Items
Learning	Team Learning Management Support for Continuous Learning Virtual Teams/Exchanged Forums in Use Communities of Practice/Shared Results Innovation Encouraged/Recognized/Rewarded
Technology	Data Warehousing Database Management SW Multi-media Repositories GroupWare Decision Support Systems Corporate Intranet Business Modeling System Intelligent Agents Neural Network

- Searching for and subscribing to relevant content
- Presenting content with sufficient flexibility to render it meaningful and applicable across multiple contexts of use

Companies are adopting more technologies to maximize the benefit of KM. However, recent global analyses of such investments highlight the fact that not all of them are necessarily successful. Too much emphasis on technology without incorporating the other critical elements (i.e., business strategy under leadership, organizational structure, and learning) can easily result in failed KM implementation.

Technologies Important to Knowledge Management

The KM technology market has introduced many products and portal solutions that deliver the major functions of KM systems. Many companies implement KM tech-

Figure 9-2

Four pillars interrelationship.

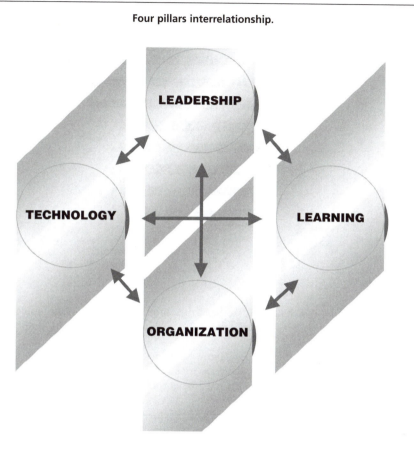

nology with a "half-cooked" approach, convincing themselves that buying a million dollars' worth of "neat" technologies will give them a measurable return on investment.

However, not all of organizations implementing KM technology are successful because some do not understand the business practices and cultural and organizational changes that must be made at the same time. The key factors for the higher return on the investment of KM technology are choosing the right technologies for given business contexts and the effective utilization of knowledge using those technologies. To choose the appropriate technologies, the KM technologies and the specific role of each of them must first be reviewed.

The result of the study conducted by International Data Corporation, sponsored by *Knowledge Management Magazine*, lists messaging and e-mail, document management, and search engines as the most important technologies in the current KM initiatives (Figure 9-3).

The survey undertaken by Radicati Group identified information technologies that play important roles in KM processes: Intranets, document management systems,

Figure 9-3

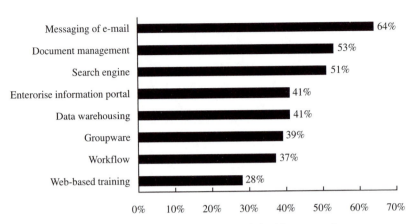

Technology important to KM initiative.

Source: IDC's 1999 Knowledge Management Survey

information retrieval systems, push technologies and intelligent agents, groupware and workflow systems, help-desk applications, and data warehousing and data mining tools.

Calabrese (2000) identified important technologies to KM as one of the key subelements of KM, data warehousing, database management software, multimedia repositories, groupware, decision support systems, corporate Intranet, business modeling systems, and intelligent agents.

It is important to see beyond the grand promise of a single technology, and to understand how creative deployment of existing technologies can couple with new entrants in the market to benefit the organization. The role of each of these technologies is as follows:

- *Document management systems* are repositories of important corporate documents and valuable tools for creating and processing complex documents. The contents of documents, together with the ways in which they are organized and accessed, form an explicit corporate intellectual asset.
- *Data warehouse* is a platform with integrated operational data of improved quality to support decision-making processes within organization. *Data mining* is a technology used to extract useful information from large database-like data warehouses.
- *Enterprise information portal* is an application that enables a company to unlock internally and externally stored information and provides internal and external users with a single gateway to personalized information needed to make informed business decisions.
- *Information retrieval systems* have improved the speed and precision of finding information through natural language querying, filtering information, and creating summaries. *Push technologies and agents* provide means for users to easily capture the types of knowledge assets they need to monitor, without requiring them to learn complex search syntax.

- *Groupware* enhances the exchange of tacit knowledge by allowing formal and ad hoc conversations among knowledge workers against temporal, spatial, and social barriers.
- *Workflow systems* enable users to codify knowledge transfer processes, which are formalized and regulate the flow of information.
- *Help-desk technology* is used in many organizations as a way of responding to both internal and external customer knowledge requirements, and the knowledge accumulated in using such systems has broader application to rapid design and improvement of products and services.
- *Knowledge mapping* serves as corporate yellow pages to transfer best practices.
- *Training systems* (e.g., *performance support systems* and *simulation software*) are directly relevant to turning knowledge into productive activity to help knowledge conversion from explicit to tacit knowledge.

Ultimately, these many technologies need to be integrated under the umbrella of a formal strategy that transcends short-term requirements and vendor-specific models for knowledge resources. This strategy must be shaped by the organizational culture. Interchange standards, models for knowledge resources, and standards for measuring the value of knowledge work will be keys in this effort.

Typology of Knowledge Management Technology

Knowledge processing can be segmented into two broad classes—distributive and collaborative—each addressing different KM objectives. Together, these approaches provide a broad set of knowledge processing capabilities. They support well-structured repositories for managing explicit knowledge, while enabling interaction to integrate tacit knowledge.

Technology used in distributive processing exhibit a sequential flow of explicit knowledge into and out of the repository, whereas technologies used in collaborative processing are primarily focused on supporting interaction among people holding tacit knowledge.

Distributive technologies maintain a repository of explicitly encoded knowledge created and managed for sequential distribution to knowledge consumers within or outside the organization. These technologies exhibit a sequential flow of information into and out of a central repository, structured to provide flexible access and views of the knowledge. Knowledge producers and consumers interact with the repository rather than with each other directly (Figure 9-4).

Figure 9-4

Distributive technologies.

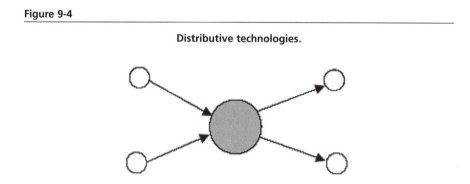

Collaborative technologies may be a simple directory of individuals within or associated with a community of knowledge. It may also take more interactive form of a knowledge brokerage, an electronic conference or discussion space where people may either search for knowledge by posing questions (e.g., "Does anyone know?") or advertise their expertise. The most collaborative form supports direct communication through discussion databases, computer conferences, and real-time collaboration technologies. These technologies directly support interaction and collaboration within and among knowledge-based teams, enabling "teams of teams" to form across knowledge communities (Figure 9-5).

The important technologies to KM identified by Calabrese and the surveys undertaken by International Data Corporation and the Radicati group are well suited to Zack's classification of KM technologies (Table 9-2).

Figure 9-5

Collaborative technologies.

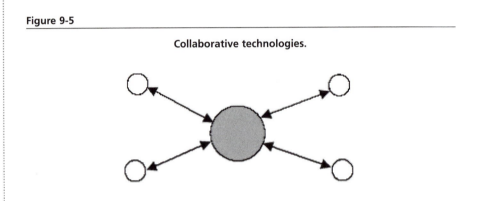

Table 9-2

Typology of KM Technology	
Distributive (Integrative)	Data Warehousing (and Data Mining Tools) Database Management Technologies Document Management Systems Electronic Publishing Information Retrieval Systems Search Engines Intelligent Agents Enterprise Information Portal (i.e. Corporate Intranet) Decision Support Systems Business Modeling Systems
Collaborative (Interactive)	Messaging or E-mail GroupWare Knowledge-mapping Tools Enterprise Information Portal (i.e. Corporate Intranet) Web-based Training Help-Desk applications Decision Support Systems Workflow Systems

Measurement of the Success of Knowledge Management Technology Implementation

The large investment in information technology (IT) that organizations must make to develop and maintain various systems, as well as in the organizational mechanisms required to mange them, dictates the need to assess whether the systems are actually doing the jobs for which they were designed. Firms regard the results of IT effectiveness evaluation to be useful in justifying further investment in IT.

Evaluating investment in technology poses a number of problems that investing in the traditional assets does not present. Standard measures of productivity ignore many important dimensions critical to customers and managers. A number of benefits are not measurable or not attributable to technology alone. These include maintaining market share, avoiding catastrophic losses, creating greater flexibility, improving responsiveness for new product lines, improving service quality, enhancing quality of work life, and increasing predictability of operations.

The focus shifts from measuring hard and quantifiable dollar benefits that will appear on the firm's income statement, to measuring indirect, diffuse, qualitative and contingent impacts that are difficult to quantify well. The Computer Science and Telecommunications Board of the National Research Council developed the survey instrument Information Technology Investment Performance (ITIP) to assess and understand the patterns of behavior that could explain why organizations were, or were not, realizing payoff from IT.

The broad categories of IT investment identified by National Research Council study are used as an outline for the survey instrument. These include basic communication and data infrastructure, mandated requirements, cost reduction programs, new products development, improvements in quality, and strategic repositioning. Respondents to the research conducted by National Research Council indicated that less successful IT implementations include a lack of strategy, failure to reengineer the process first, failure to involve customers and users, failure to secure interactive user participation, failure to use groupware tools, lack of feedback, lack of customer-driven quality metrics, unmanageable projects, failure to audit results, and failure to benchmark.

To gauge the momentum of the KM movement, International Data Corporation and *Knowledge Management Magazine* undertook an extensive electronic survey of U.S. user organizations and individuals familiar with KM. The result of the study that demonstrates the most important reasons for adapting KM (Figure 9-6) and challenges to implementing KM (Figure 9-7) were used to modify ITIP to measuring the success of KM technology investment. Park developed the Knowledge Management Technology Profile (KMTP) (Table 9-3) by modifying ITIP.

Organizational Culture

The primary challenge of KM is the need to relate KM programs to an organization's people and culture. Before an organization implements KM technologies for a successful KM implementation, it must address cultural issues. Although focusing on corporate culture and organizational change may extend the time it takes to prepare a KM program, the benefits of doing so include being better prepared for implementation and being more able to leverage existing technology.

The emergence of organizational culture as a key element of successful implementation of KM programs has generated many issues regarding the methods by which it

Figure 9-6

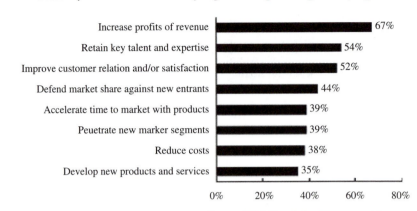

Most important reasons for adopting knowledge management program.

Source: IDC's Knowledge Management Survey

Figure 9-7

Challenges to implementing knowledge management program.

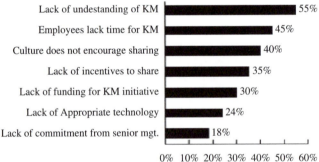

Source: IDC's 1999 Knowledge Management Survey

should be measured and the feasibility of cultural change and the direction that it should take. Researchers have made a number of efforts to understand the behavior of individuals and groups in organization using cultural concepts such as symbols, rituals, ceremonies, myths, stories, and languages. Such studies have initiated a number of discussions on issues, such as the definition of culture, a suitable methodology for investigating it, and the proper level of analysis for its study. Although debates around these issues continue, researchers have agreed that culture can be thought as a set of cognitions shared by members of a social unit.

The concept of organizational culture is derived from research in the field of organizational behavior characterized by the use of qualitative methods. Qualitative and quantitative methods are complementary approaches to the study and assessment of

Table 9-3

Culture Definition	
Becker & Geer (1970)	Set of common understandings, expressed in language
Kroeber & Kluckhohn (1952)	Transmitted patterns of values, ideas, and other symbolic systems that shape behavior
Louis (1980)	Three aspects: (1) some contact (meaning and interpretation) (2) peculiar to (3) a group
Martin & Siehl (1983)	Glue that holds together an organization through shared patterns of meaning. Three component systems: context or core values, forms (process of communication, e.g., jargon), strategies to reinforce content (e.g., rewards, training program)
Ouchi (1981)	Set of symbols, ceremonies and myths that communicate the underlying values and beliefs of the organization to its move employees
Swartz & Jordon (1980)	Pattern of beliefs and expectation shared by members that produce norms shaping behavior
Uttal (1983)	Shared values (what is important) and beliefs (how things work) that interact with an organization's structures and control systems to produce behavioral norms (the way we do things around here)
Van Maanen & Schein (1979)	Values, beliefs and expectations that members come to share

organizational process and attributes. The advantages of qualitative methods include the use of focal unit's own terms to describe itself, the intensive and in-depth information that can be obtained about a unit, and the amenability of the method for exploratory research on issues and processes about which little information exists. The advantage of quantitative methods include the ease of cross-sectional assessments and comparisons, the replicability of the assessment in different units and by other researchers or organizational development professionals, and a common articulated frame of reference for interpreting the data. Although both methods share the potential for producing cumulative bodies of information for assessment and theory testing, a quantitative approach may be more practical for purposes of analyzing data based change in organization.

The following sections will review a number of discussions on issues such as the definition and general nature of culture, and a suitable methodology for investigating it the organizational culture profile (OCP) developed by Harper, by modifying two existing instruments OCP and New Managerial Grid, will be discussed in depth.

General Nature of Culture

Culture has been treated by anthropologists and organizational researchers as a set of cognitions shared by members of a social unit (Table 9-3). These cognitions are acquired through social learning and socialization processes exposing individuals to a variety of culture-bearing elements.

These elements are the observable activities and interactions, communication, and artifacts that form the social experience. In organizations, the patterns of activities and interactions that members observe and carry out (e.g., decision making, communicating) constitute major elements of the system's structure, making structure itself an important culture-bearing mechanism in organizations. Communication, in such forms as stories, rumors, reported events, and role expectations, convey normative information about the appropriateness and desirability of behaviors. Artifacts, such as the physical plant, the equipment, and the resources used on the job (their quality and availability), and symbols that represent the organization or its members (such as a slogan and titles), have meaning and value attached to them that reinforce the way people behave and think. Culture-bearing elements are reinforcers of ways of thinking and behaving in the manner in which behaviorists use the term; reinforcers strengthen the connection between features in the environment and an individual's responses.

Culture-based cognitions are akin to what Weick has labeled the "enacted environment." Weick argued that individuals develop an organized view of the world to reduce the equivocality and uncertainty of events. This organization is accomplished by constructing meanings for events through identifying patterns. The process of interpreting and attaching meanings to these patterns typically involves the efforts of two or more people, hence the origin of the term *social construction of reality*. These social constructions, often focusing on the behaviors and interpersonal styles that are expected and rewarded by the organization, exit prior to the entry of a new member into the system. Thus, culture provides a premade and socially shared enacted environment to which the individual must accommodate in order to fit in and, in certain cases, to survive. Building on this cognitive view of culture, the assessment system proposed in this research derives from a definition of culture as "the way of thinking, behaving, and believing that members of a social unit have in common." (Cooke and Rousseau, 1988, p. 246).

Identifying Organizational Culture Style

There are some fundamental areas of agreement in the definition and the important role of culture, but less agreement exists about its measurement. To investigate person-culture fit, O'Reilly, Chatman, and Caldwell developed a survey instrument called the OCP. This survey instrument contains a set of attribute statements that can be used to assess idiographically the extent to which certain attributes characterize a target organization. In a set of related investigations using multiple sets of respondents, researchers explored the characteristics of the OCP and demonstrated its ability to assess preferences for organizational attributes.

The OCP contains 54 attribute statements that can generically capture individual and organizational attributes. The set of attribute statements was developed on the basis of an extensive review of academic and practitioner-oriented writings on organizational attributes and culture. One aspect of this review was to identify a comprehensive set of attributes that could be used to characterize organizations. An attempt was made to find items that (a) could be used to describe any organization, (b) would not be equally characteristic of all organizations, and (c) would be easy to understand. Respondents were asked to sort the 54 items into nine categories, ranging from most to least desirable or from most to least characteristic, and to put a specified number of statements on each category. Items judged to be less characteristic or uncharacteristic were placed into middle categories. While sorting the items, the respondents were asked how to describe the culture of a focal organization. To develop a profile of an organization's culture, respondents familiar with the organization were instructed to sort the 54 attributes according to the extent to which the items were characteristic of the organization. With such a procedure, separate groups of individuals can be used to assess a firm's culture.

The 9-category, 54-item Q-sort scale, with distribution [2-4-6-9-12-9-6-4-2] used by O'Reilly, Chatman, and Caldwell, was modified by Harper (2000) to agree with the 8-category, 44-item Q-sort scale, with distribution [3-5-7-7-7-7-5-3]. Such a modification still meets the general Q-sort distribution decisions based on symmetry of distribution, the number of judgment categories, and the essential shape of the symmetric distribution.

To define organizational culture style, Harper mapped 44 OCP attribute statements against the managerial grid (Figure 9-8) organization characteristics sets developed by Blake and Mouton using the method shown on Table 9-4. Harper viewed the

Figure 9-8

Managerial grid.

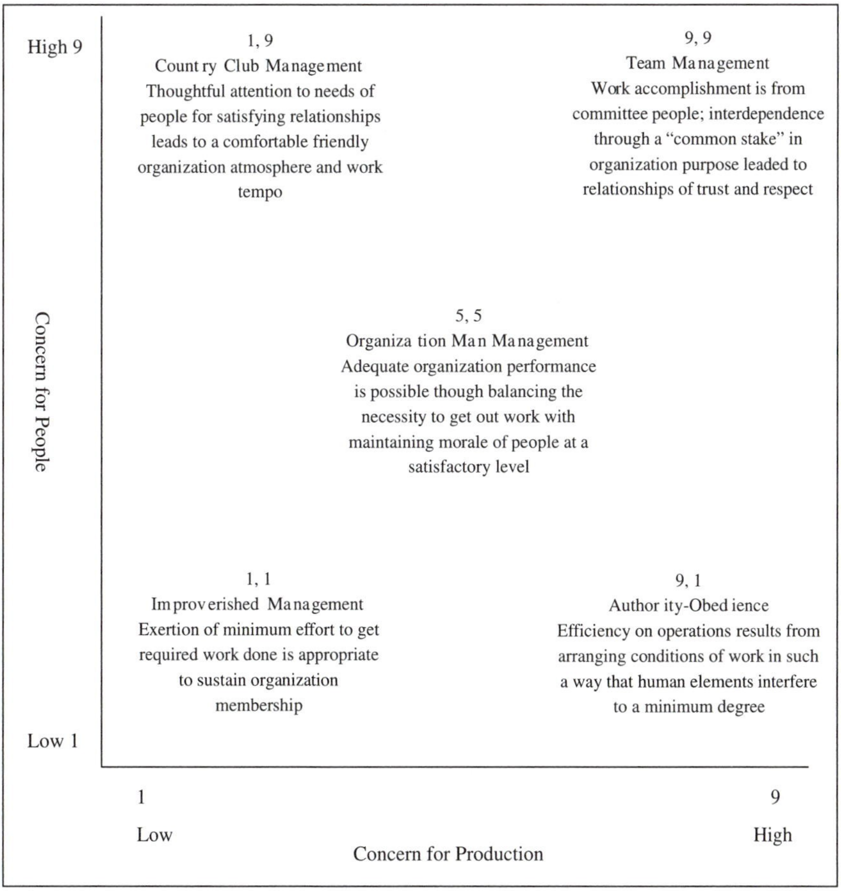

1, 9
Country Club Management
Thoughtful attention to needs of
people for satisfying relationships
leads to a comfortable friendly
organization atmosphere and work
tempo

9, 9
Team Management
Work accomplishment is from
committee people; interdependence
through a "common stake" in
organization purpose leaded to
relationships of trust and respect

5, 5
Organization Man Management
Adequate organization performance
is possible though balancing the
necessity to get out work with
maintaining morale of people at a
satisfactory level

1, 1
Improverished Management
Exertion of minimum effort to get
required work done is appropriate
to sustain organization
membership

9, 1
Author ity-Obedience
Efficiency on operations results from
arranging conditions of work in such
a way that human elements interfere
to a minimum degree

High 9

Low 1

Concern for People

1
Low

9
High

Concern for Production

Table 9-4

Culture Orientation	Cultural Attributes
9,1	Being aggressive(+), Being competitive(+), Being Innovative(–), Compliance(+), Confronting conflict directly(+), Demanding of employees(+), Fairness(–), Flexibility(–), Informality(–), Respect for the individual (–), Results oriented(+), Rule orientated(+), Sharing information freely(–), Supportiveness of employees(–), Team oriented work(–), Tolerance of failure(–)
9,9	Adaptability(+), Being competitive(+), Being Innovative(+), Being thoughtful(+), Compliance(–), confronting conflict directly(+), Enthusiasm for the job(+), Having a good reputation(+), Praise for good performance(+), Predictability(–), Problem solving(+), Respect for the individual(+), Rule orientated(–), Sharing information freely(+), Supportiveness of employees(+), Taking advantage of opportunity(+), Team oriented work(+), Tolerance of failure(+), Working closely with others(+)
5,5	Being different from others(–), Being Innovative(–), Enthusiasm for the job(+), Experimentation(–), Fairness(+), Fitting in at work(+), Flexibility(+), High expectations for performance(–), Predictability(+), Problem solving(–), Respect for the individual(+), Security of employment(+), Stability is valued(+)
1,1	Adaptability(+), Being aggressive(–), Being calm(+), Being competitive(–), Being easy going(+), Being Innovative(–), Confronting conflict directly(–), Decisiveness(–), Demanding of employees(–), Enthusiasm for the job(–), Fitting in at work(+), High expectations for performance(–), Predictability(+), Stability is values(+), Taking initiative(–)
1,9	Attention to detail(–), Being aggressive(–), Being competitive(–), Being Innovative(–), Confronting conflict directly(–), Demanding of employees(–), Developing friends at work(–), Fairness(+), Fitting in at work(+), Flexibility(+), Low level of conflict encouraged(+), Respect for the individual(+), Results oriented(–), Security of employment(+), Socially responsible(+), Supportiveness of employees(+), Trust(+)

(+) indicates the cultural attribute is positive toward that characteristic set.
(–) indicates the cultural attribute is negative toward that characteristic set.

managerial grid as sets of cultural orientations for distinct organization types. The original use of the managerial grid was to analyze interactions between significant variables of management–production and people—as a way to understand a basic conflict in a top management group. The two dimensions of the managerial grid include *concern for production* and *concern for the people*. In each case, the term *concern for* is not addressing so much with the degree to which employees' needs are being considered, but rather the degree of interest that is presented and demonstrated by the organization's management. What is significant is how management concerns itself about production and people, and how they interact. In their development of the managerial grid, Blake and Mouton defined these dimensions as follows:

- *Concern for production:* The terms *production* and *people* cover a range of considerations. Attitudes of concern toward production, for instance, may be seen in the type of policy decisions, the extent of creativity throughout the organization, procedures or processes, workload and efficiency demands, the quality of services, and the volume of output. The important aspect is that the meaning of production covers whatever the organization deems it important that people accomplish. At the lower level, concern for production may take the form of the number of things that can be counted or the time it takes to meet production schedule. But at the organizational level, it may be demonstrated in the kind of policies established, the character of direction given to major programmatic efforts, or the importance applied to finding new directions or products to sustain the organization.
- *Concern for people:* In a similar fashion, concern for people can be expressed in a number of different ways. Included might be the degree of concern for personal commitment, accountability, trust versus obedience, self-esteem, good working conditions, benefit packages, security, and social relations, or friendships with associates.

The managerial grid, depicted in Figure 9-8, shows these two concerns and the range of possible interactions between them. The horizontal axis indicates a concern for production, whereas the vertical axis indicates concern for people. Each is expressed as 9-point scale of concern, with the number 1 representing minimum concern, and the number 9 representing maximum concerns. The process of mapping the 44 OCP attribute statements, done by Harper, revolved around the sets of organization characteristics, identified by Blake and Mouton, which exhibit each of major management orientations such as [1,1], [1,9], [5,5], [9,1], and [9,9].

Relationship between Knowledge Management and Organizational Culture

The results of much research reveal sufficient evidence to establish a correlation between cultural orientation and the successful implementation of KM technology. Before an organization implements KM technologies for a successful KM implementation, it should deal with cultural issues. The success of KM technology implementation is mediated by human behavior. The specific cultural attributes are the drivers for, or barriers to, the successful KM technology implementation. Although focusing on organizational culture and change may extend the time it takes to prepare a KM program, the benefits of doing so include being better prepared for implementation, and being more able to leverage existing technology.

Organizations that are more successful in KM technology implementation have identified organization cultures that embody a mixture of both production-oriented attributes (*adaptability, being competitive, being innovative, sharing information freely, and taking advantage of opportunity*) and people-oriented attributes (*confronting conflict directly, enthusiasm for the job, having a good reputation, praise for good performance, problem solving, respect for the individual, supportiveness of employees, team oriented work, tolerance of failure, and working closely with others*) that lie within the [9,9] OCP value set. If a culture does not have high components of both orientations, those cultures with a higher people-oriented component, which consists of *developing friends at work, fairness, fitting in at work, low level of conflict encouraged, respect for the individual, security of employment, socially responsible, supportiveness of employees*, and *trust* have the second best chance of successful implementation.

The cultural attributes such *as sharing information freely, working closely with others, team oriented work, fairness, enthusiasm*, and *trust* have moderate to high positive correlation with the success of KM technology implementation. On the other hand, a number of cultural attributes having a moderate to high negative correlation with the success of KM technology implementation are identified. These attributes include *attention to detail, being competitive, being aggressive*, and *being calm*.

Many organizations are implementing KM strategies and technologies that are giving them real benefits in terms of knowledge sharing, improving customer relations, and producing new products and services. A high return on KM technology investment in sharing knowledge, improving customer relations, and producing new products and services has moderate high correlation with cultural attributes such as *team-oriented work, sharing information freely, working closely with others, trust, being innovative* and *supportive of employees*.

To maximize the benefit of KM, organizations should reduce levels of hierarchy and increase spans of control, decentralization, and the use of self-directed teaming. The organizational culture representing the attribute *autonomy* indicates a strong influence of KM technology implementation on organizational structure. KM technology could be used more effectively if users are involved in the process of designing KM technology implementation. Research reveals that the users of KM technology in the organizations that value the attribute *sharing information freely* have a higher chance to be involved in the design of a successful KM project.

The great extent to which collaborative technologies are being used have moderate high positive correlation with cultural attributes such as *working closely with others, having a good reputation, team-oriented work*, and *sharing information freely*. On the other hand, organizations that have been using distributive technologies to the great extent have identified *rule-oriented* and *result-oriented* cultural attributes. Technology is an enabler. The goals of implementing KM, such as enhancing effectiveness, facilitating innovation, and improving efficiency and competency, could be achieved by effective use of knowledge using KM technology, which provides a seamless pipeline for the flow of knowledge across organization. To maximize the benefit of KM, organizations should establish a positive organizational culture to successful implementation of KM technology by developing the cultural attributes *team-oriented work, sharing information freely, working closely with others, trust, being innovative, supportive of employees*, and *autonomy*. Organization should encourage employees to use collaborative technology more often, which are crucial methods for true knowledge sharing, by providing those positive attributes identified in this research with training programs and incentives.

Companies began a trend of increased investment in technology to improve the productivity of knowledge workers during 1980s, and this continued the 1990s. In the last 20 years, U.S. industry has invested more than $1 trillion in technology, but has realized little improvement in the efficiency or effectiveness of its knowledge workers. This failure is due to organizations' ignorance of ways in which knowledge workers communicate and operate through the social processes of collaborating, sharing knowledge, and building on each others' idea. The key factors for the higher return on the KM technology dollar are the choosing the right technologies for given business contexts, and the effective utilization of knowledge using those technologies.

Knowledge Management in a Military Enterprise: a Pilot Case Study of the Space and Warfare Systems Command

Captain Mickey V. Ross, USN, D.Sc., and William D. Schulte, Ph.D.

Introduction

What do you know about the role of knowledge management (KM) in military enterprises? To what extent can KM be commonly used in both government and commercial enterprises? Does each enterprise require different applications of KM? Another important issue that is relevant to the above debate is the role of KM technologies in achieving enterprise objectives and strategies. In recent years, the number of published articles and case studies on the impact of KM in government organizations has increased significantly.

It is clear in the scholarly literature and practical applications that there are several dimensions of KM in all organizations including organizational structure, learning culture, leadership, financial resources, content management, and technology. KM has evolved from advancements in information management, Web-based technologies, and software, hardware, and digital storage. Technology is not the most important dimension of KM; if people are too afraid to share their knowledge, they will not share. Technology enables knowledge sharing, integration, and collaboration. They also agree that KM will contribute to efficiency, effectiveness, and a sustainable competitive advantage in organizations. However, there is a lack of empirical research on these important research questions and issues.

There is clearly a great amount of anecdotal data by vendors and consultants and a growing commitment to empiric and conceptual research by scholars in KM. Anecdotal data, or case studies and stories, are great tools for communicating the value of KM technologies. Nonetheless, there is a need to grow the body of knowledge on the impact of Knowledge Management Technologies (KMTs). We know more now than we did only 5 years ago. Concurrently, interest and research in public sector KM have also grown substantially (Forman, 2003; Saussois, 2003; Scott, 2003; Pilichowski and Landel, 2003; Burton, 2003; Barrados, 2003; Holmes, 2003). Scholars and practitioners in U.S. military enterprises have led much of that research.

For example, the chief information officer (CIO) of the Department of the Navy (DON) developed an information management strategic plan to build a knowledge-sharing culture and apply innovative information technology to enable knowledge transfer across the Navy enterprise. The vision was to transform the DON into a Knowledge Centric Organization (KCO) that enhances competitiveness. As a KCO, people are connected, and the right information is delivered to the right people at the right time to improve learning, effectiveness, productivity, and innovation in the enterprise (Hanley, 2001).

Knowledge Management Research in the U. S. Federal Government

According to Dr. Charles Bixler (2002):

> The events of Sept. 11 changed the world forever. As a result of the terrorist attacks on America, there is an increased demand for timely, integrated information, knowledge and rapid analysis to meet current and future security demands of federal, state and local government agencies. Government agencies now require the next generation of processes and systems to meet the new change requirements.

KM is now a part of the national management strategy. President George W. Bush has included KM in his recent presidential management agenda. According to the President's Management Agenda (PMA),

> The Administration will adopt information technology systems to capture some of the knowledge and skills of retiring employees. KM systems are just one part of an effective strategy that will help generate, capture and dissemination knowledge and information that is relevant to the organization's mission (OMB, 2002, p. 13).

Public sector KM leaders have been engaged in a debate about how to make KM work. There has been a growing need to understand KM's competitive advantage benefits. Both public and private sector managers are focusing on performance from KM. According to Mitchell (2002), KM frameworks and theories are interesting ideas but they are not the same as showing a return on investment. Other authors have suggested that KM offers the public sector methods to improve practices and processes, enhance employee capabilities, improve customer service, and decrease costs. For example, the Goddard Space Center of the National Aeronautics and Space Administration (NASA) developed several KM initiatives to achieve those competitiveness goals (Liebowitz, 2002).

Another study reported that the first wave of interactive government services was e-government (Hoenig, 2001). Most of these have seen e-commerce applications and portals overlaid on top of massive, outdated organizations and aging information technology (IT) systems. According to Hoenig (2001), government executives and CIOs should use IT systems for understanding and learning, smart searching and problem solving, applying next-generation KM theory, developing packages expertise and interaction, building secure, modular Web-based systems and services, and instilling collaboration within government organizations. The U.S. federal government CIO council rose to this challenge several years ago.

Federal Knowledge Management Working Group

Four years ago, forward-thinking professionals from federal civilian and military organizations formed the Knowledge Management Working Group (KMWG). The group brought together representatives from more than 30 agencies to begin developing and sharing the world's largest storehouse of knowledge and expertise on KM.

According to the KMWG Web site (km.gov),

> The Federal Chief Information Officers Council (CIO Council) established the Knowledge Management Working Group (KMWG) as an interagency body to bring the benefits of the government's intellectual assets to all Federal organizations, customers, and partners. The KMWG is charged with identifying best practices in KM within and beyond Federal agencies; encouraging the dissemination of information related to the KM discipline; and ensuring the development of competency profiles for agency Chief Knowledge Officers.

The Web site provides a wealth of documentation on KM in the government sector. According to the site,

> Initiatives sponsored by the Knowledge Management Working Group are accomplished through Special Interest Groups (SIGs). The number and focus of Special Interest Groups reflects current needs and resources, and therefore changes periodically. Currently the KMWG has eight Special Interest Groups: 1) Communities of Practice, 2) Government-wide Communities of Practice, 3) Content Management, 4) KM Education, Learning and Development, 5) KM.GOV Content and KM Technology, 6) KM Stories, 7) Public Policy and Outreach, and 8) KM Surveys (Serepca, 2002).

The KMWG was chartered to have co-chairs who served at the request of the CIO Council. The first co-chairs of the group were Dr. Shereen Remez (chief knowledge officer [CKO], Government Services Administration [GSA]) and Alex Bennet (CKO, DON). When Dr. Remez left government service in 2001, Elsa Rhoads (Knowledge Management Architect, Pension Benefit Guaranty Corporation) joined Alex Bennet as co-chair. In January 2002, Giora Hadar (Federal Aviation Administration [FAA]) and Nat Heiner (CKO, U.S. Coast Guard) took the reins of service (km.gov Web site). The KMWG Charter was adopted on March 1, 2000. A copy of the original charter is presented in Figure 10-1.

Department of the Navy Knowledge Management Strategy

> The Department of the Navy (DON) has been a leader in KM implementation. For the DON, KM is essential to achieving Knowledge Superiority–the shared understanding that provides a decisive edge in war fighting. DON distributed over 20,000 copies of their Knowledge-Centric Organization (KCO) toolkit (a virtual resource on CD) across the U.S. Government. The toolkit provided a holistic resource for creating a KCO, an organization that connects people to the right information at the right time for decision and action; and learns, collaborates and innovates continuously. Working through a KM Community of Practice, the DON deployed KCO assist teams to help organizations evolve (www.cio.gov).

Although there are many definitions of KM, the DON identifies KM as a process for optimizing the effective application of intellectual capital to achieve organizational objectives. This is built on a holistic approach to intellectual capital, which includes human capital, social capital, and corporate capital. The DON information management (IM)/IT vision is a knowledge-centric organization. The DON CIO developed

Figure 10-1

Copy of the knowledge management working group charter.

KNOWLEDGE MANAGEMENT
STATEMENT OF INTENT

The economy of the United States is successful because of the intellectual capital of its people. Knowledge creation, sharing and use are cornerstones of our economic strength and vitality. Industry is successfully building these cornerstones into their enterprises, and focusing them on producing customer delight. The U.S. government has recognized the value of these cornerstones in providing effective government, i.e., better and faster government services to our ultimate customer, the citizen.

To facilitate knowledge creation, sharing and use, a common understanding of the conceptual framework and the corresponding competencies of Knowledge Management are needed. In recognition of this need, the Knowledge Management Working Group of the Federal Chief Information Officers Council is partnering with academia and industry associations currently offering KM certification programs to define a conceptual framework and a set of principles, definitions and taxonomies for Knowledge Management. This set is intended to serve as the criteria for accredited government certification programs and to provide the guidance for academic and industry associations who are interested in supporting certification of government employees.

The undersigned are committed to building a common framework and understanding of Knowledge Management for the government.

Giora Hadar, FAA

Alex Bennet, DON CIO

Harriett Riofrio, OSD (C3I)

Robert Neilson, NDU

Shereen Remez, GSA

Carolyn Offutt, EPA

Elsa Rhoads, PBGC

Date: 13 October 2000

---

the KCO framework to assist Navy and Marine organizations to support the implementation of KM within their organizations. As depicted in Figure 10-2, the KCO has five dimensions: technology, process, content, culture, and learning.

According to DON CIO leadership (Bennett, 2000), the KCO benefits all levels of an enterprise including: enhanced job performance, increased collaboration opportunities, facilitated learning, enhanced mission performance, improved decision making, greater use of expertise, process improvements, reduced duplication, leveraging orga-

Figure 10-2

U.S. Department of the Navy chief information officer knowledge centric organization framework.

nization knowledge, increased innovation and creativity, and aligning strategic directions.

Measuring Knowledge Management in the Department of the Navy

The operating principles and practices of KM show how the KCO was developed at the DON. The DON was the only public sector organization to be recognized as a world-class leader in managing knowledge to deliver superior performance in the 2002 North American Most Admired Knowledge Enterprise (MAKE) study (Chatzkel, 2000). An example of their initiatives included an "E-sailors" program that involved software routines embedded in the systems architecture that monitored their orders. This provided the DON with greater situational awareness and facilitated competency capture and KM (Fitzgerald, 1999).

The DON CIO has led the development of an IM/IT strategy to build a knowledge-sharing culture to benefit from innovative KMTs to transfer knowledge across the globally distributed enterprise. The IM/IT vision is to

Transform the DON into a Knowledge Centric Organization (KCO) where people can make and implement efficient and agile decisions. An organization becomes a KCO by connecting people to each other when helpful, and delivering the right information, and only the right information, at the right time to enhance learning, innovation, effectiveness and productivity (Hanley, 2001).

According to the DON, KM provides two primary benefits to the enterprise. They include improving performance through increased effectiveness, productivity, quality, and innovation. In addition, KM increases the financial value of the enterprise by managing human capital or knowledge as an asset as valuable as traditional financial and tangible capital.

To measure these benefits, the KCO framework applies three specific constructs to measure performance from a KM initiative: outcomes, outputs, and system metrics. Outcome metrics measure overall organizational characteristics, including increased productivity and revenue. Output metrics measure project traits, including effectiveness of lessons learned. Finally, system metrics measure the effectiveness, usefulness, functionality, and responsiveness of KMTs (Hanley, 2001). Examples of each of the measures include the following summarized in Tables 10-1, 10-2, and 10-3.

Purpose of Study

The overall goal of this research was to lay the foundation for developing a more effective KMT solutions and providing a foundation for KMT innovations in military and government agencies.

Table 10-1

Summary of Common KM Performance Metrics
Common measures: These measures can be used for all KM initiatives: *Outcome* • Time, money, or personnel time saved as a result of implementing initiative • Percentage of successful programs compared to those before KM implementation
Output • Usefulness surveys where users evaluate how useful initiatives have been in helping them accomplish their objectives • Usage anecdotes where users describe (in quantitative terms) how the initiative has contributed to business objectives
System • Latency (response times) • Number of downloads • Number of site accesses • Dwell time per page or section • Usability survey • Frequency of use • Navigation path analysis • Number of help desk calls • Number of users • Frequency of use • Percentage of total employees using system
From Metrics Guide for KM Initiatives, DON, CIO, August 2001.

Table 10-2

	Best Practice, Lessons Learned, Communities, and Expertise KM Performance Metrics		
KM Initiative	Key System Measures	Key Output Measures	Key Outcome Measures
Best Practice Directory	• Number of downloads • Dwell time • Usability survey • Number of users • Total number of contributions • Contribution rate over time	• Usefulness survey • Anecdotes • User ratings of contribution value	• Time, money, or personnel time saved by implementing best practices • Number of groups certified in the use of the best practice • Rate of change in operating costs
Lessons Learned Database	• Number of downloads • Dwell time • Usability survey • Number of users • Total number of contributions • Contribution rate over time	• Time to solve problems • Usefulness survey • Anecdotes • User ratings of contribution value	• Time, money, or personnel time saved by applying lessons learned from others • Rate of change in operating costs
Communities of Practice or Special Interest Groups	• Number of contributions • Frequency of update • Number of members • Ratio of the number of members to the number of contributors (conversion rate)	• Number of "apprentices" mentored by colleagues • Number of problems solved	• Savings or improvement in organizational quality and efficiency • Captured organizational memory • Attrition rate of community members versus non-member cohort
Expert or Expertise Directory	• Number of site accesses • Frequency of use • Number of contributions • Contribution/update rate over time • Navigation path analysis • Number of help desk calls	• Time to solve problems • Number of problems solved • Time to find expert	• Savings or improvement in organizational quality and efficiency • Time, money, or personnel time saved by leveraging expert's knowledge or expertise knowledge base

From Metrics Guide for KM Initiatives, DON, CIO, August, 2001.

Table 10-3

Portal, Tracking, Collaborative, e-Learning, and Yellow Pages KM Performance Metrics

KM Initiative	Key System Measures	Key Output Measures	Key Outcome Measures
Portal	• Searching precision and recall • Dwell time • Latency • Usability survey	• Common awareness within teams • Time spent "gathering" information • Time spent "analyzing" information	• Time, money, or personnel time saved as a result of portal use • Reduced training time or learning curve • Customer satisfaction
Lead Tracking System	• Number of contributions • Frequency of update • Number of users • Frequency of use • Navigation path analysis	• Number of successful leads • Number of new customers and value of new work from existing customers • Value of new work from existing customers • Proposal response times • Proposal "win" rates	• Revenue and overhead costs • Customer demographics • Cost and time to produce proposals • Alignment of programs with strategic plans
Collaborative Systems	• Latency during collaborative process • Number of users • Number of patents/trademarks produced • Number of articles and presentations	• Number of projects • Time lost due • Number of new products • Value of sales from products created in the last 3–5 years (a measure of innovation) • Average learning curve • Proposal response times and "win" rates	• Reduced costs of product development, acquisition, or maintenance • Reduction in the number of delays • Faster response to proposals • Reduced learning curve for new employees
Yellow Pages	• Number of users • Frequency of use • Latency • Searching precision and recall	• Time to find people • Time to solve problems	• Time, money, or personnel time saved as a result of the use of yellow pages • Savings or quality and efficiency
e-Learning Systems	• Latency • Number of users • Number of courses taken per user	• Training costs	• Savings or improvement in organizational quality and efficiency • Improved employee satisfaction • Reduced training costs • Reduced learning curve

Metrics Guide for KM Initiatives, DON, CIO, August, 2001.

Implications for scholarly community include the following:

- Providing a foundation for introducing KM into military organizations and government agencies.
- Contributing to the body of knowledge in the broader scholarly community.
- Identifying, assessing, and prioritizing critical issues in government and military organizations that determine the success or failure of KM.

Potential impacts on military enterprises include the following:

- Identify and prioritize problem areas in which KMTs will contribute to military organizations.
- Identify and prioritize the requirements necessary to institute KMT solutions in military organizations.
- Identify and prioritize the benefits (tangible and intangible) of KMTs to military organizations.

To achieve the purpose of this research agenda, this study focused on a case study enterprise in the military domain, the U.S. Navy's Space and Warfare Systems Command (SPAWAR).

SPAWAR's mission is to provide the military fighter with knowledge superiority by developing, delivering, and maintaining effective, capable, and integrated command; control; communications; and computer, intelligence, and surveillance systems. Moreover, although the name and organizational structure have changed several times over the years, the basic mission of helping the Navy communicate and share critical information has not. SPAWAR provides IT and space systems for today's DON and DOD activities, while planning and designing for the future. SPAWAR's workforce comprises approximately 7,800 military and civilian employees, working to develop, deliver, and maintain the C4ISR (Command, Control, Communications, Computers, Information, Surrivielance, Reconiscense), IT, and space systems for the DON and DOD. The following is a copy of the message from the SPAWAR Commander, RADM Ken Slaught, DON.

> This Strategic Plan presents overarching guidance and goals that will provide value for our customers. I enjoin every member of the Corporation to understand and support this Strategic Plan and make it part of his or her "day job." Although our customers encompass more than just the Fleet, Sailors and Marines must always be at the heart of our efforts. Thus, our Strategic Plan must be focused to provide value for the war fighter in the Fleet. Our Strategic Plan provides a framework to meet four broad objectives:
>
> - To achieve our vision for the future
> - To improve mission performance
> - To tell our story to our customers, stake holders, and partners
> - To motivate and educate the SPAWAR workforce
>
> Our Strategic Plan is aligned with the Top Five priorities of the Chief of Naval Operations. Namely, we aim to
>
> - Win the war for manpower
> - Improve current readiness
> - Prepare for future readiness
> - Enhance our quality of service
> - Achieve Navy-wide alignment

Accordingly, to deliver value to our customers and stakeholders while maintaining alignment with the CNO's priorities, our strategies are both external- and internal-looking. These six strategies are to

- Provide an integrated capability
- Speak with one voice
- Improve our processes
- Enhance our workforce and workplace
- Promote interoperability and commonality
- Lead C4ISR, IT, and space innovation

Additionally, our efforts must emphasize personnel development to transform advanced technologies into combat capability utilizing best business practices. Similarly, the priorities of our customers and stakeholders—our partners—must be our priorities. We will reach out to our customers and stakeholders and update them on our progress in helping them achieve their goals and objectives. We will jointly explore means to meet or exceed expectations. The SPAWAR Corporation manages over $4.5 billion in fiscal resources and is made up of the following components:

- SPAWAR Headquarters, San Diego, CA
- Systems Center Charleston, SC
- Systems Center Chesapeake, VA
- Systems Center San Diego, CA
- Space Field Activity, Chantilly, VA
- Information Technology Center, New Orleans, LA

Our corporation has over 7,800 employees, which includes over 500 reservists distributed in 21 Reserve units across the country. In partnership with Naval Sea Systems Command and Naval Air Systems Command, I expect us to create synergies and deliver value to our customers. We will measure our performance based on objective, measurable criteria. We will establish and continuously evaluate a balanced set of performance measures—these will serve as success indicators for our strategies. We will manage to our metrics and share them with our customers and stake holders. Each fiscal year we will issue an annual report, which will quantify how we have executed our Strategic Plan. I will consider this plan a success when we provide our customers with the following:

- Effective, integrated capability on schedule and at an affordable price
- Fully supported products
- Dependable service from a forward-thinking, trusted agent

(Slaught, 2001, [SPAWAR 2001 Annual Report]).

Space and Naval Warfare Systems Center San Diego (SSC San Diego) is the U.S. Navy's research, development, test and evaluation, engineering, and fleet support center for command, control, and communication systems and ocean surveillance. SSC San Diego provides information resources to support the joint war fighter in mission execution and force protection. SSC San Diego is one of five field activities of Space and Naval Warfare Systems Command (SPAWAR). SPAWAR and its systems centers provide much of the tactical and nontactical IM technology required by the DON to complete its operational missions.

In addition, according to SPAWAR's leadership, science and technology acquisition needs include the following: faster acquisition process, access to expanded information content, architecture hardware/software integration, and technology insertion processes.

Emerging naval strategies and visions provide a framework for transformation. These visions outline efforts to achieve transformational war-fighting capabilities by capitalizing on innovative concepts and describing the processes under which future innovations will be developed and integrated into the naval forces. Tomorrow's Navy and Marine Corps will produce and exploit a battlefield within which naval, air, and ground elements form a unified force (SSC San Diego Web site [www.spawar.navy.mil], 2001).

Location of Pilot Study: SSC Charleston

Based on the description of SPAWAR mission, strategies, and objectives, there is clearly a need to understand the impact of KM technologies on SPAWAR's competitive advantage. This study adds value to that investigation. This line of research began with field research conducted in the summer of 2000 at the SPAWAR Charleston Center under the auspices of the DON CIO. The following is a summary of the results from that pilot study of the value of KM in a military enterprise (Ross 2000).

During 2000 and 2001, the DON CIO and SPAWAR's Systems Center in Charleston, South Carolina (SSC-CHS) collaborated on a pilot study to implement KM at SSC-CHS. This joint effort focused on SSC-CHS's desire to increase the organization's efficiency and productivity by promoting knowledge sharing and learning throughout the organization. The research added to a larger objective of SPAWAR's headquarters to develop KMT solutions.

In August 2000, The DON CIO KCO and the SSC-CHS KM team began collaboration on the KM implementation project. A workshop was held to conduct a benchmark study on SSC-CHS's beliefs, KM state of readiness, and KM objectives. Following initial presentations on the CKO model and implementation plan, two surveys were distributed to 20 SSC-CHS KM leaders. The DON CIO developed these surveys for use throughout the Navy and Marine Corps to help gauge the existing KM status of an organization. One survey focused on assessing the readiness of the organization. The second survey measured beliefs in the relative importance of the dimensions of the KCO framework (Figure 10-3).

The results of questions 1 through 12, where the sequences of the averages are bottom to top, are summarized in Figure 10-3. The respondents to this pilot research study concluded the following:

- SSC-CHS does not think KM is well understood throughout their organization;
- Are not sure if there is sufficient funding to accomplish the KM objectives (Table 1-1) at SSC-CHS
- Recognize the importance of teamwork in KM
- Believe the organization has adequate resources to support IT
- Believe that SSC-CHS has sufficient KM tools to achieve their objectives.

The KM framework survey results are illustrated in Figure 10-4. Each research question was a pair-wise comparison of the five dimensions of the DON KM framework.

The key results of this part of the pilot survey drawn from the beliefs of the SSC-CHS respondents included the following:

- Most people do not think leadership is as important as the other components.
- Culture is considered a very important component and was overwhelmingly chosen against all the other components.

Figure 10-3

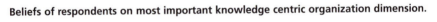

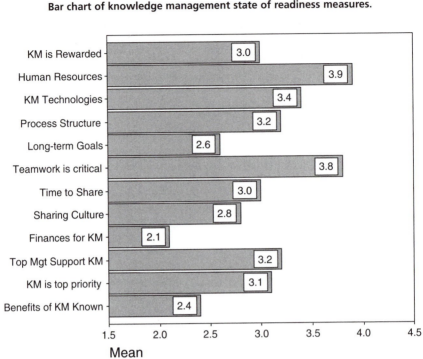

Bar chart of knowledge management state of readiness measures.

Figure 10-4

Beliefs of respondents on most important knowledge centric organization dimension.

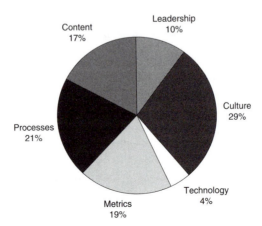

Table 10-4

Findings and Selected Objectives from the SSC-Charleston Pilot Study	
Objective Category	**Selected Objectives**
Business Development	• Capture business opportunities • Identify new markets • Increase expertise in business development and marketing strategies
Project Management (PM)	• Develop customized Flexible data visualization and analysis • Increase synergy among projects (Lessons Learned) • Improve resource management • Reduce delays • Improve PM process modeling • Leverage contractor skills and Lessons Learned • Contract issues
Personnel	• Improve training • Leverage experts • Share Lessons Learned • Advance career development and mobility • Define core knowledge requirement
Form use	• Improve how to use forms • Know when to use forms • Increase automation of forms • Develop solutions to obtain the information on the form, not the form
Data calls	• Understand critical data and where the data resides • Understand actions that are required from data
Adapted from Ross and Kantner, 2000.	

- Most people do think technology is the least important component.
- Metrics were considered very important but less than culture.
- Processes were considered very important but less than culture.
- Managing content was seen as not as important as the other components except for a unanimous opinion of its greater value compared with that of technology. The management of content, a component of leadership, when combined with leadership, rivals culture as a very important belief.

The results of the pilot study demonstrated that the SSC-CHS KM team had an informed understanding of the benefits of KM and their organization's state of readiness for KM. Moreover, the results showed that SSC-CHS leadership was aware that KM cannot be achieved only with technology. In addition, the study identified potential KM projects and suggestions for future research on KM in SPAWAR. The objectives for SSC-CHS identified in the study are summarized in Table 10-4.

The objectives in Table 10-4 revolve around the core competencies of SSC-CHS, including systems engineering, software/hardware design and development, operations and maintenance, and systems integration and installations. In addition, results indicate that for each objective category KMT solutions must allow easy and low-cost ways to update new knowledge. SSC-CHS pilot study participants also indicated that multiple levels of knowledge, which independently can be used by many people collectively, might create a security violation, suggesting that KMT solutions must be able to manage multilevel knowledge security.

Conclusions and Suggestions for Future Research from the Pilot Study

This workshop accomplished its objectives and created a benchmark for the implementation of the KCO model at SSC-CHS. The findings suggested future research and the development of a KM implementation strategy. Some of the suggestions included identification of possible KM pilot problems; assessment of the readiness for KM across the organization; identification of the stage of KCO development; increasing awareness of KM; identification of KM champions; creation of communities of practice; compiling of interviews with SPAWAR leadership to obtain level of commitment; and story-telling to get support for KM in the organization.

Additional recommendations from the study included providing customer support in building the KCO through knowledge mapping, skills and knowledge audit, performance measures, incentives for involvement, knowledge-sharing processes, knowledge base creation, training guidelines, communication plans, and knowledge transfer. Other suggestions included supporting SSC-CHS in sustaining a KCO built through dialogue, feedback, performance measurement, gap analysis, and ongoing strategic planning.

Future research was discussed, including Table 10-4 objectives as well as the efficiency, effectiveness, and sustainable competitive advantage of KM for the SPAWAR enterprise. SSC-CHS desired to investigate the impact of KM on competitive advantage. This research provided a sound foundation for further investigation into the impact of KMTs on efficiency, functionality, and sustainability at SPAWAR, which is the subject of recent research by the authors. Research findings will be published in the near future in academic and practitioner journals and books.

Knowledge Management Criteria

Vittal Anantatmula, D.Sc., CCE

Introduction

Recent advances in information and communication technologies have made it easy to store and transfer knowledge. Globalization, increasing international competition and a free market philosophy are driving forces for these advances in technology. Many organizations have realized that creation, transfer, and management of knowledge are critical for success today.

In the current economy, knowledge has become a key success factor. In a traditional economy, the factors of production have diminishing returns, whereas explicit knowledge is subject to increasing returns (Grant, 2000). Through knowledge management (KM) practices, implicit knowledge, which can be transformed into explicit knowledge, should also produce increasing returns.

Many products include intelligent information to enhance product or service quality to meet customer needs better. From microwaves to cars, and from telephones to personal computers, these smart machines continue to deliver better service. Technology and information are associated with most of our routine activities. In organizations, information and technologies are better used than ever before to produce smart machines and services that are more efficient. Walters and Macrae (2003) sum it up by stating that organizations now operate in the knowledge economy and knowledge is the ultimate competitive advantage (Figure 11-1).

The global capital market is rapidly changing the political, regulatory, and economic barriers that have prevented creation and productive use of knowledge (Manasco, 1997). The current economy has the benefit of technologies, such as the Internet, wireless communications, satellites, networks, videoconferencing, and so forth, to exchange ideas and knowledge within and among organizations at a great speed, thereby increasing the pace of economic activities. In today's business world, money is moving at lightning speed, and skilled workers have options to move from

The chapter is drawn from a paper entitled, "Outcomes of Knowledge Management Initiaitves," which has been accepted for publication in the *International Journal of Knowledge Management* 2005; 1(2): 50–67.

Figure 11-1

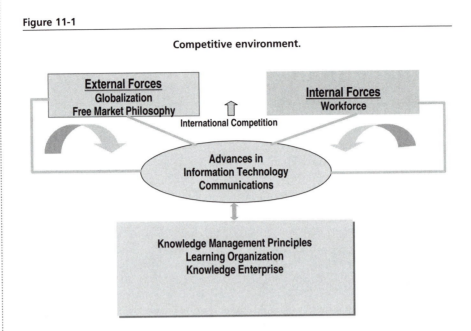

Competitive environment.

one organization to another. Losing the knowledge worker is a major concern today and underlines the importance of KM.

Acknowledging the importance of knowledge, Drucker (1993) argues that compared with previous economic development periods, knowledge has become the primary factor of production in the current economy, and traditional factors of production—land, labor, and capital—are becoming restraints rather than driving forces. Drucker (2001) further contends that managing information is a critical and challenging task and in many companies, could be a key to developing a competitive advantage.

Among the advantages, KM provides an opportunity for organizations to develop processes that would help to prevent them from continually reinventing the wheel. Intellectual capital, in particular, offers a unique competitive advantage to an organization, as it cannot be replicated easily by other organizations. A recent benchmarking study by the American Productivity and Quality Center (APQC) suggested that if companies tap the vast treasure of knowledge, know-how, and best practices that lie within their organizations, it would benefit them financially in millions of dollars and yield huge gains in speed, customer satisfaction, and organizational competence.

Definition of Knowledge and Related Terms

Data, information, and knowledge are often used in a similar vein. It is important to understand the distinction between knowledge and information, as these words are commonly used interchangeably. Figure 11-2 depicts the knowledge hierarchy.

Allee (1997) suggests that data float in a larger sea of information, and data become information through linking and organizing with other data. Information becomes knowledge when it is analyzed, linked to other information, and compared with what is already known.

Figure 11-2

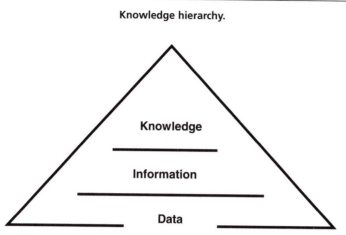

Knowledge hierarchy.

The Oxford English Dictionary provides the following definitions for data, information, and knowledge. These definitions underline the hierarchic relationship among the three terms.

- Data (2): Facts, specifically numerical facts collected together for reference or information.
- Information (2, 3a): Communication of knowledge or news of some fact, subject, or event.
- Knowledge (5a): The fact of knowing a thing, state, etc., familiarity gained by experience.

The distinction is that data represent facts, which are organized into information; when used by someone to solve a problem, information in turn becomes personal knowledge (Ellis, 2003). When we convert it to explicit knowledge, it becomes an intellectual asset that can be shared.

Thus, knowledge is derived from thinking, and it is a combination of information, experience, and insight. Deriving knowledge from information requires human judgment and is based on context and experience.

Knowledge Management

There are several definitions of KM. KM is the systematic, explicit, and deliberate building, renewal, and application of knowledge to maximize an enterprise's knowledge-related effectiveness and returns from its knowledge assets (Wiig, 1993). Ultimately, KM should focus on leveraging relevant knowledge assets to improve organizational performance (Stankosky and Baldanza, 2001).

The primary focus of KM is the use of information technology and tools, business processes, best practices, and culture to develop and share knowledge within an organization and connect those who possess knowledge with those who do not. Ultimately, leveraging relevant knowledge assets to improve organizational performance is what KM is all about.

Publications on the theme of KM are on the rise, and KM is getting attention in the business world. In addition, the increasing gap between the book value and the market value of some business entities indicates the increasing importance of knowledge-

Figure 11-3

Knowledge enterprise model.

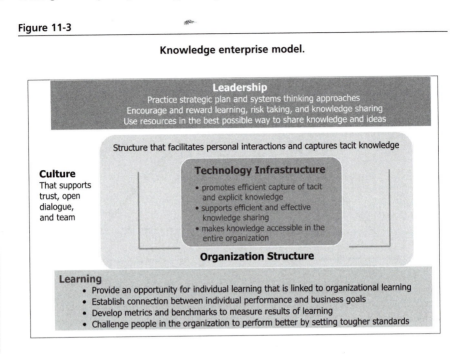

based intangible assets (Marr, 2003) and KM. Ultimately, KM should be a support in achieving desired business results.

Usually, management efforts in an organization are geared toward survival, while making a profit and KM efforts are no different. There are several key characteristics that should exist in a learning organization (Figure 11-3).

Leadership in the knowledge enterprise is responsible for practicing strategic planning and systems thinking approaches, making best use of resources, fostering a culture that encourages open dialogue and team learning, and finally, for encouraging and rewarding risk taking, learning, and knowledge sharing. The enterprise should have a structure that facilitates personal interactions and supports communities of practice to capture tacit and explicit knowledge within the organization. Similarly, technology infrastructure should promote efficient capture of explicit knowledge and support knowledge sharing within and outside the organization.

Finally, the knowledge enterprise should provide an opportunity for individual learning and link it to organizational performance. Such enterprises should develop metrics to measure the results of learning and challenge people to perform better by setting tougher targets.

Missing Commonly Accepted Principles

Several organizations are attempting to use KM to improve organizational performance, but commonly accepted KM principles are not yet developed. "The big problem with knowledge management (KM) has been lack of focus—lots of grand visions; little practicality. KM strategies now need to be built on more secure foundations," says leading expert Fons Trompenaars, of Trompenaars Hampden-Turner (Fairchild, 2002). This recent observation is in agreement with Stankosky and Baldanza's observation that, "although the thrust behind KM is to improve efficiency, effectiveness, and innovation, there are still no organized, commonly accepted KM principles or references to rely upon." According to a research study (Marr, 2003), KM is perceived as a fad by some organizations, because the concept is understood as information management, and was associated with technologic solutions, such as Intranet and databases. With such a narrow focus, an organization's knowledge management efforts and their expected outcomes will also have a narrow focus.

Among the commonly accepted knowledge management principles or references that are missing, an important one is the criteria for measuring success associated with knowledge management.

Research on Knowledge Management Criteria

Inherent intangible characteristics of knowledge assets make them difficult to measure (Ahn and Chang, 2002). Unlike materials or equipment, the core competencies and distinctive abilities of employees are not listed in balance sheets (Austin and Larkey, 2002). As a result, factors that contribute substantially to a firm's success elude traditional means of quantification, thereby presenting significant challenges to performance measurement of knowledge management.

A research study (Bassi and Van Buren, 1999) suggested that the lack of understanding of how to measure and evaluate impacts of intellectual capital is a major obstacle to turn investments toward promoting intellectual capital into a source of competitive advantage. Similarly, Ernst and Young's Center for Business Innovation survey identified measuring the value and performance of knowledge assets as the second most important challenge faced by companies behind the challenge of changing people's behavior (Van Buren, 1999).

Instead of trying to measure knowledge directly, which may not be possible to measure, a different approach is to measure its contribution to business performance, and it is still considered as a major research agenda (Ahn and Chang, 2002). Major consulting organizations agree with this approach, as indicated by another case study, which indicated that measuring effectiveness and contributions of knowledge management is a key concern for consulting organizations (Wikramasinghe, 2002).

A survey of 100 FTSE (index used by London Stock Exchange and Financial Times) companies was attempted to establish levels of engagement with knowledge management, the organizational implications, and evidence of impact on performance (Longbottom and Chourides, 2001). The survey results suggested that performance measures are not well developed, but links to balance scorecard frameworks are suggested.

Another research study indicated that since knowledge management activities are integral to other management activities and processes, measuring knowledge management is about how and when knowledge management is integrated into organizational activities, which can be measured (Fairchild, 2002). It is important to identify these activities, and determine contributions of knowledge managements to these activities. The study suggested that organizations should require less precision and more interest in trends than exact figures using a balance scorecard approach, such as customer and employee satisfaction, and intellectual capital.

All the research findings discussed above lead us to the conclusion that knowledge management results are difficult to measure. It should also be considered that there is no common or standard nomenclature for describing knowledge assets, let alone an accepted economic model of valuing them. This knowledge gap is the focus of the current research effort. Specifically, the research effort is aimed to establish criteria for measuring efforts associated with knowledge management.

Literature Review

The *Oxford English Dictionary* defines criterion as, "a test, principle, rule, canon, or standard, by which anything can be judged or estimated." A criterion can be considered a standard that allows us to establish preferences among alternatives. Establishing criteria for knowledge management is important, because we cannot determine its results unless we have criteria against which to measure.

When asked, *How do you measure success?*, Carla O'Dell, president of benchmarking organization APQC, said that there is no room for woolly targets and the value of KM strategies can only be measured by the benefits to a specific task. (Gubbins, 2003).

The literature research findings are elusive about the criteria for evaluating knowledge management success. The research question is *What should be the criteria for measuring knowledge management success?* The main research objective is to establish the criteria for measuring success associated with KM.

On the basis of extensive literature review, several factors were identified to be included in the list of criteria All of them have direct references, not necessarily as criteria, but under different terms such as "benefits," "impact," "focus," "performance factors," "metrics," "results," "strategies," and "value." Of the literature sources, eleven references were listed in Table 11-1, based on their relevance to KM (Anantatmula, 2004). As some of the references were less obvious and implicit, they had to be expanded and similar ones had to be identified from the list of criteria through analysis and inferences. Because the list was developed for the use of the survey questionnaire only, the inferences will not have any significant influence on the final research.

On the basis of the literature findings (Griffin and Houston, 1980; Jianh and Klein, 1999), a research model (Figure 11-4) was developed that shows that the criteria for measuring KM success is derived from an organization's mission, objectives, and goals. As a result, top management supports KM efforts. In turn, top management support is associated with providing adequate funds and with functional managers participating in efforts associated with KM initiatives. In addition to establishing the criteria for measuring KM efforts, associations and relations described in the research model are also examined.

Research Methodology

The research used two different research tools for data collection and analysis, with occasional use of in-depth interviewing and personal discussions. They are as follows:

1. Delphi technique
2. Survey questionnaire

The Delphi technique used a few KM experts to address the research questions, and is aimed at reaching consensus in response to these questions. The Delphi technique uses a group of experts to deliberate a research issue or a problem anonymously (i.e., without having a direct interaction among the group members). Members of the group are not informed of the identity of the other group members. The Delphi technique does not need face-to-face interaction and it does not have the disadvantages of conventional groups because it provides anonymity and controlled feedback. However, the Delphi technique has certain disadvantages: It is a slow process, and to some extent, swiftness of the decision-making process is controlled by participating individuals (Anantatmula, 2004).

Table 11-1

Literature Review Summary of KM Criteria

Criteria	KPMG	Skyrme	Perkmann	Wiig	Ofek & Sarvary	Kelly	BoozAllen & Hamilton	BP Amoco	Ruggles	Longbottom et. al	Allee	Delphi
Better decision making	•											•
Better customer handling	•	•							•			•
Faster response to key business issues	•					•	•	•		•		
Improved employee skills	•	•	•				•					
Improved productivity	•		•				•					
Increased profits	•			•		•	•	•				•
Sharing best practices	•		•				•	•	•	•	•	•
Reduced costs	•	•		•	•			•	•	•		•
New or better ways of working	•		•					•	•	•	•	•
Increased market share	•			•		•		•				•
Creation of new business opportunities	•			•						•		
Improved new product development	•			•		•		•		•		
Better staff attraction/ retention	•	•						•				

Table 11-1 (cont'd)

Criteria	KPMG	Skyrme	Perkmann	Wiig	Ofek & Sarvary	Kelly	BoozAllen & Hamilton	BP Amoco	Ruggles	Longbottom et. al	Allee	Delphi
Increased share price	•							•				
Enhanced product or service quality		•		•	•	•	•			•		•
Creation of more value to customers		•		•	•	•	•			•		•
Enhanced intellectual capital											•	•
Improved communication								•				•
Increased innovation		•	•							•	•	•
Improved business process			•								•	•
Improved learning/ adaptation capability		•			•	•	•	•	•		•	
Return on investment of KM efforts								•				
Increased market size				•		•		•	•			
Entry to different market type								•				
Increased empowerment of employees		•		•				•				•
Enhanced collaboration in organization												•

Figure 11-4

Research model.

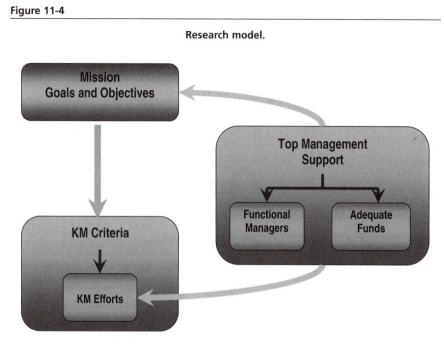

Because both these techniques address identical research questions in different forms, the Delphi technique research effort is designed to complement the survey questionnaire. Identified criteria from the Delphi technique are added to the list in Table 11-1 and used for the survey questionnaire. The summary findings of the Delphi technique were also used to refine the survey questionnaire.

With its initial design, and then based on the pilot test feedback, the survey questionnaire is designed with the following features:

- There are only 19 questions divided in three parts, which used only four pages, making the questionnaire simple and less time-consuming.
- A brief note about the purpose of the questionnaire is provided in the cover letter.
- Definitions are provided for important terms used in the questionnaire.
- An information sheet is included to obtain consent and ensure confidentiality of the responses.
- Instructions and questions are simple and easy to understand.
- Respondents are given an option to receive research findings.

The survey consists of 17 close-ended and two open-ended questions. Many of the close-ended questions have multiple choices, which use the Likert scale. The primary research question has three parts to respond to the following:

- Identify the criteria that are used to measure KM success
- Importance of each criterion
- Effectiveness of each criterion

The *Oxford English Dictionary* defines importance (1a) as, "having some degree of gravity, weight, or consequence," and effectiveness (2) as, "concerned with or having the function of carrying into effect, executing, or accomplishing." The importance of the criterion gives the evidence of significance or consequence, whereas effectiveness denotes the capability of being used to a purpose. Thus, effectiveness addresses efficacy and usefulness of the criterion. A criterion that is important may or may not be effective. If a criterion is chosen as both important and effective, it is considered the favored one.

The questionnaire was aimed at a target population consisting of professionals and practitioners of KM. Those surveyed are from government, nonprofit, and for-profit organizations. The survey instrument was used to solicit responses from a number of KM professionals around the world; 153 valid responses were received. Statistical analysis of the results reveals the most favored criteria for measuring efforts associated with KM efforts.

Research Results

Professional profiles of respondents and profiles of organizations provide valuable information about the context in which the research findings are applicable. Of those surveyed, nearly all the respondents have some KM experience, with 79% respondents having more than 3 years of experience and 42% with 6 or more years of experience in KM (Figure 11-5). When asked to rate themselves on expertise in KM, only 3.3% of respondents rated themselves as novice and more than two thirds of them considered themselves to be either experts or close to being experts. Some of those surveyed hold positions such as chairman/CEO, president/CEO, founder/CEO, chief knowledge officer, managing director, director KM, director, KM architect, KM consultant, senior knowledge strategist, principal, and principal strategy officer.

Through descriptive statistical analysis, it was evident that respondents have KM experience, that they consider themselves knowledgeable about KM, and that they are involved in decision making about KM initiatives in their respective organizations. Finally, their roles and responsibilities appear to be consistent with their organizational profiles.

Only 78% of the respondents represented provided their contact information, which provides a geographic profile of the respondents. Another question that addresses the geographic characteristics of organizations suggests that 35% of organi-

Figure 11-5

Respondents' knowledge management experience profile.

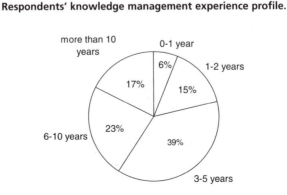

zations are multinational. While respondents represent organizations from 21 different countries, 52 of 147 organizations are multinational, indicating that the data represent organizations that have a presence in more than 21 countries.

Research results indicated that whereas 48% of respondents represented for-profit organizations, government and nonprofit organizations were represented by 21% and 26% of respondents, respectively. Of the organizations represented, 31.5% had 100 employees or fewer, whereas 36.2% organizations had 2,500 or more, and 24.8% of them had 10,000 or more employees. In terms of revenue, 47% of organizations had more than $1 million revenue, with 21% of them having more than $1 billion. Revenue is not applicable for 37% of organizations.

In summary, the demographic profile suggests that respondents to the survey questionnaire are KM professionals and practitioners and they represent the following:

- Different types of organizations in terms of number of employees
- Different types of organizations in terms of revenue
- Different types of organizations (i.e., government, for-profit, and nonprofit organizations)
- Organizations with various types of business
- Organizations with different geographic characteristics (i.e., single location, several locations, and multinational types)
- Organizations from many countries

Because almost all of the respondents indicated that they have KM experience and that they have answered KM-related questions nos. 2 to 10, we can assume that most of these organizations are involved in implementing KM. Filtered responses (based on KM experience and expertise) and total responses were used to establish the most favored KM criteria.

Knowledge Management Criteria

The main question of the survey presents a list of 26 criteria. Respondents were asked to choose whether they had used any of them for measuring KM success in their organizations. They were also asked to assign an importance and effectiveness score for each criterion on a 5-point scale. The importance of the criterion gives the evidence of significance or consequence, whereas effectiveness denotes the capability of being used to a purpose (i.e., for measuring KM success).

Establishing KM criteria is the main purpose of the research study. To ensure validity and inject rigor, it was important to use different methods to establish them. These methods include:

- Favored criteria based on mean values of importance and effectiveness for all of the responses.
- Favored criteria based on mean values of importance and effectiveness for filtered data based on respondents' expertise in KM.
- Favored criteria based on their use (yes/no responses).

The second method was operationalized by filtering the data based on respondents' experience in KM. Three sets of data are used for analysis and are based on the following:

1. All the responses ($N = 152$)
2. Respondents who have ≥ 3 years of experience ($n = 118$)
3. Respondents who have ≥ 6 years of experience ($n = 62$)

Because only 26 respondents indicated that they have 10 or more years of KM experience, that category was not used for filtering the data.

The sample mean value of the criterion importance is uniformly less than the sample mean value of effectiveness for all of the criteria. It may indicate that respondents are relatively unsure about the effectiveness of each criterion. Also, the perceived difference between importance and effectiveness is not significant. As we move from data set 1 to 3 (described above for filtering the data), the sample mean value of effectiveness decreased, indicating that respondents with more experience are more certain about the effectiveness of the KM criteria.

To determine the criteria for measuring KM success, an *x-y* scatterplot of mean values of importance and effectiveness of each criterion was used (Figure 11-6).

Similar *x-y* plots were developed for all the three data sets. The plot was divided on the basis of the quartile values. The first quartile represents high importance—high effectiveness of criteria—whereas the last quartile represents low importance—low effectiveness of criteria.

The first quartile can be seen as respondents' most favored criteria as they are both important and effective. In the same vein, the criteria placed in the last quartile of the scatterplot are considered the least favored criteria. These results suggest that respondents would use the most favored criteria and would not use the least favored criteria to measure KM efforts.

Respondents were asked to choose whether they had used any of the criteria for measuring KM success in their organization. All 26 criteria received responses in the range of 140 to 147. Thus, as an average, each criterion received 143 responses. Consistent with quartiles used earlier, a percentage of this average response is used to classify the criteria into three groups:

Figure 11-6

Scatterplot (x-y) of knowledge management criteria (all responses).

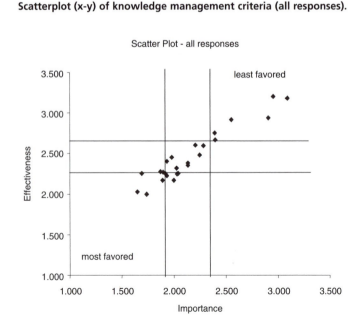

Scatter Plot - all responses

- Criteria with 75% (of average response rate) or more "yes" responses
- Criteria with 75% (of average response rate) or more "no" responses
- Criteria with "yes/no" responses (remaining)

The first set of criteria (with 75% yes responses) can be construed as respondents' most favored criteria. Similarly, the second set of criteria can be considered as respondents' least favored criteria. The qualifying number of responses for the first and second sets of criteria is 107 or more.

Table 11-2

KM—Most Favored Criteria			
All Responses	**≥3 Years Experience**	**≥6 Years Experience**	**Based on Use**
• enhanced collaboration	• enhanced collaboration	• enhanced collaboration	• enhanced collaboration
• improved communication	• improved communication	• improved communication	• sharing best practices
• improved employee skills	• improved employee skills	• improved employee skills	• better decision making
• improved productivity	• improved productivity	• enhanced product or service quality	• new or better ways of working
• better decision making			• improved employee skills
			• improved communication

Table 11-3

KM—Least Favored Criteria			
All Responses	**≥3 Years Experience**	**≥6 Years Experience**	**Based on Use**
• increased share price	• increased share price	• increased share price	• Increased share price
• increased market size	• increased market size	• increased market size	• Increased market share
• increased market share	• increased market share	• increased market share	• Increased market size
• entry into different market	• entry into different market	• entry into different market	
• increased profits	• increased profits	• increased profits	
• better staff attention/ retention	• better staff attention/ retention	• reduced costs	
• ROI on KM efforts		• ROI on KM efforts	

Based on different methods used to establish the criteria for measuring KM success discussed in this section, the common criteria to all the methods are as follows:

Most Favored Criteria
- Enhanced collaboration within organization
- Improved communication
- Improved employee skills

Least Favored Criteria
- Increased share price
- Increased market share
- Increased market size

It is interesting to note that the least favored criteria can be quantified and easily measured, whereas the most favored criteria are difficult to measure, and cannot be easily tied to bottom-line results. It can be concluded that KM efforts have internal focus, and they may have indirect impact on business results, specifically market performance.

Other criteria that are associated with business results—increased profits, reduced costs, improved new product development, return on investment of KM efforts, and enhanced product or service quality—are not among the most or least favored criteria. It is important to understand that these results do not mean that KM efforts would not lead to results associated with the least favored criteria. However, these criteria preferences may vary for different types of organizations, and these issues will be analyzed in the next section.

Knowledge Management and Organizations

Management initiatives toward KM efforts—top management support, provision of adequate funds, and participation of functional managers—are strongly aligned with each other, and with the notion that criteria for measuring KM success are based on organizations' mission, objectives, and goals.

Descriptive statistics indicated that KM efforts received top management support. Nevertheless, these results were uncertain about provision of adequate funds and participation of functional managers in KM efforts.

Although most respondents agreed that the criteria for measuring KM success are based on an organization's mission, objectives, and goals, the pair-wise correlation analysis indicated that the aligned criteria are not necessarily the most favored criteria. Some of the criteria, which are related to business performance and growth, are easily measurable and are aligned with the mission, objectives, and goals of an organization. The pair-wise correlation analysis suggested that top management support is aligned with factors relating to business performance and the delegation of power. Participation of functional managers in KM efforts is aligned with many criteria effectiveness, which signifies its value to KM efforts.

Knowledge Management and Types of Organizations

Respondents were asked to identify their organization from the following options, the percentage of responses for each one is mentioned below.

- Federal or state government: 21%
- Nonprofit organization: 26%

- For-profit organization: 48%
- Other: 5%

One-way analysis of variance (ANOVA) was used to determine whether the sample mean value difference in mean values of criteria is different for each type of organization or not. These results indicate that the criteria for measuring KM efforts are different for different types of organizations. The most favored criteria for each type of organization are as follows:

Government
- Improved communication
- Improved productivity

Nonprofit
- Improved communication
- Enhanced collaboration within organization
- Improved learning, adaptation capability

For-Profit
- Enhanced collaboration within organization
- Improved employee skills
- Enhanced product or service quality

It is interesting to note that among the three types of organizations, only government and for-profit organizations do not have any common criteria. Nonprofit organizations have one criterion in common with government and for-profit organizations. Although government and nonprofit organizations focus on internal performance only, for-profit organizations focus on both on internal and external performance.

Improving communication is a common criterion for both the government and the nonprofit organizations. Key tenets of KM are maintaining, applying, and creating knowledge. These tenets can be implemented through effective communication. Additionally, improved productivity is identified as the most favored KM criterion for government organizations. True to their altruistic purpose, nonprofit organizations favored learning, adaptability, and enhanced collaboration as the KM criteria, in addition to communication.

Enhanced collaboration is a common criterion for nonprofit and for-profit organizations. For-profit organizations favored both external and internal measures. The most favored criteria focused on improving employee skills, greater collaboration among people and processes within an organization, and providing better product or service quality to their customers.

Research Contributions

The primary objective of this research project was to establish criteria to measure success or failure associated with KM efforts. To achieve this, measurement criteria were first developed. Then the measurement criteria were tested in an exploratory study to ascertain the validity of the test criteria, and to establish a baseline for future research that might use these criteria. The availability of the criteria and the foundation for measurement would be of significant value to the body of knowledge in the KM area.

The primary focus of KM is to use information technology and tools, business processes, best practices, and culture to develop and share knowledge within an organization and connect those who possess knowledge to those who do not.

The literature shows, and the research conducted confirms, that the criteria for measuring KM success agree with this primary focus and underscore their emphasis on improving employee skills through better communication and greater collaboration within the organization. The research identified enhanced collaboration within organization, improved communication, and improved employee skills as the top three most favored criteria. The other two criteria, improved productivity and better decision making, are the results of the first three criteria.

Knowledge Management and Organization Goals

In principle, KM criteria must be guided by an organization's goals, and bottom-line results. If KM initiatives do not contribute to an organization's business and organizational performance, top management would not support such initiatives. Thus, it is important to relate research findings to bottom-line results.

The research revealed that KM efforts result in soft measures, which are not directly tied to end results. These results also imply that KM outcomes are difficult to measure. However, efforts focused on improving these soft measures lead to gains in efficiency, effectiveness, and innovation, which in turn have a significant effect on what organizations look for (Figure 11-7). The figure shows the most favored KM criteria for different types of organizations. These criteria are color-coded based on organizational type. Some of them are common to more than one organization type.

KM efforts toward *enhancing collaboration* are specific to both nonprofit and for-profit organizations. These efforts are translated into improving business processes, systems, and team performance. In turn, these successes will result in increased innovation, better decision making, and improved team performance.

Improved communication, which is common to both government and nonprofit organizations, leads to improved learning, a greater awareness of mission critical information, and the transformation of individual knowledge to organizational knowledge and vice versa. Together, these factors will improve organizational processes and decision making systems.

Improved productivity as a result of knowledge management efforts is specific to government organizations, and will lead to efficiency gains, improved employee satisfactions and morale.

KM efforts, which focus on *improving employee skills* and *enhancing product or service quality*, are specific to for-profit organizations. Gains in product or service quality are directly related to both organizational and market performance. Improved employee skills translate into efficiency and effectiveness gains.

Improved learning and adaptation ability as a result of KM efforts is specific to nonprofit organizations. These efforts will lead to the transformation of individual knowledge to organizational knowledge and vice versa. It will also result in more informed and better decision making, improved processes, and systems.

Finally, KM efforts related to these most favored criteria lead to improving efficiency, effectiveness, and innovation. As a result, KM efforts will ultimately lead to

Figure 11-7

Knowledge management criteria (business results).

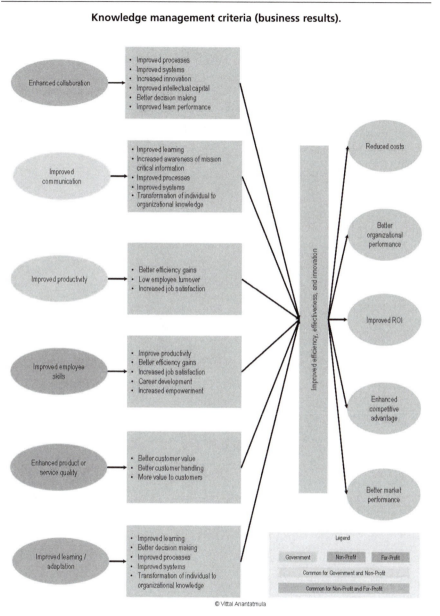

© Vittal Anantatmula

improved organizational and market performance, competitive advantage, return on investment, and reduced costs.

Research results also indicate that having KM criteria is necessary, but not sufficient alone to achieve expected results of KM efforts. The research findings should help government, nonprofit, and for-profit organizations in identifying focus areas of KM efforts, and evaluating their KM initiatives.

Conclusions

Knowledge, as a source of competitive advantage, will continue to gain strategic importance, and organizations will be compelled to apply knowledge to improve performance. KM will continue to evolve to develop industry and organization-specific systems and processes.

Through future research efforts, the most favored criteria identified through this research can be further developed into detailed measures of KM success.

A Framework of Intangible Valuation Areas

Annie Green, D.Sc.

The framework of intangible valuation areas (FIVA) represents a dynamic relationship between strategic objectives of knowledge management and value drivers of intangible assets. FIVA provides a view of intangible assets within the context of the business enterprise, supports their valuation based on a common set of business dimensions, and supports the surfacing of measurement and performance indicators of intangible assets based on a common set of business dimensions.

Introduction

> When nearly two thirds of the companies in the world's largest economy have accepted the need for change, we no longer have an interesting new trend, but a revolution. (Edvinsson and Malone, 1997, p. 7).

Businesses have transcended through a myriad of changes as they have evolved through the agricultural, industrial, and information ages. These evolutionary changes have significantly changed the way businesses operate and have affected the relative value of its existing value components. Intangible assets have surfaced as a major value contributor—accounting for up to 70% of the value of a business enterprise (Sullivan, 2000; Hope and Fraser, 1997)—and yet, they are not adequately represented in current accounting methodologies. Intangible assets, as a value contributor of today's business enterprise, have obviated previous accounting methodologies.

Intangible assets, the strategic key to a business enterprise's future, are invisible with respect to traditional bottom-line thinking and corporate practice (Rivette and Klein, 2000). Current accounting methods do not convey the relevant and timely information that is critical to the survival and success of today's business enterprises (Lev, 2001). Before the knowledge era, businesses lived in a world of tangibles, which work well with current accounting practices; however, things are different in today's world of intangibles. A major difference is the significance of intangible assets in the market valuation of the business enterprise and the methods used to account for the value contributed by them (Sullivan, 2000; Edvinsson and Malone, 1997; Reilly and Schweihs, 1999; Sveiby, 1997). Business valuations are currently viewed via a double-entry accounting method that is based on tangible-asset valuations. These accounting methods do not recognize intangible assets, which prevents most businesses from knowing their true value (Brookings, 1996). There are numerous intangible-asset models being developed to supplement traditional accounting methods (Shand, 1999; Sveiby, 2001; Bontis, 2000; Hurwitz et al., 2002). However, these valuations models service only one organization—usually the one that it was designed for or that designed it (Bontis, 2000). Current intangible-asset models tend to focus on one or two classes of intangibles for specific firms (Hurwitz et al., 2002), are primarily anecdotal (Bontis, 2000; Shand, 1999), and are based on individual organizations or researchers who have established intangible-asset initiatives that are documented and developed from previous models without advancing or testing them (Bontis, 2000). There is a business need to view intangible assets within the context of the business enterprise and to value them on a common set of dimensions (Stewart, 2001). The accounting of intangible assets needs to be defined and standardized. The significance contributions of a defined and standard approach to intangible-asset valuation are as follows:

- The identification of a discrete set of common value drivers of intangible assets
- The presentation of intangible asset management (IAM) within the context of the business/enterprise value chain
- The establishment of a common taxonomy that contributes to the accountability of intangible assets of a business enterprise
- The definition of an evolutionary path that serves as a base case by which a business can measure its IAM position and progress
- The identification of leverage areas that provides a business with strategic focal points

Today's businesses need to evolve into the knowledge economy, with a methodology and valuation system that enables the identification, capture, and valuation of intangible assets that is aligned with the strategic goals of the business. Today's business enterprise needs a comprehensive methodology that supports the following:

- The dynamic development and use of knowledge in an effective manner in the execution of business activities (Sullivan, 1998)
- The establishment of tools and indicators to manage innovation and increase earnings within the business enterprise (Sullivan, 1998)
- The use of knowledge in future development of a business enterprise value chain (Von Krogh et al., 1998)
- The introduction of a more fluid value network model in the value creation process of a business enterprise (Allee, 2000)
- The cultivation of intellectual capital (IC) in the context of the business strategy (Stewart, 1999)
- The establishment of strategies that concentrate on knowledge value exchanges and intangible benefits (Allee, 2000)

There are many efforts by researchers and individual companies to develop methods and tools to account for intangible assets (Sveiby, 2001; Bontis, 2000; Hurwitz et al., 2002; Shand, 1999). However, these methods are not consistent, standard, or validated enough to be used by industry at large (Stewart, 2001; Bontis, 2000; Shand, 1999).

The industry is in an economic transformation from an industrial economy to an information-based economy (Toffler, 1980). This transformation is significantly changing the value components of today's business enterprise. Investors are uninformed and managers are operating with significant uncertainty in their decision making due to a lack of knowledge of intangible-value drivers (Stewart, 2001). Industry is scrutinizing the viability of existing intangible-assets models (Bontis, 2000; Shand, 1999). The service industry, which appears to be the main benefactor of intangible-assets management, is experiencing significant growth (Hope and Hope, 1997; Blair and Wallman, 2000; Sveiby, 1997; Triplett and Bosworth, 2000). These factors, along with others, are business drivers that support the business enterprises' need to have methods and techniques to account for and measure intangible assets.

The business enterprise of today is not effective at accounting for and valuing a significant portion of its valuation components. Leaders of America's most successful companies recognize that intangible assets rather than physical assets give rise to a new ecology of competition (Rivette and Klein, 2000). They also realize that intangible assets can provide tangible bottom-line results if the drivers of value are extracted.

Background

Today's businesses are currently in a dislocation phase between the second- and third-wave economies (Hope and Hope, 1997). The *first wave* of economic evolution, the agricultural economy, lasted from 8000 B.C. to the mid-eighteenth century and was driven by physical labor. The *second wave*, the industrial economy, led the way as industry transitioned to the twentieth century and was driven by machines and blue-collar workers. The industrial wave is currently transitioning to the *third wave*, the information economy, which is driven by information technology (IT) and knowledge workers (Toffler, 1980). The transition from the industrial to the information age has highlighted the reality that accepted management principles and practices that worked in the first and second waves are not adequate for the competitive environments of the third wave (Hope and Hope, 1997).

The following defines the evolution of intangible assets as a value component in today's knowledge economy:

The old economy—The traditional value scheme and its role in the valuation of the business enterprise.

The evolving economy—The drivers of change to the traditional valuation scheme and the impact of the changes on the valuation of the business enterprise.

The new economy—What valuation components are needed to transition the traditional valuation scheme to an effective new valuation scheme to be used in the valuation of today's business enterprise.

The Old Economy

The value components that brought success throughout the industrial wave are now ineffective with the competitive environment of the new millennium (Hope and Hope, 1997). Tangible assets are the value drivers of the old economy and generally accepted accounting principles (GAAP) is the structure that supports the valuation of tangible assets.

Tangible Assets

Five hundred years ago, Frater Luca Bartolomes Pacioli developed double-entry bookkeeping methods (ACAUS, 1999). This was the first accounting text (Stewart, 1994). The current accounting system is based on the Pacioli scheme of double-entry bookkeeping. Current belief is that Pacioli's scheme does not work in the information age, because it only includes the costs of material and labor (Stewart, 1994), not the value components introduced by the information wave.

The Generally Accepted Accounting Principles

The following paragraph summarizes the discussion of the history of disclosure practices and conventions published by Robert E. Litan and Peter J. Wallison, in *The GAAP Gap Corporate Disclosure in the Internet Age* (Litan and Wallison, 2000, pp. 13–25). Accounting has been in existence for centuries. The role of government in the U.S. economy was minimized until the depression following the stock market crash of 1929. The Securities Act of 1933 and the Securities and Exchange Act of 1934 formed the legal basis of disclosure policy and provided the Securities Exchange Commission (SEC) with the authority to set accounting standards or to delegate that authority. The SEC delegated the authority to the American Institute of Certified Public Accountants (AICPA), who produced what is known today as Generally Accepted Accounting Principles (GAAP). AICPA held this authority until 1973. In 1974, the Financial Accounting Standards Board (FASB) was established to oversee the refinement of GAAP. Also in 1973, the International Accounting Standards Committee (IASC) was formed because of the need for globalization of economic activity to set standards that would allow easy comparison of the financial performance of firms headquartered in different countries. Most countries, except Canada and the United States, adopted the standards of the IASC. The GAAP does not account for intangible assets and is not effective in the current business environment (Eccles et al., 2001; Lev, 2001; Barth, 2000; Skyrme, 1999; Brookings, 1996; Edvinsson and Malone, 1997; Sullivan, 1998; Sveiby, 1997; Stewart, 2001).

An Evolving Economy

The information wave began in 1960; it will extend for decades to come (Toffler, 1980). Current economic theory dictates the valuation of resources in the market place, but supply-and-demand of IC in the market place has not been fully developed (Barth, 2000). Standard accounting practices present major hurdles in achieving IC valuation (Eccles, 2001; Lev, 2001; Barth, 2000; Skyrme, 1999; Brookings, 1996; Edvinsson and Malone, 1997; Sullivan, 1998; Sveiby, 1997).

Significant research and studies have been performed to support the status of intangible assets in today's economy. Dr. Margaret Blair of the Brookings Institute did a study of thousands of nonfinancial companies over a 20-year period. The study findings indicate that a typical firm's value associated with tangible assets decreased from 80% in 1978 to 30% in 1998, whereas its value associated with intangible assets increased from 20% in 1978 to 70% in 1998 (Sullivan, 2000). Hope and Fraser (1997) identified IC as a critical metric in determining the economic value of a company and presented IC and KM as representing 50% to 90% of the market value of today's business. Tobin's q ratio, which measures the relationship between a company's market value and its replacement value, is high in companies in which IC is abundant (Bontis, 1998a). The five top-valued companies (as of 1997) on the New York Stock Exchange have a market value approximating 13 times their book value. Microsoft and Coca-Cola, the two leading companies, have market values at 21 and 26 times the book value, respectively (Sullivan, 1998). *Fortune* magazine commissioned Baruch Lev and associate Mark Bothwell to calculate the knowledge capital of the brawniest nonfinancial companies in America. IC for companies like General

Electric, Pfizer, Microsoft, which lead the list of the top 50 U.S. companies, forms an incredible percentage of market capitalization (Stewart, 2001).

Stewart's 2001 article, *Accounting Gets Radical*, discusses methods of valuing knowledge capital. Stewart applauds the efforts because he recognizes the need for these types of valuation methods. However, Stewart "flips the coin" and expresses concern that these methods be validated before being absorbed and instantiated into industry. The SEC, members of the financial community, accounting professions, and policy makers are joining the efforts to supplement annual financial reports with knowledge measures (Sullivan, 1998). The Brookings Institute, PricewaterhouseCoopers (PWC), and the FASB are voicing their discontent with the current standard for reporting IC and have started initiatives to research and provide acceptable solutions (Stewart, 2001). The market-to-book ratio among the largest 500 companies in the United States (Standard and Poors [SandP] 500) has continuously increased since the early 1980s, reaching a value of approximately 6 in March 2001. For every dollar on the balance sheet, there are 5 dollars representing intangible assets not accounted for on the balance sheet (Lev, 2001).

The surge of intangibles is related to two economic factors: intensified business competition due to globalization of trade and deregulation in key economic sectors (e.g., telecommunications, electric power suppliers, financial services), and the advent of information technologies (Lev, 2001). These changing economic factors have evolved the information wave (Toffler, 1980), which is dominated by service organizations (Hope and Hope, 1997; Blair and Wallman, 2000; Sveiby, 1997; Triplett and Bosworth, 2000). In the United States, 1995 is the year companies *serving* industry outnumbered those in industry (Sveiby, 1997). Capital accumulation has more than doubled in the last 10 years, and the bulk of this growth is attributed to IT (Bosworth and Triplett, 2000). The technology sector has grown from 10% of the SandP-500 index in 1991 to over 30% of the index in 2000 (Bosworth and Triplett, 2000). IT, a large segment of the service industry, is a major driver of this economic change (Hope and Hope, 1997). With the steady increase of the service industry comes the delivery of high-end skilled services and professional services that significantly involves intangibles (Blair and Wallman, 2000).

The New Economy

The postindustrial economy or information age would be better described as the *knowledge economy* (Litan and Wallison, 2000). The term *knowledge economy* reflects the major component—knowledge—that is the key driver of value for the fastest growing companies in the information wave, or knowledge economy (Litan and Wallison, 2000). Knowledge management (KM) drives the knowledge economy, and "knowledge" within the business enterprise is used to positively affect the performance of a business enterprise (Sullivan, 1998). "Knowledge," or the collective intelligence of people within a business enterprise, is believed to be the largest intangible asset in a business enterprise (Sullivan, 1998).

Although knowledge is identified as the largest intangible asset in an organization (Sullivan, 1998), the sum of measures of individual capabilities (knowledge, skill, and experience of the company's employees and managers) does not include all the intangible assets within a business enterprise. The business enterprise must also capture the dynamics of an intelligent business enterprise in a changing competitive environment (Edvinsson and Malone, 1997). Emphasizing only new technologies and focusing only on information disregards the social periphery—context, background, history, common knowledge, and social resources (Brown, 2000). The social periphery, the communities, organizations, and institutions are vital to how people live and work (Brown, 2000). Intangibles include the people and the social periphery that surrounds them. "Knowledge is a fluid mix of framed experience, values, contextual information, and expert insight that provides a framework for evaluating and incorporating new experience and information. In organizations, it often becomes embedded not only in documents or repositories, but also in organizational routines, processes, practices, and norms" (Davenport and Pruzak, 1998, p. 5). In the new economy, intangibles are capital, assets, and investments and are capitalized or monitored from an asset point of view (Wiig, 1994).

New Valuation and Management Components

Innovation, service, quality, speed, and knowledge are the defining factors in the knowledge economy (Hope and Fraser, 1997). In the knowledge economy, a business enterprise creates value through intangibles such as "innovation, employee skill and imagination, customer loyalty, contractual relationships with suppliers and distributors, and better internal and external communications, trademarks, know-how, patents, software, brands, research and development, strategic alliances, and product differentiation" (Litan and Wallison, 2000, p. 26). Intangible assets are the new valuation components in the knowledge economy and are to be included in the value chain of a business enterprise. KM and IAM are the management components that support the accounting of intangible assets within the business enterprise.

Intellectual Capital/Intangible Assets

IC is the possession of the "knowledge, applied experience, organizational technology, customer relationships and professional skills" (Edvinsson and Malone 1997, p. 44) that provide a business enterprise with competitive advantage in the marketplace, IC value is tightly coupled with the business enterprise's ability to transform intangible assets into financial returns (Edvinsson and Malone, 1997). IC is the key to corporate competitiveness and survival, and today's business enterprise seeks to become a knowledgeable and more intelligent enterprise (Sullivan, 1998).

IC is not new; it has been in existence for a while, it has been named "goodwill" (Brookings, 1996). There are many interpretations (and misinterpretations) of goodwill, which can be grouped into two categories—accounting interpretations and economic interpretations (Reilly and Schweihs, 1999). The accounting interpretation of goodwill is generally under GAAP, and is rarely recorded on the company's financial statements. To the accountant, intangible value in the nature of goodwill is the total value (i.e., the acquisition purchase price) of the business less the value of the businesses tangible assets (Reilly and Schweihs, 1999). The economist's interpretation defines intangible-asset goodwill as the capitalization of all of the economic income from a business enterprise that cannot be associated with any other asset (tangible or intangible) of the business. The economist quantifies all of the economic income and allocates or assigns portions of the total economic income to each of the assets (tangible or intangible) that contribute to the production of that income (Reilly and Schweihs, 1999). The economist's interpretation is less global than the accountant's interpretation and is more useful in the identification and valuation of specific intangible-asset goodwill (Reilly and Schweihs, 1999). IC is a critical metric for determining the economic value of a company, and companies should account for profitability of these investments, or monitor how well these investments contribute to revenues, improved operating costs, and net incomes.

Knowledge Management

The purpose of KM is to create a more collaborative environment, reduce duplication of effort, and encourage the sharing of knowledge to ultimately save time and money (Berkman, 2001). KM's goal is to build and leverage knowledge—to facilitate the creation, accumulation, deployment, and application of quality knowledge (Wiig, 1994). KM promotes the growth of behaviors that lead to innovation and discovery, knowledge creation, and improved knowledge use (Wiig, 1994). "Knowledge management is the process of capturing a company's collective expertise wherever it resides—in databases, on paper, or in people's heads—and distributing it to wherever it can help produce the biggest payoff" (Hibbard, 1997, 46). KM in the new economy is the core to the use of intangible assets to positively affect the performance of a business enterprise (Sullivan, 1998).

Intangible Asset Management

Intangible asset measurement programs have evolved over the last two decades to supplement the weaknesses of traditional accounting methods. These efforts have demonstrated value in specific cases; however, no widely applicable standards of intangible-asset measurement have emerged to quantify their benefits (Shand, 1999; Sullivan, 1998). There is no shortage of proposed methods and theories to measure intangible assets or IC (Sveiby, 2001). Numerous measurement systems target improved categorization of knowledge-based activities (Shand, 1999). Karl Erik Sveiby (2001) has categorized 21 intangible measurement approaches by extending the work of Luthy (1998) and Williams (2000). Sveiby (2001) established four categories of measurement approaches and assigned each of the 21 models to a single category. Additional models have been developed (Andriessen, 2004), thereby providing a way to further validate or enhance taxonomy of intangible assets.

These methods all have advantages and disadvantages. However, industry appears to be leaning toward the balanced-scorecard approach to reporting nonfinancial measures. A survey conducted by Dialog Software and Paul Bergquist, the editor of *The Balanced Scorecard Newswire* indicated that 76.9% of the respondents believe that implementing a balanced scorecard does influence their company's bottom line—although 70.7% of the respondents of this survey have not taken action in implementing a balanced scorecard. A survey conducted by PWC's Management Barometer (www.barometersurveys.com) indicated that 61% of the respondents had completed, or almost completed, formal causal models that link together key financial and nonfinancial factors. The attributes of the models of the second survey, causal and linkage of financial and nonfinancial factors, are in alignment with Kaplan and Norton's (1996) definition of the original balanced-scorecard construction. Surveys conducted by the Dialog Software and PWC support the direction that the scorecard method has a significant presence in industry. The scorecard type of models identifies the various components of intangible assets and generates indicators that are reported as scorecards or graphic interfaces (Sveiby, 2001). Classification schemes, describing major components of intangible assets have been a consistent trend of researchers of intangible-asset models (Williams, 2000). The decomposition of the components of intangible-asset models provides the capability to trace the indicators and indices to their source(s).

Strategic Alignment of Intangible Assets

A business enterprise that is fully informed—transforming enterprise data and information into enterprise intelligence and intangible assets.

Knowledge within the business enterprise needs to be managed like traditional factors of labor, capital, and raw materials (Von Krogh et al., 1998). The new valuation components of the knowledge economy must be aligned with the scope and context of the business enterprise. A business enterprise needs to articulate the link between strategy and the knowledge required to execute the strategy (Allee, 2000; Zack, 1999b). Strategy develops and sustains competitive advantages for a business (D'Aveni et al., 1995) and builds future competitive advantages (Hamel and Prahalad, 1994). Competitive advantage depends on the command of, and access to, effective utilization of its resources and knowledge (Barney, 2001; Hamal and Prahalad, 1994; Porter, 1980). This provides the business with the capability to implement cost or differentiation advantages (Barney, 2001; Porter 1980) or both (Hamel and Prahalad, 1994). Strategy is the identification of the desired future state of the business, the specific objectives to be obtained, and the strategic moves necessary to realize that future (Boar, 1994). Strategy includes all major strategic areas, such as markets, suppliers, human resources, competitive advantages, positioning, critical success factors, and value chains (Boar, 1994; Porter, 1980; Alter, 2002). The value chain is a key component in the strategic planning framework (Boar, 1994) and is the critical path to delivery of its business products and services. The value chain provides the alignment of enterprise value drivers to its vision and its subsequent valuation components. The value chain supports the business in identifying how intangible assets could or should bring value to the business (Sullivan, 2000). Aligning intangible assets with the value chain of a business enterprise provides a first step in aligning knowledge to its business strategy. The linkage between strategy, knowledge, and performance of a business is the strategic context of the business (Zack, 1999b).

A paradigm shift is needed, such that a business enterprise is viewed as multiminded sociocultural system that includes employees who collaborate to serve themselves and their environment (Gharajedaghi, 1999). To establish this view, there needs to be a concept of something familiar and similar to represent the complex business enterprise (Gharajedaghi, 1999). The value chain provides a systematic way to divide a business enterprise into its discrete activities ([Porter 1985], [Alter 2002]). The value chain is a concept that could be used to examine the groupings of business activities and to establish boundaries that align with drivers of value (Porter, 1985). A business enterprise vision is one of its most important pieces of intangible assets. Vision is planned by strategy, and executed by values that drive day-to-day decision-making (Sullivan, 2000). The economic value of an intangible asset drives the decision to further invest, hold onto it, or dispose of it (Sullivan, 2000). An intangible economic value is the measure of the utility it brings to the business enterprise (Sullivan, 2000). Today's businesses are unaware if they have people, resources, or business processes in place to execute and succeed in their strategy (Bontis, 1998a). The alignment of the firm's intangible assets with its vision and strategy is a powerful idea. Indeed, the idea of alignment underlies virtually all management theories, concepts, fads and fashions. The power of the concept of alignment is that companies can focus their resources and activities on a set of objectives for achieving them faster, or without unnecessary effort (Sullivan, 2000).

Value chain creation begins with a review of the business enterprise vision and strategy and the roles for its intangible assets (Sullivan, 2000). The value chain

- Enables businesses to shift their resources to capture potential value (McNair and Vandermeersh, 1998).
- Provides a framework to view how a company can build and sustain a competitive advantage over its competitors that ensures long-term profitability and survival (Morecroft and Sterman, 2000).
- Is a unique combination of activities that together create competitive value-added products or services for a company (Koulopoulos, 1997; McNurlin and Sprague, 1998; Von Krogh et al., 1998).
- Consists of tasks and activities that are organized into workflow applications that eliminate waste—unnecessary and redundant tasks and automation of routine tasks (Koulopoulos, 1997; Alter, 2002).
- Consists of and represent business components that are interdependent (Von Krogh et al., 1998).
- Is dynamic—it is re-created daily by its components and their relationships (Alter, 2002; Porter, 1980).

Consequently, to define and manage intangible assets, it must be aligned with the strategy of the organization, and understood what is to be done with them. (Stewart, 1999). Incorporating intangible assets into a business enterprise's value chain is the start of aligning intangible assets to its value creation and its business strategy.

A major strategic challenge confronting the value creation process in a knowledge economy is the reconfiguring of businesses from a value chain structure to a more fluid value network model (Allee, 2000). The traditional value chain is an industrial age model that is gradually being superseded by the value network, a new enterprise model (Allee, 2000). The nature of value within the business enterprise has changed, and new assets cannot be measured with old tools (Parker, 1996). Industry experts advise that the value chain model must be changed to reflect the new business enterprise, of which intangible assets are critical (Parker, 1996; Bontis, 1998b). The network value chain is a concept that could be used to expand the existing value chain concept to include intangible assets (Allee, 2000).

The Framework of Intangible Valuation Areas

FIVA proposes a framework for facilitating the systematic and repeatable identification of intangible assets. The FIVA methodology leverages the efforts of existing intangible-asset models and existing value chain models. Included in the design approach to the FIVA methodology is the analysis of existing intangible-asset balance scorecard valuation models, and value chain models to discern their value components. The value components extracted from the models are aligned with performance-based activities of the business enterprise. The value components are synthesized to define a common taxonomy of value drivers of intangible assets (Table 12-1). The valued components are defined and validated by industry experts. The FIVA is constructed on the basis of the analytic hierarchy process (AHP) model to facilitate a ranking of value components in relative order of importance, based on defined strategic KM objectives. The AHP model represents decisions in a hierarchic form (Saaty, 1980). FIVA is a validated framework for organizing and studying the breadth of intangible assets that can be used to surface and organize intangible-asset measurement and performance indicators.

The FIVA framework is designed to align the value drivers of intangible assets with KM objectives. The framework is designed to facilitate the ranking of the KM objectives and value drivers of intangible assets in relative order of importance. The hierar-

Table 12-1

Value Drivers of Intangible Assets	
VALUE DRIVER	**DEFINITION**
1 Customer	The economic value that results from the **associations** (e.g., loyalty, satisfaction, longevity) an enterprise has built with consumers of its goods and services.
2 Competitor	The economic value that results from the **position** (e.g., reputation, market share, name recognition, image) an enterprise has built in the business market place.
3 Employee	The economic value that results from the **collective capabilities** (e.g., knowledge, skill, competence, know-how) of an enterprise's employees.
4 Information	The economic value that results from an enterprise's ability to **collect and disseminate its information and knowledge** in the right form and content to the right people at the right time.
5 Partner	The economic value that results from **associations** (financial, strategic, authority, power) an enterprise has established with external individuals and organizations (e.g., consultants, customers, suppliers, allies, competitors) in pursuit of advantageous outcomes.
6 Process	The economic value that results from an enterprise's ability (e.g., policies, procedures, methodologies, techniques) to **leverage the ways in which the enterprise operates and creates value** for its employees and customers.
7 Product/Service	The economic value that results from an enterprise's ability to **develop and deliver its offerings** (i.e., products and services) that reflects an understanding of market and customer(s) requirements, expectations and desires.
8 Technology	The economic value that results from the **hardware and software** an enterprise has invested in to support its operations, management and future renewal.

chic structure of AHP provides a decision hierarchy to allow objectives, sub-objectives, and alternatives to be compared on a pair-wise basis with respect to the element in the next level of hierarchy using a ratio scale.

The design of FIVA uses a bottom-up structuring that identifies the advantages and disadvantages of each value driver of intangible assets to identify the KM objectives (Figure 12-1). Table 12-2 shows four KM objectives.

The combination of the value drivers of intangibles (alternatives) and the KM objectives (criteria) are modeled as depicted in Figure 12-2. The FIVA model provides significant insight into the value components that contribute toward the achievement of a specific KM objective. The design of the FIVA model supports a dynamic mix of value components based on the business environment.

FIVA represents a dynamic relationship between strategic objectives of KM and value drivers of intangible assets and is an initial step toward the development of a

Figure 12-1

Structuring bottom up (clustering).

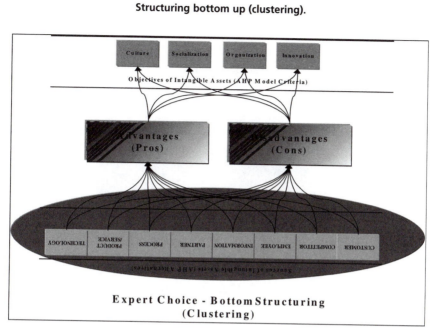

E x p e r t C h o i c e - B o t t o m S t r u c t u r i n g
(C l u s t e r i n g)

Table 12-2

KM Objectives of Intangible Assets	
OBJECTIVE	**OBJECTIVE DESCRIPTION**
Innovation	The **generation of new ideas** to improve the efficiency and effectiveness of identifying and implementing new products, new services, advance skills, improved activities and best practices for economic gain.
Organization	The **structuring of resources** to improve the efficiency and effectiveness of capturing, transferring and sharing knowledge throughout the enterprise for economic gains.
Socialization	The **establishment of interactions between resources** to improve the efficiency and effectiveness of capturing, transferring and sharing knowledge throughout the enterprise for economic gain.
Culture	The **establishment of an environment of visions and values to improve** the efficiency and effectiveness of collaboration, creativity, communication, trust and sharing throughout the enterprise for economic gain.

network and dynamic model to value and report intangible assets. FIVA leverages existing works, and to move the discipline of intangibles forward, it provides a view of intangible assets within the context of the business enterprise and supports their valuation based on a common set of business dimensions.

FIVA provides a concept of something familiar and similar to represent the complex business enterprise. It provides a systematic way to divide a business enterprise

Figure 12-2

Framework of Intangible Valuation Areas (FIVA) model.

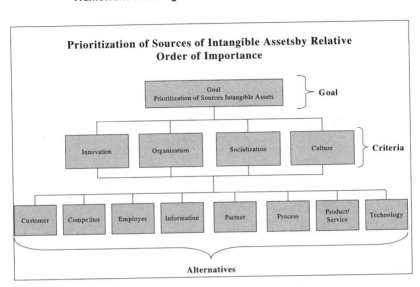

into its discrete activities and is a concept that could be used to examine groupings of business activities and to establish boundaries that align with drivers of value, both tangible and intangible. FIVA incorporates intangible assets in the value chain of a business enterprise, providing a first step of aligning intangible assets to value creation with its business strategy. The alignment of FIVA with strategic objectives and intangible value drivers provides a mechanism by which companies can focus their resources and activities on a set of KM objectives for the purpose of achieving them more effectively and efficiently. It provides a more fluid value network model to reflect the new business enterprise, and is an initial step toward the development of a network and dynamic model to value and report intangible assets.

FIVA is a concept that allows a business to identify and link performance measurements/indicators to its intangible value drivers and subsequently capture measures to monitor and evaluate leading and lagging indicators in the achievement of its KM strategy. FIVA provides a methodology to have command of, and access to, effective utilization of business resources and knowledge, which support the business's capability to implement cost and differentiation advantages.

FIVA—Empiric Evidence

A single-sector study, with results isolated to IT firms was conducted in the Washington Metropolitan Area (Washington, Maryland, and Virginia) (Green, 2004). The target audiences of the study were chief executive officers (CEOs) and chief financial officers (CFOs), and the study emphasized the scorecard-type model, as classified by Sveiby (2001). The results of the study support the presence of characteristics within the business environment that influence the value components of the firm, and that these value components are related to the business strategy. The findings of the study support the hypothesis that a one-size-fits-all solution to valuing the intangible assets within the business environment is not feasible. This study provides a base case to evaluate other industries and a structure to focus on measurements and indicators of the value components of a business enterprise.

The target audience of CEOs and CFOs were selected because they are relatively equal in judging performance and valuation components for the business enterprise. Their roles are instrumental in the performance health of the business enterprise as per the following:

- The strategic management system is the personal responsibility of the CEO and the senior executive team. Development of a balanced scorecard must start with an active dialogue between the CEO and the CFO, and the CEO is the "process owner" of the balanced scorecard (Kaplan and Norton, 1996).
- The CEO selects activities that are most important to obtaining value, and most frequently required in the management of the firm's IC (Sullivan, 2000).
- The only executive, who can be responsible for the totality of intangible resources, from patents to company reputation, is the CEO (Zack, 1999b).

The relationship between the CFO and the CEO is tightly coupled. The International Federation of Accountants (IFAC), in *The Role of the Chief Financial Officer (CFO) in 2010* (2002), discussed the viewpoint of CEOs, who indicate that the role of the CFO is moving toward one of acting as guardian of information, and acting as a steward and compliance officer.

The CFO helps shape the future of the business and contributes to organizational mission—97% develop long-term plans and 88% help to manage the future of the company as researched by Heidrick and Struggles (1998). *CFOs: Strategic Business Partners Survey* by Heidrick and Struggles (1998) highlighted that the role of the CFO has changed dramatically, and that the CFO plays a much more integrated role and acts as a strategic business partner to the CEO. The CFO is a logical custodian of the balanced scorecard process (Kaplan and Norton 1996, 290)

Summary of Findings

The results of my research (Green, 2004) identified three samples of experts. Each sample represented approximated one third of the respondents (33% CEO, 34% CFO, and 31% "Other Executives"; 2% [one respondent]) did not select a position. Respondents from the survey identified the core business area, main business orientation, company ownership, annual revenue, number of employees, and existence or absence of KM programs/systems and a chief knowledge officer (CKO) for their organization.

Analysis of data supports the prioritization of KM business objectives and highlights that value drivers of intangible assets are a dynamic mix based on a business's strategy and environment. Table 12-3 provides a summary of the findings. These results indicate that the relative importance of KM objectives can vary on the basis of the decision maker. The decision maker's priorities regarding KM objectives within the business enterprise are influenced by the amount of revenue and the size of the firm. The relative importance of value drivers of intangible assets is subject to vary based on the KM objective, the decision maker, the main business orientation, the company ownership, the annual revenue, and the size of the firm. Findings provide empiric evidence to support intangible-asset valuation methods need to accommodate a dynamic mix of KM objectives and their subsequent intangible-asset value drivers.

Table 12-3

Business Components that Influence KM Objectives and Intangible Asset Value Drivers		
	KM Objectives	**Value Drivers**
	Influence the selection of KM Objectives	Influence the contribution of value drivers with respect to the KM Objective
Decision Maker (Position CEO, CFO, "Other Executives")	✓	✓
Main Business Orientation (Service, Product)		✓
Company Ownership (Private, Public)		✓
Annual Revenue	✓	✓
Number of Employees (size of company—small, medium, large)	✓	✓
KM System Program (Exists or Does Not Exist)		

The study provides empiric evidence that IT firms that use a standard and consistent taxonomy of intangible assets could increase their ability to identify and account for more intangible assets for measurement and valuation. Three of the four models evaluated did not adequately represent all of the value drivers of intangible assets that were represented in the validated and prioritized taxonomy of intangible value drivers. The results indicate that the relative importance of the intangible-asset value drivers not represented in the three existing intangible-asset models are of significant importance to the value contribution of intangible assets within IT firms.

The study also provides empiric evidence that the balanced-scorecard model, developed by Kaplan and Norton, does adequately represent all of the value drivers of intangible assets that are represented in the validated and prioritized taxonomy of intangible value drivers. The results indicate that the balanced-scorecard model is a flexible and adaptive model that can represent the fluid and dynamic mix of the value contribution of intangible assets given a business's KM objectives and the business environment within IT firms.

The results of this study support that IT firms that use intangible asset models based on a standard and consistent intangible-asset taxonomy could account for more intangible assets for measurement and valuation and provide a base-case for IT firms; however, the model could be used to investigate other industries.

FIVA—Surface Performance Measures and Indicators

FIVA is a framework for organizing and studying the breadth of intangible assets that can be used to surface and organize intangible-asset measurement and perfor-

Figure 12-3

Surface and organize intangible asset measurement and performance indicators for each value driver.

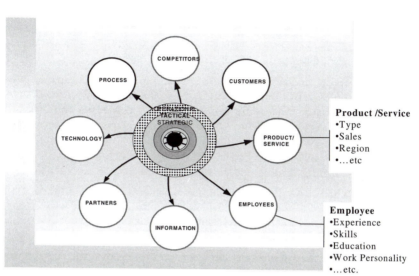

Product /Service
•Type
•Sales
•Region
•...etc

Employee
•Experience
•Skills
•Education
•Work Personality
•...etc.

mance indicators (Figure 12-3). It reflects the realities of the business enterprise and is designed to accommodate the explicit functions of the business enterprise. It provides a gateway to construct integrated enterprise models to the routine and special statistical, financial, forecasting, management science, and other quantitative models that provide analysis capabilities for decision-making. Enterprise decision-making models are described in terms of syntax (what the allowable expressions are), semantics (what they mean), and proof theory (how can we draw new conclusions given some statements in the logic). Solving problems in a particular domain generally requires knowledge of the objects in the domain and knowledge of how to reason in that domain. Enterprise models are divided into four major categories: strategic, tactical, operational, and model-building blocks and routines (Turban and Aronson, 1998) as follows:

- Strategic models: Support top management's strategic planning responsibilities (long term)
- Tactical models: Used mainly by middle management to assist in allocating and controlling the organization resources (intermediate term)
- Operational models: Used to support the day-to-day working activities of the organization—usually daily to monthly time horizon (short term).
- Model-building blocks and routines: The integration of strategic, tactical and operational models

These models are established on the basis of the knowledge needs of those making decisions, reflect the realities of the business enterprise, and must accommodate the explicit functions of the business enterprise.

In the business enterprise domain, intangible assets are a critical metric for determining the economic value of a company, and companies should understand their contribution to its capacity—the value-creating ability of an organization, an ability that takes in a wide variety of resources (McNair and Vangermeersch, 1998).

Capacity (Measurement and Performance Indicators)

> The work of organizations includes taking stock of the resources at one's command and planning the fullest use of them all. (J. Blackstone, 1989)

The essence of capacity is the need to use resources to their fullest capacity. When resources are not used to their fullest capacity, this produces waste. Waste erodes profits and degrades organizational performance. Capacity is defined for every resource, and each resource has a driver (Figure 12-4). These drivers represent the measures of capacity for the resource thus establishing the resource as an asset. This approach to capacity provides the following:

- A path to enterprise intelligence
- The extent to which enterprise intelligence is a unique attribute of the enterprise
- Determination of how enterprise intelligence is measured or evaluated
- Determination of the nature of mechanisms capable of intelligence

Capacity cost management establishes a consensus within an organization on determining capacity and the baseline measures used to capture this capability. Having agreed on the basis capacity of the enterprise, the enterprise can establish the following:

- Estimates of the cost of a unit of capacity
- How to track and report the utilization of existing capacity
- How to improve company performance in key functional areas

Unutilized capacity that cannot be "stored" is waste. Minimizing wasted capacity, regardless of whether that waste is stored in unnecessary inventory, reflected in pure idleness, hidden by rework, or buried in standards, is the ultimate goal of capacity cost management (McNair and Vangermeersch, 1998).

Capacity is tied to the decision-making process of the organization and capacity utilization is a primary goal of the operational, tactical, and strategic decision-making process. This relationship provides a basis for taking action to improve performance, and the marriage of these two creates a strong foundation for the construction of enterprise intelligence. This union provides an approach to intelligence and establishes a mechanism for an IAM system to measure the achievements of the enterprise by using the capacity of an organization as its measurement of performance. The IAM system establishes a common language of intelligence and knowledge as it pertains to the value drivers of the enterprise and in the context of the enterprise's decision-making processes. This common language (McNair and Vangermeersch, 1998) includes the following:

- **Resource capability:** The amount and type of work a resource can support—resources are what an organization buys and use to support its activities and outputs.
- **Baseline capacity measures:** The capability to do work—the amount of work the resources can support.
- **Capacity deployment:** Measurements of the deployment of capacity deemed to be available for use.

Figure 12-4

Capacity drives the intelligent enterprise.

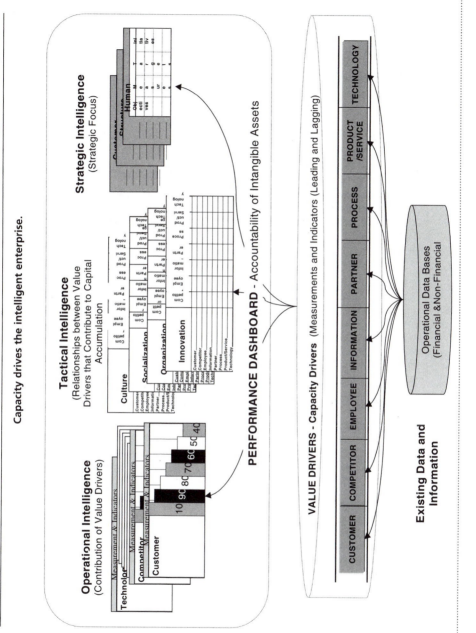

- **Capacity utilization measures:** Tracking and reporting actual performance against plans and the profit and cost implication of this performance.
- **Timeframe of analysis:** Provide operational, tactical and strategic views of capacity—views reflect the changing timeframe and context of decisions that affect available capacity and it deployment.
- **Organizational focus and capacity cost management:** The unit of analysis, the focus of the organization—the value drivers of the enterprise.

Integrating Value, Capacity, and Learning

Value, capacity, and learning are key factors in the equation for determining organizational performance. The following are major points to consider:

1. The **value** chain of an enterprise is the critical path to delivery of business products and services. This path needs to be clearly defined. If the value chain is not visible, how can a decision be made about what, where, when, who and why a change is necessary?
2. The **capacity** of an organization is the ultimate driver to its success. Profit has two views: the increase of revenue or the decrease of expenses. When viewing the bottom line, anything achievable must be measurable, and the final unit of measure within the business enterprise is the dollar. A business must be aware of the cost of its activities in order to understand where the waste is.
3. Change is inevitable, and to err is human; however, to repeat the same mistake or non—value-adding activity repeatedly, without any consideration of change or improvement, is lethal. Organizational **learning** is critical, as it is the ability to recognize when something is not efficient and/or effective.

Enterprise Knowledge Representation—Key to Success

FIVA leverages the current enterprise environment and provides a foundation that facilitates the integration of fundamental types of models to each other to provide a holistic approach to implementing IAM in an enterprise environment. The way a problem is presented is important for the manner in which a solution is proposed. Problem representation is the transformation of a problem until it takes on an easy aspect, or translating the problem into a form that is easily recognizable.

> Knowledge must be represented efficiently, and in a meaningful way. Efficiency is important, as it would be impossible to represent explicitly every fact that you might ever need. There are just so many potentially useful facts, most of which you would never even think of. You have to be able to infer new facts from your existing knowledge, as and when needed, and capture general abstractions, which represent general features of sets of objects in the world" (Cawsey, 1998, p. 3).

Facts in a knowledge representation scheme should be related to facts in the real world. The knowledge representation scheme for the business enterprise needs to be clear and precise, with a well-defined syntax and semantics; and the knowledge model must adequately demonstrate the relationship and/or interactions between value drivers within the enterprise. FIVA speaks the language of the business environment.

Data: the Foundation of Intelligence

> Access to data is very powerful. The reason, for example, that Thoreau became able to tell the calendar date of the year from the flowers and trees of Walden was

that he accumulated the necessary data. He had personally tramped through the woods and see how each plant behaved from season to season (Bailey 1996, p. 136).

Data are formed into information, which is transformed into knowledge. The challenge is to be able to retrieve these data within a specific domain and in a useful form for its intended use. Companies should be thinking strategically about how to work with existing business systems and data to extract information and knowledge that provide the correct views and insights into organizational performance.

Conclusion

Leverage the knowledge of Albert Einstein, whose insight was that the world that has been made as a result of the level of thinking thus far and creates problems that cannot be solved at the same level of thinking at which they were created. Consider approaching knowledge and intangibles with a sober and humble realization that laying the foundation for the next economy should be the starting point. There is an overabundance of knowledge and models to achieve intangible-asset management, but perhaps what needs to be identified is a way to co-create intangible-asset management for the knowledge era. Perhaps industry is spending too much time on redesigning the old corporate accounting structures to find time to capitalize current efforts and deliver results. Maybe industry should define the nonfinancial components of a business and integrate them with the financial components to build a holistic business enterprise model. After all, financial systems are not a static model; they are a dynamic mixture of the financial components that drive value within the business environment, and a company prepares its financial statement and balance sheet on what it knows it has, and not on what it perceives it has. FIVA provides the necessary breadth to establish a comprehensive valuation methodology that could be leveraged across all industries. Let us define and standardize intangible-asset valuation to facilitate the systematic and repeatable identification, documentation, and valuation of intangible assets, and enable visibility of intangibles so that stake holders of business enterprises are able to make cognizant decisions about its future renewal and growth.

Research is now under way at George Washington University (GW) to address the identification problem of intangible assets. Building on the theory and principles of FIVA, Andreas Andreou (*aandreou@gwu.edu*), a doctoral candidate at GW, aims to identify the knowledge assets that are supported by the value drivers of the FIVA model. Consistent with the value network concept (Allee, 2000), Andreou's research is driven by the interaction between the eight value drivers that generate 28 different business value-exchanging activities. The scope of the research is on the development of a knowledge asset index for the value exchange activities resulting from the interaction between the value driver, the employee, and the other value drivers. His focus will be on high-tech business services, a growing sector of the services industry and the knowledge economy. This sector comprises information, professional, scientific, and technical services, among others. The suggested index, human capital knowledge asset performance index (HCKAPI), is developed by answering the two following questions: (a) what strategic imperative (i.e., performance focus area) does the organization need to achieve or focus on for each business activity and (b) what are the critical success factors (CSFs) that employees need to manage that cause that strategic imperative?

The proposed research is unique, in that the index is developed on the basis of theoretic and empiric analysis using knowledge elicitation interviews. In addition, the test of the proposed model will be based on formative indicators versus reflective indicators on which current models are based (Bontis, 1998a, 2004; Bontis et al., 2000; Bontis and Fitzenz, 2002; Chen et al., 2004). Nick Bontis, a pioneer in the research concerning the structural relationship of IC components, proposes that the use of formative indicators can illuminate better what items (e.g., knowledge assets) are causing or forming a construct, such as a value driver. In addition, he proposes that more empiric research studying the interplay between the IC components could be useful (Bontis, 2000).

Andreou's research is completed as far as the development of the proposed index based on theory. The identified performance focus areas, and their related knowledge assets, cover the spectrum of IC components. An indicative list of performance focus areas and knowledge assets includes (a) environmental scanning (i.e., the ability to reduce environmental uncertainty) with knowledge assets such as community intelligence, political intelligence and social intelligence; (b) value-added information (i.e., ability to add value and reduce noise in information) with knowledge assets as motives, self-concepts, perceptions, cognitive processing abilities and content knowledge; and (c) customer intimacy (i.e., the ability to provide customers what they exactly need at value), with knowledge assets such as interpersonal relations between employees and customers, understanding of customer needs and goals and understanding of customer's business and industry. The next step of the research involves the conduct of knowledge elicitation sessions with the personnel of the companies participating in the research in order to finalize the index. Upon finalization of the index, a wide-scale questionnaire survey will be conducted to gather data in order to test the structural relationship of the model components. The study is to be completed in spring 2005. There are both theoretical and practical contributions from the study. First, it will complement quantitative studies with empiric qualitative research in developing a theory that seeks to understand the process of IC valuation/management and assertions of causations. Second, it will contribute to our understanding of the factors that drive knowledge worker productivity. Understanding knowledge worker productivity could improve market efficiency and close the gap between market and book value. At the same time, it could improve organizational capacity through more effective and efficient recruitment, management, training, development, and retention of best talent.

Bibliography

Chapter 1

Despres, C. and Chauvel, D. (2000). *Knowledge Horizons*, Woburn, MA: Butterworth-Heinemann.

Chapter 2

Amabile, Teresa M. (1998). "How to Kill Creativity." *Harvard Business Review*, Boston, MA: Harvard Business School Press. Volume 75, Number 6, September–October.

Bailey, Robert W. (1996). *Human Performance Engineering: Designing High Quality Professional User Interfaces for Computer Products, Applications, and Systems*, Upper Saddle River, New Jersey: Prentice-Hall, Inc.

Baldanza C. and Stankosky M. (2000). "Knowledge Management: An Evolutionary Architecture Toward Enterprise Engineering." Paper presented to NO. CSE, May (2000).

Barton, Lawrence. (1993). *Crisis in Organizations: Managing and Communicating in the Heat of Chaos*, Cincinnati, Ohio: Southwestern Publishing Company.

Bensaou, M. and Earl, Michael. (1998). "The Right Mind-set for Managing Information Technology." *Harvard Business Review*, Boston, MA: Harvard Business School Press. Volume 76, Number 5, September–October.

Brinkman, Rick and Kirschner, Rick. (1994). *Dealing with People You Can't Stand: How to Bring Out the Best in People at their Worst*, New York: McGraw-Hill, Inc.

Calabrese FA. (2000). "A Suggested Framework of Key Elements Defining Effective Enterprise-Wide Knowledge Management Programs." Doctoral Dissertation. Washington, D.C.: George Washington University.

Chapanis, Alphonse. (1996). *Human Factors in Systems Engineering*, New York: John Wiley and Sons, Inc.

Czaja, Ronald and Blair, Johnny. (1996). *Designing Surveys: A Guide to Decisions and Procedures*, Thousand Oak, CA: Pine Forge Press.

Davenport, Thomas. (1999). "Knowledge Management and the Broader Firm: Strategy, Advantage, and Performance." In: *Knowledge Management Handbook*, Liebowitz, Jay, ed. Boca Raton, FL: CRC Press.

Despres, Charles and Chauvel, Daniel. (1999). *A Traumatic Analysis of The Thinking in Knowledge Management*, Sophia Antipolis, France: The Theseus Institute.

Drucker, Peter F. (1998). "The Coming of the New Organization." *Harvard Business Review on Knowledge Management*, Boston, MA: Harvard Business School Publishing.

Drucker, Peter F. (1997). "The Future that has Already Happened." *Harvard Business Review*, Boston, MA: Harvard Business School Publishing Corporation. Volume 75, Number 6.

Eisner, Howard. (1997). *Essentials of Project and Systems Engineering Management*, New York: John Wiley and Sons, Inc.

Eisner, Howard. (1988). *Computer Aided Systems Engineering*, Englewood Cliffs, New Jersey: Prentice Hall.

Foy, Patricia S. (1999). "Knowledge Management in Industry." *Knowledge Management Handbook*, Liebowitz, Jay, ed. Boca Raton, FL: CRC Press.

Gates, Bill and Hemingway, Collins. (1999). *Business @ the Speed of Thought*, New York: Warner Books.

Goleman, Daniel. (1998). "What Makes a Leader?" *Harvard Business Review* Boston, MA: Harvard Business School Press. Volume 76, Number 6.

Hammer, Michael. (1996). *Beyond Reengineering*, New York: HarperCollins.

Hammer, Michael and Champy, James. (1993). *Reengineering the Corporation: A Manifesto for Business Revolution*, New York: Harper Business.

Hammer, Michael and Stanton, Steven. (1999). "How Process Enterprises Really Work." *Harvard Business Review* Boston, MA: Harvard Business School Press. Volume 77, Number 6.

Hickins, Michael. (1999). "*A memoir: management association*" *Management Review*.

Leonard, D. (1995). "Wellsprings of Knowledge–Building and Sustaining the Sources of Innovation." *Harvard Business Journal*, Boston, MA: Harvard Business School Press.

Manganelli, Raymond L. and Klein, Mark M. (1994). *The Reengineering Handbook: A Step-By-Step Guide to Business Transformation*, New York: American Management Association.

Mintzberg, Henry. (1998). "Covert Leadership: Notes on Managing Professionals." *Harvard Business Review*, Boston, MA: Harvard Business School Press. Volume 76, Number 6, November–December.

Mintzberg, Henry and Van Der Heyden, Ludo. (1999). "Organigraphs: Drawing how companies really work." *Harvard Business Review*, Boston, MA: Harvard Business School Press. Volume 77, Number 5, September–October.

Morten, Hansen T., Nohria, Nitin, and Tierney, Thomas. (1999). "Whats your Strategy for Managing Knowledge?" *Harvard Business Review* Boston, MA: Harvard Business School Press. Volume 77, Number 2, March–April.

Murray A and Calabrese F A. (2000). EMSE 270 Lecture Materials.

Nonaka, I. (1998). "The Knowledge-Creating Company." *Harvard Business Review on Knowledge Management*, Boston, MA: Harvard Business School Press.

Pascale, Richard, Millemann, Mark, and Gioja, Linda. (1997). "Changing the Way we Change." *Harvard Business Review*, Boston, MA: Harvard Business School Press. Volume 75, Number 6, November–December.

Pauchant, Thierry C. and Matroff, Ian I. (1992). *Transforming the Crisis Prone Organization: Preventing Individual, Organizational, and Environmental Tragedies*, San Francisco, California: Jossey-Bass Inc.

Proctor, R. W. and Van Zandt, T. (1994). *Human Factors in Simple and Complex Systems*, Boston, MA: Allyn and Bacon.

Prokesch, Steven E. (1997). "Unleashing the Power of Learning: An Interview by Tish Petrolium's John Browne." *Harvard Business Review*, Boston, MA: Harvard Business School Publishing, Volume 75, Number 5, September–October.

Rivette, Kevin G. and Kline, David. (2000). "Thinking About Discovering New Value in Intellectual Property." *Harvard Business Review* Boston, MA: Harvard Business School Press. Volume 78, Number 1, January–February.

Salant, Priscilla and Dillman, Don A. (1994). *How to Conduct Your Own Survey*, New York: John Wiley and Sons, Inc.

Sanders, M. S. and McCormick, E. J. (1997). *Human Factors in Engineering Design* (7th Edition). New York: McGraw Hill Inc.

Senge, Peter M. (1990). *The Fifth Discipline–The Art of Learning Organization*, New York: Bantam Doubleday Dell Publishing Group.

Senge, Peter M. (1994). *The Fifth Discipline Field Book*, New York: Bantam Doubleday Dell Publishing Group.

Senge, Peter M. (1999). *The Dance of Change—The Challenge of Sustaining Momentum in Learning Organizations*, London, England: Doubleday Broadway Publishing Group, Random House.

Schulte, William D. (1999). Doctoral Dissertation, "The Effect of International Corporate Strategies and Information and Communication Technologies on Competitive Advantage and Firm Performance." Washington D.C.: The George Washington University.

SPSS Base 8.0 User's Guide. (1998). Chicago, IL: SPSS.

SPSS Base 8.0 Applications Guide. (1998). Chicago, IL: SPSS.

SPSS Base 8.0 Data Analysis Guide. (1998). Chicago, IL: SPSS.

Stankosky, Michael A. (2000). "A Theoretical Framework." *KM World*, 2000; 9(1).

Turban, Efraim and Aronson, Jay E. (1998). *Decision Support Systems and Intelligent Systems, fifth edition*, Upper Saddle River, New Jersey: Simon and Schuster Company.

Wah, Louisa. (1999). "Management Review." *American Management Association.*

Weintraub, Sarah. (1998). *The Hidden Intelligence: Innovation Through Intuition*, Woburn, MA: Butterworth-Heinemann.

Wenger, C. Etienne and Snyder, M. William. (2000). "Communities of Practice: The Organization of Frontier." *Harvard Business Review*, Boston, MA: Harvard Business School of Publishing. Volume 78, No. 1.

Winograd, Terry and Flores, Fernando. (1987). *Understanding Computers and Cognition*, Norwood, New Jersey: Ablex Publishing Corporation.

Zisman, Michael. "Start Talking and Get to Work." **http://www.lotus.com/solutions**

Chapter 3

Bixler, Charles H. (2000). Dissertation Research: "Creating a Dynamic Knowledge Management Maturity Continuum for Increased Enterprise Performance and Innovation." Washington, D. C.: The George Washington University.

Cochran, W., Vedhanayagam, A. and Blagg, B. (1997). "Knowledge Based Systems as a Technology Enabler for Business Process Re-Engineering." *Knowledge Management and Its Integrated Elements*, Liebowitz, Jay and Wilcox, Lyle C. eds. Boca Raton, FL: CRC Press.

Drucker, Peter F. (1988). "The Coming of the New Organization" *Harvard Business Review* 1988;66(1):4–11.

Eccles, Robert G. and Nohria, Nitin. (1992). *Beyond the Hype–Rediscovering the Essence of Management*, Boston, MA: Harvard Business School Press.

Ellis, Lynn. (1997). *Evaluation of the RandD processes: Effectiveness Through Measurements*, Boston, MA: Artech House.

Hansen, Morten T. et al. (1999). "What's Your Strategy for Managing Knowledge?" Harvard Business Review 1999;77(2):106–116.

Holsapple, C. and Joshi, K. (1997). *Knowledge Management: a Three-Fold Framework*. Kentucky Initiative for Knowledge Management Paper No. 104.

Leonard, D. (1995). *Wellsprings of Knowledge–Building and Sustaining the Sources of Innovation*, Boston, MA: Harvard Business School Press.

Liebowitz, Jay. (1999). *Knowledge Management Handbook*, Boca Raton, FL: CRC Press.

Malhorta, Y. (1998). *Toward a Knowledge Ecology for Organizational White-Waters*. Keynote Presentation for the 1998 Knowledge Management Fair, BRINT Institute.

Nonaka, I. (1998). *The Knowledge-Creating Company*. Harvard Business Review on Knowledge Management. Boston, MA: Harvard Business School Press.

O'Dell, Carla. (1996). "A Current Review of Knowledge Management Best Practices." Conference on Knowledge Management and the Transfer of Best Practices. London: Business Intelligence.

Price Waterhouse Change Integration Team. (1995). *Better Change–Best Practices for Transforming Your Organization*, Bristol, VT: Irwin Professional Publishing.

Probst, Gibert J. and Bettina, S. T. (1997). *Organizational Learning–The Competitive Edge of the Future*, London, England: Prentice Hall.

Prusak, Laurence. (1997). *Knowledge in Organizations*, Newton, MA: Butterworth-Heinemann.

Roos, J., Roos, G., Edvinsson, L., Dragonetti, N. (1998). *Intellectual Capital*, New York: University Press.

Sena, James A. and Shani, A. B. (1999). "Intellectual Capital and Knowledge Creation: Towards an Alternative Framework." *Knowledge Management Handbook*, Liebowitz, Jay, ed. Boca Raton, FL: CRC Press.

Stewart, Thomas A. (1997). *Intellectual Capital*, Middlebury, VT: Bantam Doubleday Dell Publishing Group.

Wiig, K. Fall (1997). "Knowledge Management: Where Did It Come From and Where Will It Go?" *Expert Systems with Applications*, Pergamon Press/Elsevier, Vol. 14.

Chapter 4

Alazmi, Mutiran, and Mohamed Zairi. (2003). Knowledge management critical success factors. *Total Quality Management* 2003;14(2):199–204.

Ashkanasy, Neal M., Lyndelle E. Broadfoot, and Sarah Falkus. (2000). Questionnaire Measures of Organizational Culture. In: *Handbook of Organizational Culture and Climate*, edited by N. M. Ashkanasy, C. P. M. Wilderom and M. F. Peterson. London: Sage Publications, Inc.

Babbie, Earl. (1998). *The Practice of Social Research, 8th ed.* Belmont, California: Wadsworth Publishing Company.

Baldanza, Carolyn, and Michael A. Stankosky. (1999). "Knowledge Management: An evolutionary architecture toward enterprise engineering." Paper read at International Council on Systems Engineering (INCOSE), Mid-Atlantic regional conference, September, 15.

Bassi, Laurie J. (1999). Measuring knowledge management effectiveness. In: James W. Cortada and John A. Woods (Eds.) *The Knowledge Management Yearbook 1999–2000* (USA, Butterworth-Heinemann), pp. 422–427.

Bennet, David, and Alex Bennet. (2001). The Rise of the Knowledge Organization. In *Knowledge Management: The Catalyst for Electronic Government*, edited by R. C. Barquin, A. Bennet and S. G. Remez. Vienna, Virginia: Management Concepts.

Berkman, Eric. (2001). When Bad Things Happen to Good Ideas. *Darwin Magazine*, april 2001.

Bixler, Charles H. (2000). Creating a Dynamic Knowledge Management Maturity Continuum for Increased Enterprise Performance and Innovation. Doctoral Dissertation, Engineering Management and Systems Engineering, The George Washington University, Washington, D.C.

Bixler, Charles H. (2001). "Don't always believe the 'experts'". *KM World*, 2001;10(9).

Calabrese, Francesco. (2000). "A suggested framework of key elements defining effective enterprise knowledge management programs." Doctoral dissertation, Engineering Management and Systems Engineering, The George Washington University, Washington, D.C.

Cameron, Kim S. and Robert E. Quinn. (1999). *Diagnosing and Changing Organizational Culture*. Boston: Addison-Wesley.

Chait, Laurence P. (2000). Creating a Successful KM System. *IEEE Engineering Management Review* 2000;28(2):92–95.

Chiem, Phat X. (2001). In the Public Interest. *Knowledge Management Magazine*, August, 2001.

Choi, Yong Suk. (2000). "An Empirical Study of Factors Affecting Successful Implementation of Knowledge Management." Doctoral Dissertation, University of Nebraska, Lincoln, NE.

Cronbach, L. J. (1951). Coefficient alpha and the internal structure of tests. *Psychometrica* 1951;16:297–334.

Davenport, Thomas, David W De Long, and Michael C. Beers. (1998). Successful Knowledge Management Projects. *Sloan Management Review* 1998:43–57.

Davenport, Thomas and Larry Prusak (1998). *Working Knowledge* (Cambridge, MA, Harvard Business Press).

Denning, Stephen. (2000). *The Springboard: How Storytelling Ignites Action in Knowledge-Era Organizations*, Boston: Butterwoth Heinemann.

Digman, Lester A. (1990). *Strategic Management: Concepts, Decisions, Cases, 2nd ed.* Homewood, IL: BPI/Irwin.

Dyer, Greg, and Brian McDonough. (2001). "The State of KM." *Knowledge Management Magazine*, May, 2001.

Eisenhart, Mary. (2001). "Washington's Need to Know." *Knowledge Management Magazine*, January, 2001.

Eisner, Howard. (2000). *Reengineering Yourself and Your Company: From Engineer to Manager to Leader*: Artech House Technology Management and Professional Development Library.

Eugene, Amy C. (2001). "KM in Education (Readers offer responses and suggestions)." *Knowledge Management Magazine*, August.

Evered, R. and M. Louis. (1981). Alternative Pespectives in Organizational Science: Inquiry From the Inside and Inquiry From the Outside. *Academy of Management Review* 1981; 6:385–395.

Federal Chief Information Officers' Council Knowledge Management Working Group Charter (2001). [Web Page]. Federal Chief Information Officer's Council (2001) [cited March (2001)]. Available from KM.gov/documents/charter.html.

Finneran, Tom. (1999). *A Component-Based Knowledge Management System*, Robert S. Seiner htty://www.tdan.com/i009hy04.htm. Accessed 1 June 2001.

Goffee, Rob, and Gareth Jones. (1998). *The Character of a Corporation*: How your company's culture can make or break your business. London: Harper Collins.

Graham, Ricci. (2001). "Benchmarking Jackson State." *Knowledge Management Magazine*.

Hansen, Morten T., Nitin Nohria, and Thomas Tierney. (1999). "What's your strategy for managing knowledge?" *Harvard Business Review* 1999:106–116

Harrison, R. (1979). Understanding your organization's character. *Harvard Business Review* 1979;50(5):119–128.

Hatcher, Larry, and Edward J. Stepanski. (1994). *A Step-by-Step Approach to Using the SAS System for Univariate and Multivariate Statistics*, Cary, NC: SAS Institute Inc.

——. (2002). *Homeland Security Act*. 107, H.R. (5005).

Haxel, G. (2001). Foreword. In: Kai Mertins, Peter Heisig, Jens Vorbeck, Kai Mertens (Eds.) *Knowledge Management Best Practices In Europe* (Springer).

Heising, P. (2001). *Business Process Oriented Knowledge Management*. In: Kai Mertins, Peter Heisig, Jens Vorbeck, Kai Mertens (Eds.) *Knowledge Management Best Practices In Europe* (Springer).

Hooijberg, Robert, and Frank Petrock. (1993). On Cultural Change: Using the Competing Values Framework to Help Leaders Execute a Transformation Strategy. *Human Resource Management* 1993;32(1):29–50.

Hoyt, Bradley J. (2001). *KM Technology and Tools Listing* [Web Page]. Hoyt Consulting, November 21 (2001) [cited November 6 (2001)]. Available from **http://www.kmnews.com**.

Jennex, M. E. and Lorne Olman. (2004). "Assessing Knowledge Management Success/ Effectiveness Models." Paper read at 37th Hawaii International Conference on System Sciences.

Kemp, Jeroen, Marc Pudlatz, Philippe Perez, and Aracelli Munoz Ortega. (2001). "KM Technologies and Tools." European KM Forum.

Kemp, Linda L., Nenneth E. Nidiffer, Louis C. Rose, Robert Small, and Michael Stankosky. (2001). Knowledge Management: Insight from the Trenches. *IEEE Software* 2001; 18(6):66–68.

Knowledge Management Review. (2001). Briefings: KM Survey. *Knowledge Management Review* 2001;4(5):8–9.

Kotter, John P. and James L. Heskett. (1992). *Corporate Culture and Performance*. New York The Free Press.

Liebowitz, Jay. (1999). Key ingredients to the success of an organization's knowledge management strategy, *Knowledge and Process Management*, 6(1), pp. 37–40.

Liebowitz, Jay. (2002). A Look at NASA Goddard Space Flight Center's Knowledge Management Initiatives. *Software, IEEE* 2002;19(3):40–42.

Liebowitz, Jay. (2004). *Addressing the Human Capital Crisis in the Federal Government: A Knowledge Management Perspective*, Burlington, MA: Elsevier.

Lundberg, Craig C. (1990). Innovative Organisation Development Practices: Part II–Surfacing Organisational Culture. *Journal of Managerial Psychology* 1990;5(4):8.

Manasco, B. (1999). *The Knowledge Imperative Leverage it or Lose it*, http://webcom.com/ quantera/empires5.html. Accessed 12 October 2001.

Marwick, A. D. (2001). Knowledge Management Technology. *IBM Systems Journal* 2001; 40(4):814–830.

McDermott, Richard, Stephanie Carlin, and Alexandria Womack. (1999). Creating a Knowledge-Sharing Culture: American Productivity and Quality Center.

McDermott, Richard, and Carla O'Dell. *Overcoming the 'Cultural Barriers' to Sharing Knowledge*. APQC Web page (2000) [cited July 23, (2001). Available from **http://www.apqc.org**.

McKellar, Hugh, and Sandra Haimila, eds. (2002). *KM World Buyers' Guide*. Fall (2002) Edition, *Buyers' Guide*: KM World and Information Today.

Meek, V. L. (1988). Organizational Culture: Origins and Weaknesses. *Organizational Studies* 1988;9:453–473.

Moore, Andy, et al. (2001). "Best Practices in Enterprise Knowledge Management: The Next Generation of KM Solutions." *Special Supplement to KM World*, 2001.

Morey, Daryl. (1998). *Knowledge Management Architecture*, http://www.brint.com/members/online/120205/kmarch/kmarch.html. Accessed 4 August 2001.

O'Neill, Regina M. and Robert E. Quinn. (1993). "Applications of the Competing Values Framework." *Human Resource Management* 1993;32(1):1–7.

Ott, Steven J. (1989). *Organizational Culture and Perspective*, Chicago, IL: Dorsey Press.

Park, Heejun. (2001). "Assessing the Success of Knowledge Management Technology Implementation as a Function of Organizational Culture." Doctoral Dissertation, Engineering Management and Systems Engineering, The George Washington University, Washington, D.C.

Payne, Roy L. (2001). "A Three Dimensional Framework for Analyzing and Assessing Culture/Climate and its Relevance to Cultural Change." In: *The International Handbook of Organizational Culture and Climate*, edited by C. L. Cooper, S. Cartwright and P. C. Earley. New York: John Wiley and Sons, Inc.

Peckenpaugh, Jason. (2004). Feds Win! *Government Executive*, 2004:35–44.

Pettigrew, Andrew M. (2000). Foreward. In: *Handbook of Organizational Culture and Climate*, edited by N. M. Ashkanasy, C. P. M. Wilderom and M. F. Peterson. London: Sage Publications, Inc.

The President's Management Agenda. Fiscal Year (2002). Washington, D.C.: Executive Office of the President.

Quinn, Robert E. (2001). OCAI Tool Using Likert Scale. Greenbelt, MD, November 27.

Quinn, Robert E. and Gretchen M. Spreitzer. (1991). "The psychometrics of the competing value culture instrument and an analysis of the impact of organizational culture on quality of life." *Research in Organizational Change and Development* 1991;5:115–142.

Remez, Shereen G. (2001). The GSA Story. In: *Knowledge Management: The Catalyst for Electronic Government*, edited by R. C. Barquin, A. Bennet and S. G. Remez. Vienna, Virginia: Management Concepts.

Ribière, Vincent M. (2001). "Assessing Knowledge Management Initiative Success as a Function of Organizational Culture." Doctoral Dissertation, Engineering Management and Systems Engineering, The George Washington University, Washington D.C.

Ricadela, Aaron. (2001). *Priorities Shift At The Top* [Web Page]. InformationWeek.com (2001) [cited September 17 (2001)]. Available from **http://www.informationweek.com**.

Roman, Juan. (2004). "An Empirical Study of Knowledge Management in the Government and Nonprofit Sectors: Organizational Culture Composition and its Relationship with Knowledge Management Success and the Approach for Knowledge Flow." Doctoral Dissertation, Engineering Management and Systems Engineering, The George Washington University, Washington D.C.

Roman, Juan, Vincent M. Ribiere, and Michael Stankosky. (2004). "Organizational Culture Types and their Relationship with Knowledge Flow and Knowledge Management Success: An empirical study in the U.S. Government and Nonprofit Sectors." *Journal of Information and Knowledge Management* 2004:3(2).

Rousseau, D. M. (1990). "Assessing Organizational Culture: The case for Multiple Methods." In: *Organizational Climate and Culture*, edited by B. Schneider. San Francisco: Jossey-Bass.

Sackmann, Sonja. (2001). "Cultural Complexity in Organizations: The Value and Limitations of Qualitative Methodology and Approaches." In: *The International Handbook of Organizational Culture and Climate*, edited by C. L. Cooper, S. Cartwright and P. C. Earley. New York: John Wiley and Sons, Inc.

Schein, Edgar H. (1992). *Organizational Culture and Leadership, 2ⁿᵈ ed.* San Framcisco, California: Jossey-Bass.

Schulz, Martin. (2001). "The Uncertain Relevance of Newness: Organizational Learning and Knowledge Flows." *Academy of Management Journal* 2001;44(4):661.

Sekaran, Uma. (1992). *Research Methods for Business, 2ⁿᵈ ed.*, New York: John Wiley and Sons, Inc.

Shand, Dawne. (1998). "Harnessing Knowledge Management Technologies in RandD." *Knowledge Management Review* 1998;(3):20–26.

Skyrme, David. (2000). *Knowledge Management: Making Sense of an Oxymoron,* http://www.skyrme.com/pubs/knwstrat.htm. Accessed 13 November 2001.

Skyrme, David and Debra Amidon. (1999). The knowledge agenda. In: James W. Cortada and John A. Woods (Eds.) *The Knowledge Management Yearbook 1999–2000* (USA, Butterworth-Heinemann), pp. 108–125.

Stankosky, Michael, and Carolyn Baldanza. (2001). "A System Approach to Engineering a Knowledge Management System." In: *Knowledge Management: The Catalyst for Electronic Government,* edited by R. C. Barquin, A. Bennet and S. G. Remez. Vienna, Virginia: Management Concepts.

Stankosky, Michael, and Carolyn Baldanza. (2001). "A System Approach to Engineering a Knowledge Management System." In: *Knowledge Management: The Catalyst for Electronic Government,* edited by R. C. Barquin, A. Bennet and S. G. Remez. Vienna, Virginia: Management Concepts.

Streels, N. (2000). Success factors for virtual libraries, *Wilton,* 23(5), pp. 68–71.

Trussler (1999). The rules of the game. In: James W. Cortada and John A. Woods (Eds.) *The Knowledge Management Yearbook 1999–2000* (USA, Butterworth-Heinemann), pp. 280–286.

Tucker, Robert W., McCoy, Walt J. and Evans, Linda C. (1990). "Can Questionnaires Objectively Assess Organizational Culture?" *Journal of Managerial Psychology* 1990;5(4):4–8.

Weidner, Douglas. (2002). "Using Connect and Collect to Achieve the KM Endgame." *IT Professional* 2002;4(1):18–24.

Wiig, Karl. (1996). *On the Management of Knowledge—Position Statement,* http://www.km-forum.org/what_is.htm. Accessed 12 December 2001.

Yeung, Arthur K. O., J. Wayne Brockbank, and David O. Ulrich. (1991). "Organizational Culture and Human Resources Practices: An Empirical Assessment." *Research in Organizational Change and Development* 1991;5:59–81.

Chapter 5

Aulakh, P., Kotabe, M. and Sahay, A. (1996). "Trust and performance in cross-border marketing partnerships: A behavioural approach." *Journal of International Business Studies.* 1996; 27(5)1005–1032.

Barth, S. (2000). "KM Horror Stories." *Knowledge Management Magazine* 2000;3:37–40.

Ciancutti, A. and Steding, T. L. (2000). *Built on Trust. Gaining Competitive Advantage in Any Organization.* Chicago, IL: Contemporary Books.

Cohen, D. and Prusak, L. (2001). *In Good Company. How Social Capital Makes Organizations Work.* Boston, MA: Harvard Business School Press.

Cook, J. and Wall, T. (1980). "New work attitude measures of trust, organizational commitment and personal need non-fulfilment." *Journal of Occupational Psychology* 1980;53:39–52.

Cummings, L. L. and Bromiley, P. (1996). "The Organizational Trust Inventory (OTI)." In: *Trust in Organizations; Frontiers of Theory and Research,* R. M. Kramer and T. R. Tyler, eds. Thousand Oaks, CA: Sage Publications.

Davenport, T., De Long, D. W. and Beers, M. C. (1998). "Successful Knowledge Management Projects." *Sloan Management Review* 1998;39:43–57.

Davenport, T. and Prusak, L. (1998). *Working Knowledge. How organizations manage what they know.* Boston, MA: Harvard Business School Press.

De Furia, G. L. (1996). *A Behavioral Model of Interpersonal Trust.* Unpublished Doctoral dissertation, St. John's University, Springfield, LA.

——. (1997). *Facilitator's guide to the interpersonal trust surveys*. San Francisco, California: Pfeiffer and Co.

De Long, D. W. and Fahey, L. (2000). "Diagnosing cultural barriers to knowledge management." *Academy of Management Executive* 2000;14(4):113–127.

Deal, T. E. and Kennedy, A. A. (1982). *Corporate Cultures: The Rites and Rituals of Corporate Life*. Boston, MA: Addison-Wesley.

Ford, D. (2001). "Trust and Knowledge Management: The Seeds of Success." (Working Paper WP 01-08), Kingston: Queen's KBE Centre for Knowledge-Based Enterprises.

Gilbert, J. and Li-Ping Tang, T. (1998). "An examination of organizational trust antecedents." *Public Personnel Management* 1998;27(3):321–338.

Goffee, R. and Jones, G. (1998). *The Character of a corporation. How your company's culture can make or break your business*. London: Harper Coilins.

Holowetzki, A. (2002). *The relationship between knowledge management and organizational culture: An examination of cultural factors that support the flow and management of knowledge within an organization*. Unpublished Master of Science, University of Oregon, Beaverton.

Hubert, C. (2002). *Knowledge Management: It's About Engaging Your Culture, Not Changing It*. Retrieved July, 17, 2004, from **www.apqc.org/portal/apqc/site/content?docid=(1074)92**

Jennex, M. E. and Olfman, L. (2004). *Assessing Knowledge Management Success/Effectiveness Models*. Paper presented at the 37th Hawaii International Conference on System Sciences.

Kinsey Goman, C. (2002a). *Five Reasons People Don't Tell What They Know*. Retrieved February, 5, 2003, from **http://destinationkm.com/articles/default.asp?ArticleID=960**

Kinsey Goman, C. (2002b). What leaders can do to foster knowledge sharing. *Knowledge Management Review* 2003;5(4):10–11.

KM Review survey reveals the challenges faced by practitioners. *Knowledge Management Review* 2001;4:8–9.

KPMG Consulting. (2000). *Knowledge Management Research Report*.

Lewis, J. D. (1999). *Trusted Partners. How Companies Build Mutual Trust and Win Together*, New York: The Free Press.

Microsoft. (1999). *Practicing Knowledge Management*. Seattle, WA: Microsoft Inc.

Nyhan, R. C. and Marlowe, H. A. J. (1997). Development and Psychometric Properties of the Organizational Trust Inventory. *Evaluation Review* 1997;21(5):614–635.

Park, H., Ribière, V. and Schulte, W. D. (2004). Critical Attributes of Organizational Culture Promoting Knowledge Sharing and Technology Implementation Successes. *Journal of Knowledge Management* 2004;8(3):106–117.

Pauleen, D. and Mason, D. *(2002) New Zealand Knowledge Management Survey: Barriers and Drivers of KM Uptake*. Retrieved January 10, 2004, from **http://www.nzkm.net/mainsite/NewZealandKnowledgeManagementSurveyBarriersandDriv.html**

Rao, M. (2002). *Eight Keys to Successful KM practice*. Retrieved February, 1, 2003, from **http://www.destinationkm.com/articles/default.asp?ArticleID=990**

Ribière, V. and Roman-Velazquez, J. A. (2005). "KM Strategic Approaches to Knowledge Flow." In: D. G. Schwartz (Ed.), *Encyclopedia of Knowledge Management*. Hershey, PA: Idea Group.

Ribière, V. and Tuggle, F. D. (2005). "The role of organizational trust in knowledge management tools and technology use and success." *International Journal of Knowledge Management* 2005:1(1).

Rolland, N. and Chauvel, D. (2000). "Knowledge Transfer in Strategic Alliances." In: *Knowledge Horizons*, C. Despres and D. Chauvel, eds. Burlington, MA: Butterworth-Heinemann, 225–236.

Rotter, J. (1967). "A new scale for the measurement of interpersonal trust." *Journal of Personality* 1967;35:651–665.

Rousseau, D., Sitkin, S., Burt, R. and Camerer, C. (1998). "Introduction to special topic forum. Not so different after all: A cross-discipline view of trust." *Academy of Management Review* 1998;23(3):393–404.

Schein, E. H. (1992). *Organizational culture and leadership, 2nd ed*. San Francisco, CA: Jossey-Bass.

Schein, E. H. (1999). *The corporate culture survival guide*. San Francisco, CA: Jossey-Bass.
Smith, H. A. and McKeen, J. D. (2003). *Instilling a knowledge-sharing culture*. Retrieved July 17, 2004, from **http://business.queensu.ca/kbe/docs/Smith-McKeen%(2003)-11.pdf**
Welch, J. (1993). Jack Welch's lessons for success. *Fortune* 1993;127:86.
Wilson, M. B. (1993). *A New Method For Assessing Cook and Wall's Informal Theory of organizational Trust: A Coast Guard Sample*. Unpublished Doctoral Dissertation, The George Washington University, Washington, D.C.
Zand, D. E. (1997). *The leadership Triad—Knowledge, Trust, and Power*. Oxford, U.K.: Oxford University Press.

Chapter 6

Banerjee, Parthasarathi and Richter, Frank-Jurgen. (2001). "Intangibles in Competition and Cooperation Euro-Asian Perspectives." New York: Palgrave.
Barkema, Harry G., Bell, H. J., Pennings, Johannes M. (1996). "Foreign Entry, Cultural Barriers and Learning." *Strategic Management Journal* 1996;17(2):151–166.
Bond, Michael Harris, Hofstede, Geert. (1989). "The Cash Value of Confucian Values." *Human Systems Management* 1989;8(3):195–199.
Chow, Paula K., Chow, Gregory C. (1997). "Asia in the Twenty-First Century Economic, Social-Political, Diaplomatic Issues." Hackensuck, NJ: World Scientific.
Commercial Times, November 20, 2001.
Copper, John Franklin. (1999). "Taiwan: Nation-state or province?" Boulder, CO: Westview Press.
Davis, Herbert J., Schulte, William D. (1997). "National Culture and International Management in East Asia." London: International Thomson Business Press.
Denning, Stephen. (1998). "Building Communities of Practice." Houston, TX: APQC.
——. (1998). Economist Intelligence Unit and Anderson Consulting.
Ernst, Dieter. (2000). "Inter-organizational knowledge outsourcing: What permits small Taiwanese firms to compete in the computer industry?" *Asia Pacific Journal of Management*, 2000;17(2):223–255.
Ferdinand, Peter. (1996). "Take-Off for Taiwan?" The Royal Institute of International Affairs.
Government Information Office. Executive Yuan, Taiwan, R. O. C., http://www.ey.gov.tw/web/english/
Grant, Robert M., Baden-Fuller, Charles. (1995). "A knowledge-based theory of inter-firm collaboration." *Academy of Management Journal, Best Papers Proceedings*, 17–21.
Harrigan, Kathryn Rudie and Dalmia, Gaurav. (1991). "Knowledge Workers: The Last Bastion of Competitive Advantage." *Planning Review* 1991;48:4–9.
Harris, Philp R. and Moran, Robert T. (1991). "Managing Cultural Differences-High-performance Strategies for a New World of Business." Houston, TX: Gulf Publishing Company.
Hofstede, Geert, Bond, Michael Harris. (1988). "The Confucius Connection: From Cultural Roots to Economic Growth." *Organizational Dynamics* 1988;16(4):4–21.
Hofstede, Geert. (1993). "Cultural constraints in management theories." *The Executive* 1993; 7(1):81–95.
Joynt, Pat and Warner, Malcolm. (1996). "Managing Across Cultures." London: International Thomson Business Press.
Lin, Hsin-yi. (2001). News speech, WTO, Nov, 11, 2001.
Maguire, Keith. (1998). "The Rise of Modern Taiwan."Burlington, VT: Ashgate.
McBeath, Gerald A. (1998). "Wealth and Freedom: Taiwan's New Political Economy." Ashgate.
Norman, Leslie P. (2001). "Asian Trader: Taiwanese Hold Big Stakes in Mainland Companies." Barron's; Chicopee.
Nonaka, Ikujiro and Takeuchi, Hirotaka. (1995). "The knowledge-Creating Company How Japaanese Companies Create the Dynamics of Innovation." Oxford University Press.
Orton, Charles Wesley. (2001). "Bridges to fertile ground." *World Trade* 2001;14(2):64–66.
Pao, Maureen. (2001). "Tied to China's Dragon." Far Eastern Economic Review; Hong Kong.

——. (2001). "The mainland allure, Far Eastern Economic Review; Hong Kong.

Simon, Denis Fred and Hau, Michael Y. M. (1991). "Taiwan Beyond the Economic Miracle." Armonk, NY: East Gate Book.

The China Business Review, Engholm, (1994). p. 1.

Tsang, Denise. (1999). "National culture and national competitiveness: A study of the microcomputer component industry." *Advances in Competitiveness Research* 1999;7(1):1–34.

Wang, Po-Jeng. "An Exploratory Study of the Effect of National Culture on Knowledge Management Factors, Expectations and Practices: A Cross-Cultural Analysis of Taiwanese and U. S. Perceptions", Dissertation, George Washington University, 2004.

Weidenbaum, Murry. (2000). "United States-China-Taiwan: A precarious Triangle." *Challenge* 2000, September.

Weisert, Drake. (2001). Book review "Doing Business in China." by Rim Ambler and Morgan Witzel. *The China Business Review*. Washington.

Yoshida, Phyllis Genther. (2001). "Asian economies striving to enhance innovation capabilities." Research Technology Management, Washington.

Chapter 7

Anand, V., Manz, C. and Glick, W. (1998). An Organizational Memory Approach to Information Management. *Academy of Management Review*, 1998;23(4):796–809.

Argyris, C. (1996). "Toward a Comprehensive Theory of Management." In: B. Moingeon, A. Edmondson, eds. *Organizational Learning and Competitive Advantage*, Thousand Oaks, CA: SAGE.

Bluth, B. (1982). *Parson's General Theory of Action—A Summary of the Basic Theory*. Granada Hills, CA: NBS.

Bradley, S. (1993). The Role of IT Networking in Sustaining Competitive Advantage. In: S. Bradley, J. Hausman, R. Nolan, eds. *Globalization, Technology, and Competition*, Boston, MA: Harvard Business School Press.

Calabrese, F. (2000). *A Suggested Framework of Key Elements Defining Effective Enterprise-Wide Knowledge Management Programs*. The George Washington University.

Clemons, E. (1993). "Information Technology and the Boundary of the Firm: Who Wins, Who Loses, Who has to Change." In: S. Bradley, J. Hausman, R. Nolan, eds. *Globalization, Technology, and Competition*, Boston, MA: Harvard Business School Press.

Croswell, C. (1996). *Organizational Learning in Nonprofit Organizations: A Description of the Action Patterns of a Professional Association's Governing Network and Leadership Role in Turbulent Times*, Washington, D.C.: George Washington University.

Cross, R., Israelit, S. (2000). *Strategic Learning in an Knowledge Economy—Individual, Collective and Organizational Learning Process*, Woburn, MA: Butterworth-Heinemann.

Daft, R., Weick, K. (1984). "Toward a Model of Organizations as Interpretation Systems." *Academy of Management Review* 1984;9(2):284–295.

Fiol, C., Marjorie, L. and Marjorie, M. (1985). "Organizational Learning." *Academy of Management Review* 1985;10(4):803–813.

Garvin, D. (1998). "Building a Learning Organization." In: *Harvard Business Review on Knowledge Management.*, Boston, MA: Harvard Business School Press.

Johnson, C. (2000). *A theoretical model of organizational learning and performing action systems: the development and initial validation of the duality of a Parsonian action frame of reference through confirmatory factor analysis*. The George Washington University.

Lesser, E. (2000). *Knowledge and Social Capital*, Woburn, MA: Butterworth-Heinemann.

Liebowitz, J. and Wilcox, L. (1997). *Knowledge Management and Its Integrative Elements*, Boca Raton, FL: CRC Press.

Marquardt, M., Kearsley, G. (1999). *Technology-Based Learning*, Boca Raton, FL: CRC Press.

Matusik, C. and Hill, C. (1998). The Utilization of Contingent Work, Knowledge Creation, and Competitive Advantage. *Academy of Management Review* 1998;23(4):680–697.

Quinn, J., Anderson, P. and Finkelstein, S. (1998). Managing Professional Intellect: Making the Most of the Best. In *Harvard Business Review on Knowledge Management*, Boston, MA: Harvard Business School Press.

Ruggles, R. (1997). *Knowledge Management Tools*, Boston, MA: Butterworth-Heinemann.

Schwandt, D. (1994). *Organizational Learning: As a Dynamic Sociological Construct: Theory and Research*. Paper presented at the Instructional System Dynamics Conference (ISD). University of Scotland, Stirling, Scotland.

Schwandt, D. (1996). "Integrating Strategy and Organizational Learning: A Theory of Action Perspective." In: Huff, A. and Walsh, J., eds. *Advances in Strategic Management*. Stamford, CT: JAI Press.

Senge, P. (1990). *The Fifth Discipline—The Art and Practice of the Learning Organization*, New York: Currency Doubleday.

Chapter 8

Baxi, S. (2002). *Most valuable brands: Coca-Cola best, MS next*. Times News Network, July 26, 2002.

Bontis, N. (1998). "Intellectual Capital: an exploratory study that develops measures and models." *Management Decisions* 1998;3(2):63–76.

Edvinsson. L. and Malone, M. S. (1997). *Intellectual Capital: Realizing Your Company's True Value by Finding its Hidden Brainpower*, New York: Harper Business.

KPMG Consulting (2000). Knowledge Management Research Report, KPMG.

Lang, J. C. (2001). "Management of Intellectual Property Rights." *Journal of Intellectual Capital* 2001;2(1):8–26.

Nelson, R. and Winter, S. G. (1982). *An Evolutionary Theory of Economic Change*, Cambridge, MA: Harvard University Press.

Ribière, V. M. (2001). *Assessing Knowledge Management Initiatives' Success as a Function of Organizational Culture*. The School of Engineering Management and Systems Engineering, Washington D.C., The George Washington University.

Sullivan, P. H. (2000). *Value-driven intellectual capital: How to convert intangible corporate assets into market value*, New York: John Wiley and Sons, Inc..

Swart, J. and Kinnie, N. (2003). "Sharing Knowledge in knowledge-intensive firms" *Human Resource Management Journal* 2003;13(2):60–75.

Wiig K. (1997). "Management: Where did it come from and where will it go?" *Expert Systems with Applications*, Pergamon Press/Elsevier, p. 14.

Wiig K. (1997). "Integrating Intellectual Capital and Knowledge Management" *Long Range Planning* 1997;30(3):399–405.

Williams, R. L. and Bukowitz, W. R. (2001). "The yin and yang of intellectual capital management: the impact of ownership on realizing value from intellectual capital." *Journal of Intellectual Capital* 2001;2(2):96–110.

Chapter 9

Argyris, C. and Schon, D. A. (1978). *Organizational Learning: A Theory of Action Perspective*, Reading, MA: Addison-Wesley.

Baets, Walter R. J. (1989). *Organizational Learning and Knowledge Technologies in a Dynamic Environment*, Boston, MA: Kluwer Academic Publishers.

Banker, Rajiv D., Kauffman, Robert J. and Mahmood, Mo Adam (1993). *Strategic Information Technology Management: Perspective on Organizational Growth and Competitive Advantage*, London: Idea Group Publishing.

Barnard C. (1938). *The Functions of the Executive*, Cambridge, MA: Harvard University Press.

Bartlett, Jeffrey (2000). "Number Theory: New Kings Among KM Tools." *Knowledge Management* 2000;3(9):10–12.

Blackler, F. (1995). "Knowledge, Knowledge Work and Organizations: An Overview and Interpretation." *Organization Studies* 1995;16(6):1021–1046.

Blake, Robert R. and Mouton, Jane S. (1985). *The Managerial Grid III*, Houston, TX: Gulf Publishing Company.

Blake, Robert R. and Mouton, Jane S. (1978). *The New Managerial Grid*, Houston, TX: Gulf Publishing Company.

Brocka, B. and Brocka, M. S. (1992). *Quality Management Implementing the Best Ideas of the Masters*, Homewood, IL: Business One Irwin.

Bruss, Lois R. (1999). "Ten steps to achieve KM success." *KMWorld* 1999:8(4).

Brynjolfsson, Erik, and Hitt, Lorin (1996). "The Customer Counts." *InformationWeek*, September 9, 1996.

Burns, T. and Stalker, G. M. (1961). *The Management of Innovation*, London: Tavistock.

Calabrese, Francesco. (2000). *A suggested framework of key elements defining effective enterprise knowledge management programs*, Washington, D.C.: The George Washington University.

Chatman, J. (1988). *Matching People and Organizations: Selection and Socialization in Public Accounting Firms*, Berkeley, CA: Walter A. Haas School of Business, University of California.

Chatman, J. and Jehn, K. A. (1994). "Assessing the Relationship between Industry Characteristics and Organizational Culture: How Different Can You Be?" *Academy of Management Journal* 1994;37(3):522–553.

Collins, H. (1993). "The Structure of Knowledge." *Social Research* 1993;60:95–116.

Cooke, R. and Rousseau, D. (1988). "Behavioral Norms and Expectations: A Quantitative Approach to the Assessment of Organizational Culture." *Group and Organizational Studies* 1988;13:245–273.

Cyert, R. M. and March, J. G. (1963). *A Behavioral Theory of The Firm*, Englewood Cliffs, NJ: Prentice-Hall.

Deming, W. E. (1982). *Quality Productivity, and Competitive Position*, Cambridge, MA: MIT Center for Advanced Engineering Study.

Davenport, T. (1996). Jarvenpaa, S. and Beers, M. "Improving Knowledge Work Processes." *Sloan Management Review* Summer 1996, 53–66.

Davenport, Thomas H. (1992). "Managing Information in a Process Context." *Working Paper, No. 23*, Ernst and Young LLP Center for Business Innovation.

——. (1992). "Teltech: The Business of Knowledge Management." *Field Profile, No. 23*, Ernst and Young LLP Center for Business Innovation.

Davenport, Thomas, and Prusak, Laurence. (1998). *Working Knowledge. How organizations manage what they know*, Boston, MA: Harvard Business School Press.

David, S. (1982). *Managing Corporate Culture*, Cambridge, MA: Addison-Wesley.

Dodgson, M. (1993). "Organizational Learning: A Review of Some Literature." *Organization Studies* 1993;14(3):375–394.

Dyer, Greg. (2000). "KM Crosses the Chasm." *Knowledge Management* 2000;3(3):50–54.

Garvin, D. A. (1993). "Building a Learning Organization." *Harvard Business Review* 1993; 78–91.

Gay, L. R. and Diehl, P. L. (1991). *Research Methods for Business and Management*, New York: Macmillan.

Geertz, C. (1973). *The Interpretation of Culture*, New York: Basic Books.

Halal, William E. and Smith, Raymond. (1998). *The Infinite Resource: Creating and Leading the Knowledge Enterprise*, San Francisco, CA: Jossey-Bass.

Happer, George R. (2000). *Assessing Information Technology Success as a Function of Organizational Culture*, Huntsville, Alabama: The University of Alabama in Huntsville.

Hares, John and Royal, Duncan. (1994). *Measuring the Value of Information Technology*, New York: John Wiley and Sons, Inc.

Hibbard, Justin and Carrillo, Karen M. (1998). "Knowledge Revolution–Getting employees to share what they know is no longer a technology challenge, it's a corporate culture challenge." *Information Week* 1998:663.

Hibeler, R. J. (1996). "Benchmarking Knowledge Management." *Strategy and Leadership* 1996: 22–29.

Johns, A. P. and James, L. R. (1979). Psychological Climate: Dimensions and Relationships of Individual and Aggregated Work Environment Perceptions, *Organizational Behavior and Human Performance* 1979;23:201–250.

Jones, A. P., Johnson, L. A., Butler, M. C. and Main, D. S. (1983). "Apples and Oranges: An Empirical Comparison of Commonly Used Indices of Interrater Agreement." *Academy of Management Journal* 1983;26:507–519.

Khosrowpour, Mehdi. (1994). *Information Technology and Organization: Challenges of New Technology*, Harrisburg, PA: Idea Group Publishing.

Kim, D. H. (1993). "The Link between Individual and Organizational Learning." *Sloan Management Review* 1993;37–50.

KPMG Consulting. (2000). *Knowledge Management Research Report*, KMPG.

Kroeber, A. I. and Kluckhohn, C. (1952). *Culture: A Critical Review of Concepts and Definitions*, New York: Vintage.

Liebowitz, Jay. (2000). *Building Organizational Intelligence: A Knowledge Management Primer*, Boca Raton, FL: CRC Press.

Louis, M. R. (1983). "Surprise and Sensemaking: What new comers experience in entering unfamiliar organizational settings." *Administrative Science Quarterly* 1983;25:226–251.

Manasco, Britton. (1997). "Silicon Graphics Developments Powerful Knowledge Network." *Knowledge, Inc.* 1997;2(3).

Martin, J. and Siehl, C. (1983). "Organizational Culture and Counterculture: An uneasy symbiosis." *Organizational Dynamics* 1983;12(1):52–64.

Matway, Lisa and Andrews, Linda. (2000). "Collaboration: the neglected side of KM." *KMWorld* 2000;9(3):22–23.

Malhotra, Yogesh. (1998). "Knowledge Management for the New World of Business." *Asian Strategy Leadership Institute Review* 1998;6:31–34.

Malhotra, Yogesh. (1998). Deciphering the Knowledge Management Hype." *Journal for Quality and Participation* 1998;21(4):58–60.

Mitev, Nathalie N. (1994). "The Business Failure of Knowledge-based Systems: Linking Knowledge-based Systems and Information Systems Methodologies for Strategic Planning." *Journal of Information Technology* 1994;9:173–184.

National Research Council, Computer Science and Telecommunications Board. (1994). *Information Technology in the Service Society*, Washington, D.C.: National Academy Press.

O'Dell, Carla and Grayson, C. Jackson. (1998). "If Only We Know What We Know: Identification and Transfer Internal Best Practices." *California Management Review* 1998;40:154–174.

O'Reilly, Charles A., Chatman, Jennifer and Caldwell, David F. (1991). "People and Organizational Culture: A Profile Comparison to Assessing Person-Organization Fit." *Academy of Management Journal* 1991;34(3):487–516.

Ott, J. S. (1989). *Organizational Culture and Perspective*, Homewood, IL: Richard D. Irwin Co.

Ouchi, W. (1981). *Theory Z*, Reading, MA: Addison-Wesley.

Ouchi, W. and Wilkins, A. (1985). "Organizational Culture." *Annual Review of Sociology* 1985;11:457–483.

Perez, Rebecca R. and Hynes III, Martin D. (1999). "Assessing Knowledge Management Initiatives" *Knowledge Management Review* 1999;8:16–21.

Peters, T. and Waterman, R. (1982). *In Search of Excellence*, New York: Harper and Row.

Polanyi, Michael. (1958). *Personal Knowledge*, Chicago, IL: University of Chicago Press.

Popper, K. R. (1967). "Knowledge: Subjective Versus Objective." In: D. Miller, ed., *Popper Selections*, Princeton, NJ: Princeton University Press, 58–77.

Quinn, J. B. (1992). *Intelligent Enterprise*, New York: Free Press.

Quinn, J. B., Anderson, P. and Finkkelstein, S. (1996). "Managing Professional Intellect, Making the Most of Best." *Harvard Business Review* 1996;74(2):77–82.

Quinn, James Brian and Baily, Martin Neil. (1994). "Information Technology: Increasing productivity in services." *Academy of Management Executive* 1994;8(3):28–51.

Remo, Pareschi. (1988). "Information Technology for Knowledge Management." In: Uwe, M. and Borghoff, R., eds. New York: Springer-Verlag.

Roberts, Bill. (1999). "Making Beautiful Music: Culture Change, not Technology, is Key to Collaboration." *CIO* 1999(December, 15):107–114.

Rousseau, D. (1990). "Quantitative Assessment of Organizational Culture: The Case for Multiple Measures." In: B. Schneider, ed. *Frontiers in Industrial and Organizational Psychology* 1990;3:153–192.

Ruber, Peter. (2000). "Silicon Solutions." *Knowledge Management* 2000;3(3):18–20.

Senge, T. (1990). "Coach: A Teaching Agent that Learns." *Communication of the ACM* 1990; 37(7):92–99.

Smircich, L. (1983). "Concept of Culture and Organizational Analysis." *Administrative Science Quality* 1983;28:339–359.

Spek, R. and Spijkervet, A. L. (1996). "A Methodology for Knowledge Management." *Tutorial Notes of the 3rd World Congress on Expert System*, Seoul, Korea.

Stankosky, Michael A. (2000). "A Theoretical Framework." *KMWorld* 2000;9(1).

Stankosky, Michael, and Baldanza, Carolyn. (1999). "Knowledge Management: An Evolutionary Architecture Toward Enterprise Engineering." *INCOSE Mid-Atlantic Regional Conference, September 15 (1999).*

Swartz, Marc J. and Jordan, David K. (1980). *Culture: The Anthropological Perspective*, New York: John Wiley and Sons, Inc.

Swidler, A. (1986). "Culture in Action: Symbol and Strategies." *American Sociology Review* 1986;51:273–286.

Tkach, Daniel. (2000). "The Pillars of Knowledge Management." *IBM Data Management, February 16, (2000).*

Utley, D. R. (1995). *Empirical validation of Classical Behavioral Concepts With Respect to Quality Enhancement Implementation in Engineering Organizations*, Huntsville, AL: The University of Alabama in Huntsville.

Uttal, B. (1983). "The Corporate Culture Vultures." *Fortune, October, 17.*

Van Maanen, J. and Schein, E. H. (1979). "Toward a Theory of Organization Socialization." *Research on Organization Behavior* 1979;1:209–264.

Wallace, Anthony, F. C. (1970). *Culture and Personality*, New York: Random House.

Weick, Karl E. (1979). *The Social Psychology of Organizing*, Reading, MA: Addison-Wesley.

Wiig, K. (1993). *Knowledge Management Foundation*, Arlington, TX: Schema Press.

Zack, Michael H. (1999). "Managing Codified Knowledge." *Sloan Management Review* 1999:69–82.

Chapter 10

Barrados, Maria. (2003). "Can Organizations in Governments Learn?" *Organization for Economic Co-operation and Development (OECD) Symposium on the Learning Government: Managing Knowledge in Central Government*, February 3–4, 2003, Paris, France.

Bixler, Charlie. (2002). "Knowledge management: A practical solution for emerging global security requirements." *KM World* 2002;11(5):18–28.

Burton, Bruce G. (2003). "Knowledge Sharing at the U.S. Department of State." *Organization for Economic Co-Operation and Development (OECD) Symposium on the Learning Government: Managing Knowledge in Central Government*, February 3–4, 2003, Paris, France.

Chatzkel, Jay. (2002). "Conversation with Alex Bennet, Former Deputy CIO for Enterprise Integration at the US Department of Navy." *Journal of Knowledge Management* 2002; 6(5):434–444.

Fitzgerald, James R. (1999). "The Power of E-Sailors" *United States Naval Institute. Proceedings* 1999;125(7):62–63.

Forman, Mark (Chairman). (2003). *Organization for Economic Co-operation and Development (OECD) Symposium for Senior E-Government Officials*, Washington, D.C.: White House, June 9, 2003.

Hanley, Susan. (2001). *Metrics Guide for Knowledge Management Initiatives*, Washington, D.C.: Department of the Navy, Chief Information Officer.

Hoenig, Christopher. (2001). "Beyond e-government." *Government Executive* 2001;33(14): 49–56.

Holmes, James H. (2003). "Remarks by Ambassador James H. Holmes, Director Office of Ediplomacy, U.S. Department of State." *Organization for Economic Co-operation and Development (OECD) Symposium on the Learning Government: Managing Knowledge in Central Government*, February 4, 2003, Paris, France.

Liebowitz, Jay. (2002). "A look at NASA Goddard Space Flight Center's Knowledge Management Initiatives." *IEEE Software* 2002;19(3):40–42.

Mitchell, Kenneth D. (2002). "Collaboration and Information Sharing: An ROI Perspective?" *Public Manager* 2002;31(1):59–61.

The President's Management Agenda Fiscal Year 2002. Washington, D.C.: Office of Management and Budget (OMB) Executive Office of the President.

Pilichowski, Elsa and Dorothee Landel. (2003). "Conclusions from the Results of the Survey of Knowledge Management Practices for Ministries, Departments and Agencies of Central Government in OECD Member Countries, Human Resources Management Working Party, Public Management Committee, Public Governance and Territorial Development Directorate." Paris: Organization for Economic Co-operation and Development (OECD).

Ross, M. V. (2000). "SSC Charleston KM Project Workshop Presentation Summary." Washington, D.C.: Department of the Navy Office of the Chief Information Officer.

Saussois, Jean-Michel. (2003). "Knowledge Management in Government: An Idea Whose Time has Come." *Organization for Economic Co-operation and Development (OECD) Symposium on the Learning Government: Managing Knowledge in Central Government*, February 3–4, 2003, Paris, France.

Scott, Graham. (2003). "Learning Government." *Organization for Economic Co-operation and Development (OECD) Symposium on the Learning Government: Managing Knowledge in Central Government*, February 3–4, 2003, Paris, France.

Serpeca, Beth. (2002). **www.km.gov**.

SSC San Diego Executive Board. (2001). *SSC San Diego Strategic Plan*, San Diego, CA: SPAWAR Systems Center.

Slaght, Ken, RADM USN. (2001). *Message from the SPAWAR Commander August*, San Diego, CA: SPAWAR Systems Center.

Chapter 11

Ahn, J. and Chang, S. (2002). "Valuation of Knowledge: A Business Performance-Oriented Methodology." *Proceedings of the 35th Hawaii International Conference on System Sciences (2002).*

Allee, V. (1997). *The Knowledge Evolution: Expanding Organizational Intelligence*, Newton, MA: Butterworth-Heinemann.

Anantarmula, V. (2004). *Criteria for Measuring Knowledge Management Efforts in Organizations*. Unpublished dissertation, Washington, D.C.: The George Washington University.

Austin, R. and Larkey, P. (2002). "The Future of Performance Measurement: Measuring Knowledge Work." In: Neely, A., ed. *Business Performance Measurement*, Boston: Cambridge University Press.

Baldanza, C. and Stankosky, M. (2000). "Knowledge Management: An Evolutionary Architecture Toward Enterprise Engineering." *INCOSE*:13.2-1–13.2-8.

Bassi, L. and Van Buren, M. (1999). "Valuing Investments in Intellectual Capital." *International Journal of Technology Management* 1999;18(5,6,7,8):414–432.

BP Amoco. (2001). **http://bp.com**. Retrieved April, 2001.

Chourides, P., Longbottom, D. and Murphy, W. (2003). "Excellence in Knowledge Management: An Empirical Study to Identify Critical Factors and Performance Measures." *Measuring Business Excellence* 2003;7(2):29–45.

Drucker, P. (1994). *Post-Capitalist Society*, New York: Harper Business.

Ellis, K. (2003). "K-span: Building a Bridge Between Learning and Knowledge Management." *Training* 2003;40(10):46.

Fairchild, A. (2002). "Knowledge Management Metrics via a Balanced Scorecard Methodology." *Proceedings of the 35th Hawaii International Conference on System Sciences 2002.*

Fowles. (1978). *The Delphi Method.* The Department of Civil and Arechitectural Engineering, Illinois Institute of Technology: **http:///www.iit.edu/it/delphi.html.** Retrieved June, 2001.

Griffin, H. and Houston, A. (1980). "Self-Development for Managers: Making Most of Existing Resources." *Personnel Management* 1980;12(9):46.

Gubbins, M. (2003). "Enterprise–Conference call–Reap the long-term rewards of knowledge management." *Computing* 2003:20.

Jiang, J. and Klein, G. (1999). "Project Selection Criteria by Strategic Orientation." *Information and Management* 1999;36(2):63–75.

Kelley, J. (2003). *Strategic Premises and Propositions for I-Value Growth.* **http://www. transformpartners.com.** Retrieved September, 2003.

KPMG International, UK. (1999). *Knowledge Management Research Report,* United Kingdom: KPMG Consulting.

Longbottom, D. and Chourides, P. (2001). "Knowledge management: a survey of leading UK companies." *Proceedings of the 2nd MAAQE International Conference. "Towards a Sustainable Excellence?"* Versailles, France, September 26–28, 2001, 113–126.

Marr, B. (2003). "Known Quantities" *Financial Management* 2003:25–27.

O'Dell, C and Grayson CJ (1998). "If only We knew What We Know: Identification and Transfer of Internal Best Practices." *California Management Review* 1998;40(3):154–174.

Ofek, E. and Sarvary, M. (2001). "Leveraging the Customer Base: Creating Competitive Advantage Through Knowledge Management." *Management Science INFORMS* 2001; 47(11):1441–1456.

Perkmann, M. (2002). *Measuring knowledge value?: Evaluating the impact of knowledge projects. KIN Brief #7.* Warwick Business School, Leicester University, UK. **http://www. ki-network.org.** Retrieved January, 2003.

Ruggles, R. (1998). "The State of Notion: Knowledge Management in Practice." *California Management Review* 1998;40(3):80–89.

Simpson, J. A. and Weiner, E. S. C. (1989). *The Oxford English Dictionary, 2/e,* Oxford, UK: Oxford University Press.

Skyrme, D. (1997). *Knowledge Networking: Creating the Collaborative Enterprise,* Boston, MA: Butterworth-Heinemann.

Stankosky, M. and Baldanza, C. (2001). *A Systems Approach to Engineering a KM System.* Unpublished manuscript.

Sveiby, K. (1997). *The New Organisational Wealth: Managing and Measuring Knowledge-based Assets,* San Francisco: Berrett-Koehler.

The Delphi Method: Definition and Historical Background. **http://www.carolla.com/ wp-delph.htm.** Retrieved July, 2001.

Van Buren, M. (1999). "A Yardstick for Knowledge Management." *Training Development* 1999;53(5):71–77.

Wikramasinghe, N. (2002). "Practising What We Preach: Are Knowledge Management Systems in Practice Really Knowledge Management Systems." *Proceedings of the 35th Hawaii International Conference on System Science 2002.*

Wiig, K. M. (1993). *Knowledge Management Foundations: Thinking About Thinking—How People and Organizations Create, Represent, and Use Knowledge,* Arlington, TX: Schema Press.

Chapter 12

Allee, Verna. (1997). *The Knowledge Evolution, Expanding Organizational Intelligence,* Woburn, MA: Butterworth-Heinemann.

Allee, Verna. (2000). "Reconfiguring the Value Network." *Journal of Business Strategy* 2000:21(4). Available from **http://www.sveiby.com.au/Allee-ValueNets.htm.**

Alter, Steven. (2002). *Information Systems, The Foundation of E-Business, 4/e* New Jersey: Prentice Hall.

Andriessen, Daniel. (2004). *Making Sense of Intellectual Capital, Designing a Method for the Valuation of Intangibles,* Woburn, MA: Elesevier Butterworth-Heinemann.

Andriessen, Daniel and Tissen, René. (2000). *Weightless Wealth: Find Your Real Value In A Future Of Intangible Assets,* London: Prentice Hall.

Armacost, Robert L. et al. (1999). *Using the Analytic Hierarchy Process as a Two-phased Integrated Decision Approach for Large Nominal Groups.* New York: Kluwer Academic Publishers.

Association of Chartered Accontants in the United States (ACAUS). (1999). **http://www.acaus.org/history.** Retrieved October, 2002.

Barchan, Margareta. *How to Measure Intangible Assets.* **http://www.kmworld.com/resources.** Retrieved October, 2002.

Barney, Jay B. (2001). *Gaining and Sustaining Competitive Advantage,* New Jersey: Prentice Hall.

Bart, Christopher K. et al. (2000). *A Model of the Impact of Mission Statements on Firm Performance,* Hamilton, Ontario, Canada: DeGroote School of Business, McMaster University.

Barth, Steve. (2000). "KM Horror Stories" *Knowledge Management Magazine,* 2000:37–40.

Bergquist, Paul. (2002). *The Votes Are In, Results From Our First Survey.* **http://www. dialogsoftware.com/balancedscorecard/balanced_scorecard_survey1.htm.** Retrieved October, 2002.

Berkman, Eric. (2001). "When Bad Things Happen to Good Ideas." *Darwin Magazine* 2001:50–56.

Blair, Margaret M. and Wallman, Steven M. H. (2000). *Unseen Wealth, Report of the Brookings Task Force on Understanding Intangible Sources of Value.* **http://www.brookings.org.** Retrieved October, 2000.

Boar, Bernard H. (1994). *Practical Steps for Aligning Information Technology with Business Strategies, How to Achieve a Competitive Advantage,* New York: John Wiley and Sons, Inc.

Bolita, Dan. *Intellectual Assets–Corporate Value Moves from Top Minds to Bottom Lines a Price (What's in) your Head,* **http://www.kmworld.com.** Retrieved October, 2002.

Bontis, Nick, et al. (1999). "The Knowledge Toolbox: A Review of the Tools Available to Measure and Manage Intangible Resources" *European Management Journal* 1999; 17(4):391–402.

Bontis, Nick, and Fintz-enz, Jac. (2002). "Intellectual Capital ROI: A Causal Map of Human Capital Antecedents and Consequents" *Journal of Intellectual Capital* 2002;3(3): 223–247.

Bontis, Nick, William Keow, Chua Chong, and Richardson, Stanley (2000). "Intellectual Capital and Business Performance in Malaysian Industries" *Journal of Intellectual Capital* 2000; 1(1):85–100.

Bontis, Nick. (1998a). *Intellectual Capital: An Exploratory Study that Develops Measures and Models,* West Yorkshire, England: MCB University Press.

Bontis, Nick. (1998b). "Managing Organizational Knowledge by Diagnosing Intellectual Capital, Framing and Advancing the State of the Field." *Journal of the Technology Management* 1998;18:443–462.

Bontis, Nick. (2000). *Assessing Knowledge Assets: A Review of the Models Used to Measure Intellectual Models.* Doctoral Dissertation, Hamilton, Ontario, Canada: DeGroote School of Business, McMaster University.

Bontis, Nick. (2002). *World Congress on Intellectual Capital Readings, Cutting-edge thinking on Intellectual Capital and Knowledge Management from the World's Experts,* Woburn, MA: Butterworth-Heinemann.

Bontis, Nick. (2004). "National Intellectual Capital Index: a United Nations Initiative for the Arab Region." *Journal of Intellectual Capital* 2004;5(1):13–39.

Bosworth, Barry P. and Boyd, Stowe. *The Sveiby Toolkit: Web Tools for Intangible Asset Management.* http://www.kmworld.com/resources. Retrieved October, 2002.

Bosworth, Barry P. and Triplett, Jack E. (2000). *What's New About The New Economy? IT, Economic Growth and Productivity.* http://www.brook.edu/views/papers. Retrieved October, 2002.

Brimson, Jim. *Why Your Balanced Scorecard Will Not be Successful–Unless.* The Scorecard Authority. http://www.bettermangement.com. Retrieved October, 2002.

Brooking, Annie. (1996). *Intellectual Capital: Core Asset For The Third Millennium,* London: International Thomson Business Press.

——. (1999). *Corporate Memory: Strategies For Knowledge Management.* International Thomson Business Press.

Brown, John Seely and Duguid, Paul (2000). *The Social Side of Information,* Harvard Business School Press.

Brown, Juanita et al. (1999). *The World Café: Catalyzing Large-Scale Collective Learning,* Waltham, MA: Pegasus Communication. Available from http://www.pegasuscom.com. Retrieved October, 2002.

Calabro, Lori. (2001). *On Balance, Almost 10 years after developing the balanced scorecard, authors Robert Kaplan and David Norton share what they've learned,* CFO Magazine. Available from http://www.cfo.com. Retrieved October, 2002.

Cawsey, Alison. (1998). *The Essense of Artificial Intelligence,* New Jersey: Prentice Hall.

Chandrasekhar, R. et al. (1999). *Case Study: The Case of the (Un) Balanced Scorecard* http://www.zigonperf.com/resources/pmnews/bsc_case_study.html. Retrieved October, 2002.

Chen, Jim, Zhu, Zhaohui and Xie, Hong Yuan (2004). "Measuring intellectual Capital: a New Model and Empirical Study." *Journal of Intellectual Capital* 2004;5(1):195–212.

Clemen Robert T. and Terence Reilly. (2001). *Making Hard Decisions, with Decision Tools,* Pacific Grove, CA: Duxbury Thomson Learning.

Clippinger III, John Henry. (1999). *The Biology of Business, Decoding the Natural Laws of Enterprise,* Jossey-Bass Publisher.

Collingwood, Harris. (2001). "The Earnings Game, Everyone Plays, Nobody Wins", *Harvard Business Review* 2001:5–12.

Cortada, James W. (1998). *Rise of the Knowledge Worker,* Woburn, MA: Butterworth-Heinemann.

D'Aveni, Richard A. D., Harrigan, Kathryn R. and Gunther, Robert (1995). *Hypercompetitive Rivalries: Competing in Highly Dynamic Environments,* New York: Free Press.

Davenport, Thomas H. and Prusak, Laurence (1998). *Working Knowledge, How Organizations Manage What They Know,* Boston: Harvard Business School Press.

Davidson, James Dale and Lord William Rees-Mogg. (1997). *The Sovereign Individual, Mastering the Transition to the Information Age,* New York: Simon and Schuster.

DeSanctis, G. and Gallupe, R. B. (1987). "A Foundation for the Study of Group Decision Support Systems." *Management Science* 1987;33:589–609.

Dixon, Nancy. (2000). *Common Knowledge, How Companies Thrive by Sharing What They Know,* Boston: Harvard Business School Press.

Doe, John B. (1996). *Conceptual Planning: A Guide to a Better Planet, 3d ed,* Reading, MA: Smith Jones.

Downes, Larry. (2001). *Strategy Can Be Deadly (Industry Trend or Event)* The Industry Standard–May 14, 2001. Available from http://www.findarticles.com. Retrieved October, 2002.

Drucker, Peter F. (1954). *The Practice of Management,* HarperCollins Publishers.

Drucker, Peter F. (1985). *Innovation and Entrepreneurship,* London: HarperCollins Publishers.

Drucker, Peter F. (1994). "The Age of Social Transformation." *The Atlantic Monthly* 1994:53–80.

Drucker, Peter F. (2001). *The Next Society,* The Economist Newspaper and The Economist Group. http://www.economist.com. Retrieved October, 2002.

Dyer, Greg. (2000). *Knowledge Management: U.S.* Worldwide Forecast and Analysis, 1999–2004. Available from **www.idc.com**. Retrieved October, 2002.

Eccles Robert G., et al. (2001). *The Value Reporting Revolution*, New York: John Wiley and Sons, Inc.

Edvinsson, Leif and Malone, Michael S. (1997). *Intellectual Captial, Realizing Your Company's True Value by Finding its Hidden Brainpower*, London: HarperCollins Publishers.

Fitz-enz, Jac. (1995). *How To Measure Human Resources Management, Second Edition*, New York: McGraw-Hill.

Gharajedaghi, Jamshid. (1999). *System Thinking, Managing Chaos and Complexity, A Platform for Designing Business Architecture*, Woburn, MA: Butterworth-Heinemann.

Green, A. (2004). "Prioritization of Value Drivers of Intangible Assets for use in Enterprise Balance Scorecard Valuation Models of Information Technology Firms." Doctoral Dissertation, Washington, D.C.: School of Engineering and Applied Science, George Washington University.

Haeckel, Stephan H. (1999). *Adaptive Enterprise, Creating and Leading Sense-And-Respond Organizations*, Boston: Harvard Business School Press.

Hamel G. and Prahalad, C. K. (1994). *Competing for the Future*, Boston: Harvard School Business Press.

Hammer Michael and James Champy. (1993). *Reengineering the Corporation, A Manifesto for Business Revolution*, London: HarperCollins Publishers.

Harvard Management Update. (2001). *Getting a Grip on Intangible Assets, What They Are, Why They Matter, and Who Should Be Managing Them in Your Organization.* Available from **http: www.hbsp.harvard.edu/hmu/intangibles**. Retrieved October, 2002.

Hatcher, M. (1992). "A Video Conferencing System for the United States Army." *Decision Support Systems* 1992;8:181–190.

Heidrick and Struggles. *CFOs Strategic Business Partners, Results of a Survey Conducted by Heidrick and Struggles.* Available from **http://www.h-s-com**. Retrieved October, 2002.

Hibbard, J. (1997). "Knowing What We Know." *Information Week*, October 20, 1997.

Hodgetts, Richard M. (1998). *Measures of Quality and High Performance, Simple Tools and Lessons Learned from America's Most Successful Corporations*, New York: Amacom.

Hope Jeremy and Tony Hope. (1997). *Competing in the Third Wave*, Boston: Harvard Business School Press.

Hope, Jeremy, and Robin Fraser. (1997). "Beyond Budgeting, Breaking Through the Barrier to the Third Wave." *Management Accounting*, Harvard Business School Press.

Huber, G. P. (1984). "Issues in the Design of Group Decision Support Systems." *MIS Quarterly* 1984;8(3):195–204.

Hurwitz, Jason. et al. (2002). "The Linkage Between Management Practices, Intangibles Performance and Stock Returns." *Journal of Intellectual Capital*. 2002;3(1):51–61.

Huseman, Richard C. and Jon P. Goodman. *Leading With Knowledge: The Nature of Competition in the 21st Century*, Thousand Oaks, CA: Sage Publications, Inc.

International Federation of Accountants. (2002). *The Role of the Chief Financial Officer in. (2010).* Available from **http://www.ifac.org**. Retrieved October, 2002.

Kaplan, Robert S. and David P. Norton. (1996). *The Balanced Scorecard, Translating Strategy into Action*, Boston: Harvard Business School Press.

Kaplan, Robert S. (1996). "Using the Balanced Scorecard as a Strategic Management System." *Harvard Business Review* 1996:75–85.

Kaplan, Robert S. (2001). *The Strategy-Focused Organization, How Balanced Scorecard Companies Thrive in the New Business Environment*, Boston: Harvard Business School Press.

Kaydos, Will. (1999). *Operational Performance Measurement, Increasing Total Productivity*, Boca Raton, FL: St. Lucie Press.

Kern, Harris et al. (1996). *Managing the New Enterprise*, New Jersey: Prentice Hall.

Kersnar, Janet and Steven Mintz. (2000). *In the Know*, CFO Europe. Available from **http://www.cfoeurope.com/(2000)11a.html**. Retrieved October, 2002.

Klein, David A. (1998). *The Strategic Management of Intellectual Capital*, Woburn, MA: Butterworth-Heinemann.

KMWorld Magazine Archives. *An Intellectual Accounting: Why do intellectual capital measures focus on the wrong.* [cited **http://www.kmworld.com**. Retrieved October, 2002.

KMWorld Magazine News. (1999). *KM Summit News: Value Your Intangible Assets, Says Allee,* Available from **http://www.kmworld.com**. Retrieved October, 2002.

Koulopoulos, Thomas M. (1997). *Smart Companies Smart Tools, Transforming Business Processes into Business Assets,* London: International Thomson Publishing Company.

Kransdorff Arnold and Russell Williams. (1999). "Swing Doors and Musical Chairs" *Business Horizon* 1999:27–32.

Lev Baruch. (2001). *Intangibles, Management, Measurement and Reporting,* Washington, D.C.: Brookings Institution Press.

Litan Robert E. and Peter J. Wallison. (2000). *The GAAP Gap, Corporate Disclosure in the Internet Age,* Washington, D.C.: American Enterprise Institute for Public Policy Research or The Brookings Institution.

Luthy, D. H. (1998). *Intellectual Capital and its Measurements* **http:www3.bus. Osaka-cu.ac.jp/apira98/archives/htmls/25.htm**. Retrieved October, 2002.

Maisel, Lawrence S. and American Institute of Certified Public Accountants, Inc. (2001). *Performance Measurement Practices Survey Results.* Available from **http://www.aicpa.org**. Retrieved October, 2002.

Marshall, Chris et al. (1996). "Financial Risk and the Need for Superior Knowledge Management." *California Management Review* 1996;38(3):77–101.

Mavrinac, Sarah and Tony Siesfield. (1998). *Measuring Intangible Investment, Measures that Matter: An Exploratory Investigation of Investors' Information Needs and Value Priorities,* Ernst and Young Center for Business Innovation: Organisation for Economic Co-Operation and Development.

McDonough, Brian. *The Intellectual Capital Management Application Market,* KMWorld Magazine Archives. Available from **http://www.KMWorld.com/magazine** archives. Retrieved October, 2002.

McNair, C. J. and Vangermeersch, Richard. (1998). *Total Capacity Management, Optimizing at the Operational, Tactical, and Strategic Levels,* Boca Raton, FL: St. Lucie Press.

McNurlin, Barbara C. and Ralph H. Sprague, Jr. (1998). *Information Systems Management in Practice, 4/e,* New York: Prentice Hall.

Mintz, S. L. (2000). "A Knowing Glance." *CFO Magazine.* 2000:52–62.

Moore Geoffrey A. (2000). *Living on the Fault Line, Managing for Shareholder Value in the Age of the Internet,* London: HarperCollins Publishers.

Morecroft, John D. W. and John D. Sternman. (2000). *Modeling for Learning Organizations,* University Pork, IL: Productivity Press.

Ngwenyama, O. K., Bryson, N. and Mobolurin, A. (1996). "Supporting Facilitation in Group Support Systems: Techniques for Analyzing Consensus Relevant Data." *Decision Support Systems* 1996;16:155–168.

Nicholson Nigel. (2000). *Executive Instinct, Managing the Human Animal in the Information Age,* New York: Crown Publishers.

Nonaka, Ikujiro and Takeuchi, Hirotaka (1995). *The Knowledge-Creating Company: How Japanese Companies Create the Dynamics of Innovation,* Oxford: Oxford University Press.

Nonaka, Ikujiro, et al. (2000). *Enabling Knowledge Creation, How to Unlock the Mystery of Tacit Knowledge and Release the Power of Innovation,* Oxford: Oxford University Press.

Norman, Geoffrey R. and Streiner, David L. (1997). *PDQ Statistics, 2/e,* St. Louis: Mosby.

O'Dell, Carla and C. Jackson Grayson Jr. (1998). *The Transfer of Internal Knowledge and Best Practice, If Only We Knew What We Know,* New York: The Free Press.

Osterland, Andrew. (2001). Knowledge Capital Scorecard: Treasures Revealed, The Third Annual Knowledge Capital Scorecard. *CFO Magazine.* Available from **http://www.cfo.com**. Retrieved October, 2002.

Parker, Marilyn M. (1996). *Strategic Transformation and Information Technology, Paradigms for Performing While Transforming,* New York: Prentice Hall.

Patel Keyur and McCarthy, Mary Pat (2000). *Digital Transformation, The Essentials of e-Business Leadership,* McGraw-Hill.

Porter, Michael E. (1980). *Competitive Strategy, Techniques for Analyzing Industries and Competitors*, New York: The Free Press.

——. (1985). *Competitive Advantage, Creating and Sustaining Superior Performance*, New York: The Free Press.

PriceWaterhouseCoopers Management Barometer. (2002). Available from **http:www.barometer-surveys.com**. Retrieved October, 2002.

PriceWaterhouseCoopers Trendsetter Barometer. (2002). Available from **http:www.barometer-surveys.com**. Retrieved October, 2002.

Prusak, Laurence. (1997). *Knowledge in Organizations*, Woburn, MA: Butterworth-Heinemann.

Rapport, Marc. (2001). *Unfolding Knowledge, Clarifying How Your Company's Knowledge is Structured is Key to Unlocking its Value*. Available from **http://www.destinationcrm.com/km/dcrm_km_article.asp?id906**. Retrieved October, 2002.

Rayport, Jeffrey F. and Sviokla, John J. (1995). "Exploiting the Virtual Value Chain" *Harvard Business Review* 1995:75–85.

Reilly, Robert F. and Schweihs, Robert P. (1999). *Valuing Intangible Assets*, New York: McGraw-Hill.

Rivette, Kevin G. and Klein, David (2000). *Rembrants in the Attic: Unlocking the Hidden Value of Patents*, Boston: Harvard Business School Press.

Rodrigues, Jorge Nascimento. (2001). *Management is Practice*. Available from **http://gurusonline.tv/uk/conteudow/drucker4.asp**. Retrieved October, 2002.

——. (2001). *Management is Practice*. Available from **http://gurusonline.tv/uk/conteudow/edvisson.asp**. Retrieved October, 2002.

Roos, J., Roos, G., Dragonetti, N. C. and Edvinnson, L. (1997). *Intellectual Capital: Navigating in the New Business Landscape*, New York: MacMillian.

Saaty, Thomas L and Vargas, Luis G. (1994). *Decision Making in Economic, Political, Social and Technological Environments with the Analytic Hierarchy Process*, Pittsburgh, PA: RWS Publications.

Saaty, Thomas L. (1980). *The Analytic Hierarchy Process*, New York: McGraw-Hill.

Saaty, Thomas L. (2001). *Decision for Leaders, The Analytic Hierarchy Process for Decisions in a Complex World*, Pittsburgh, PA: RWS Publications.

Shand, Dawne. (1999). "Return on Knowledge" *Knowledge Management* 1999:33–39.

Skyrme David J. (1999). *Knowledge Networking, Creating the Collaborative Enterprise*, Woburn, MA: Butterworth-Heinemann.

Slywotzky, Adrian J. (1999). "Profit Patterns: A Strategic Shortcut" *Harvard Business Review*. 1999:10–12.

Stern, Joel M. and Shiely, John H. (2001). *The EVA Challenge: Implementing Value Added Change in an Organization*, New York: John Wiley and Sons, Inc.

Stewart III, Bennett, G. (1999). *The Quest for Value*, London: HaperCollins Publishers.

Stewart, Thomas A. (1994). "Your Company's Most Valuable Asset, Intellectual Capital" *Fortune* 1994:68–72.

Stewart, Thomas A. (1999). *Intellectual Capital: The New Wealth of Organizations*, New York: Bantam Dell Publishing Group, Inc.

Stewart, Thomas A. (2001). "Accounting Gets Radical", *Fortune 500* 2001:184–194.

Sullivan, Patrick H. (1998). *Profiting from Intellectual Capital, Extracting Value from Innovation*, New York: John Wiley and Sons, Inc.

Sullivan, Patrick H. (2000). *Value-Driven Intellectual Capital, How to Convert Intangible Corporate Assets into Market Value*, New York: John Wiley and Sons, Inc.

Sveiby, Karl Erik. (1997). *The New Organizational Wealth, Managing and Measuring Knowledge-Based Assets*, San Francisco, CA: Berrett-Koehler Publishers, Inc.

Sveiby, Karl Erik. (2001). *Methods for Measuring Intangible Assets*. Available from **http://www.sveiby.com.au/IntangibleMethods.htm**. Retrieved October, 2002.

Svendsen, Ann. (1998). *The Stakeholder Strategy: Profiting From Collaborative Business Relationships*, Berett-Koehlet Publishers, Inc.

Tapscott, Don. (2000). *The Evolving Value Chain*. Available from **http://www.agilebran.com/tapscott4.html**. Retrieved October, 2002.

Tissen, René, Andriessen, Daniel and Lekanne, Frank (2000). *The Knowledge Dividend: Creating High-Performance Companies Through Value-Based Knowledge Management*, New York: Prentice Hall.

Toffler, Alvin. (1980). *The Third Wave*, London: Pan Books.

Triplett, Jack E. and Barry P. Bosworth. (2000). *Productivity in the Services Sector*, American Economic Association. Available from http://www.brook.edu/views/papers/triplette/20000112.htm. Retrieved October, 2002.

Von Krogh, George, et al. (1998). *Knowing in Firms: Understanding, Managing and Measuring Knowledge*, Thousand Oaks, CA: Sage Publications Ltd.

Von Krogh, George, Ichijo Kazuo and Ikujiro Nonaka. (2000). *Enabling Knowledge Creation, How to Unlock the Mystery of Tacit Knowledge and Release the Power of Innovation*, Oxford: Oxford University Press.

Waterhouse, John H. (1999). "Measuring Up" *CA Magazine* 1999:41–44.

Weick, Karl E. (1995). *Sensemaking in Organizations*, Thousand Oaks, CA: Sage Publication, Inc.

Weick, Karl E. and Kathleen M. Sutcliffe. (2001). *Managing the Unexpected*, San Francisco, CA: Jossey-Bass.

Wiig, Karl M. (1994). *Knowledge Management, The Central Mangement Focus for Intelligent-Acting Organizations*, Arlington, TX: Schema Press.

Williams, S. Mitchell. (2000). *Is a Company's Intellectual Capital Performance and Intellectual Capital Disclosure Practices Related?: Evidence From Publicly Listed Companies From the FTSE 100*, Calgory, Canada: University of Calgary.

Working Council for Chief Information Officers. (2000). *Making the Business Case for Knowledge Management, Case Studies in Information Sharing for Business Performance Improvement*, Washington, D.C.: Corporate Executive Board.

Zach, Michael H. (1999a). "Managing Codified Knowledge" *Sloan Management Review* 1999:45–57.

Zach, Michael H. (1999b). *Knowledge and Strategy*, Woburn, MA: Butterworth-Heinemann.

About the Contributors

Dr. Vittal S. Anantatmula is the director and faculty member of the Project Management Program, School of Business of The George Washington University. He has worked in the petroleum and power industries for about 15 years as an electrical engineer and project manager. As a consultant, he worked with the World Bank, Arthur Andersen, and other international consulting firms. He is a certified cost engineer and a member of PMI an AACE. His academic qualifications include and Doctor and Master's of Science in Engineering Management, an MBA (Project Management), and a B.E. (Electrical Engineering).

Dr. Charles H. Bixler is currently the Vice President and Director of Homeland Security and Law Enforcement for DigitalNet, Inc., managing all aspects of a complex and highly dynamic government IT environment. Additionally, he is a Professorial Lecturer at The George Washington University in the School of Engineering and Applied Sciences. He has extensive experience in the area of major systems development projects, including research, development, production, and acquisition. He has over 25 years of Program Management experience, encompassing many areas of research, development, and acquisition. He was the former Director for Knowledge Management at Keane Federal Systems, Inc., and Acquisition and Procurement Manager for the Defense Contract Management Command. He has experience managing tri-service programs and developing policy for all DOD system-wide procurement. Additionally, he served in the United States Navy for 23 years, having performed the duties of Program Manager, Test Pilot, TOPGUN Instructor, and operational F-14 Fighter Pilot. He holds a Doctor of Science in Systems Engineering and Master's of Engineering Management from The George Washington University; and a Bachelors of Science in Aerospace and Mechanical Engineering.

Dr. Francesco A. Calabrese is President/CEO and co-founder of the Enterprise Excellence Management Group International, Inc. (E_xMG), a professional services and executive consulting firm which provides Integrated Knowledge Management solutions to private, public and academic sector organizations. He has over 47 years of experience in the acquisition and execution of programs encompassing engineering, information and telecommunications systems design and development. His past 12 years have been spent in senior consulting roles supporting information and telecommunication companies in their business, marketing, management, strategic planning, and most recently, knowledge management activities. His 25 plus years with Planning Research Corporation culminated in CEO duties for a $250 million, 2,500-person global Information Systems Group. He has been adjunct faculty in the School of Engineering and Applied Sciences, George Washington University (GW) since 1997, where he teaches graduate programs in Knowledge Management, Systems Engineering and Engineering Management. He holds a Doctor of Science and Master of Science from GW, and a Bachelors of Science in Civil Engineering from Drexel University.

Dr. Juan Pablo Giraldo is a Systems Engineer and Architect from the Systems Engineering and Architecture (SEA) group at IBM Global Services. He has over eleven years of experience leading the successful design, development and integration of complex solutions. He has worked in numerous initiatives fostering the reuse of intellectual assets, developing formal and informal communities of practice, and mentoring the use of collaboration technologies to identify, codify, and validate domain specific knowledge. He holds a Doctor of Science, Engineering Management and Systems Engineering and a Master's of Engineering Management, both from the George Washington University; and a Bachelors in Computer Science, Escuela Colombiana de Ingeniería (E.C.I.), Bogotá, Colombia.

Dr. Annie Green is a Knowledge Management Strategist/Architect for Keane Federal Systems. She has 20+ years of progressive experience in systems engineering, business process re-engineering, requirements engineering, project management and methodology development. Annie has serves as an adjunct professor at George Washington University for 15 years and is the lead professor for the KnowledgeWare Technologies course in the knowledge management program. She holds a Doctor of Science from the George Washington University.

Dr. Kevin J. O'Sullivan is an Assistant Professor of management at the New York Institute of Technology. He has over 16 years of IT experience in multinational firms and consulting both in the private and public sector in American, Middle Eastern, European and Far Eastern cultures. He has delivered professional seminars to global Fortune 100 organizations on subjects such as global collaboration, knowledge management, information security and multinational information systems. His research and development interests include knowledge management, intellectual capital security and information visualization. His doctorate is from the George Washington University.

Dr. Heejun Park is an Assistant Professor of Engineering Management in the School of Engineering at Yonsei University in South Korea. Prior to joining Yonsei University, he was an Assistant Professor at Marymount University in the US and Soongsil University in South Korea. His areas of research are the systems approach to organizational learning and knowledge management, technology management and engineering economics. He received his Doctorate and M.S. in Engineering Management, and a B.S. in Computer Science from the George Washington University.

Dr. Vincent Ribière is an Assistant Professor of Information Systems at the Management School of the New York Institute of Technology. He teaches and conducts research in the area of knowledge management and information systems. He is a Program Director at the George Washington University Institute for Knowledge and Innovation. He presented various research papers at different international conferences on knowledge management, organizational culture, information systems and quality, as well as published in various journals. He was an Assistant Professor at American University, teaching in Information Technology. He received his Doctorate of Science in Systems Engineering and Engineering Management with a specialty in Knowledge Management from the George Washington University.

Dr. Juan A. Román-Velázquesz works at the National Aeronautics and Space Administration (NASA) Goddard Space Flight Center as a Project Manager and New Business Liaison in the Office of the Associate Center Director. He is responsible for planning, organizing, and directing projects and proposal activities for science and technology missions. Prior to this, he served as Engineering Technology Program Manager for Space Sciences responsible for the development and management of R&D efforts in support of future Large Aperture Telescopes missions. He has written technical and management articles in several journals. He received his Doctorate of Science in Engineering Management and Systems Engineering with a concentration on Knowledge Management from The George Washington University, a master of Science in Engineering Management from The University of Maryland, and a Bachelors of Science in Mechanical Engineering from the University of Puerto Rico, Mayagüez Campus. He is a member of the Goddard Space Flight Center KM Working Group, George Washington University Institute for Knowledge and Innovation, the Knowledge and Innovation Management Professional Society (KMPro) and a Certified Knowledge Manager (CKM).

Dr. Mickey V. Ross is a Captain, U.S. Navy, and currently the Commanding Officer, and Supervisor of Shipbuilding Puget Sound. He is responsible for over $140m in contracts, over 100 civilian and military personnel, and engineering oversight; providing the Northwest Fleet with optimal warfighting capability, utilizing the private sector industrial base for submarine and surface ship repair and modernization. His previous post was as the Shore Installations Manager, responsible for over $300m for the Space and Naval Warfare Systems (SPAWAR) Command Installations and Logistics Directorate in San Diego. There, he established shore customers a streamlined installation process for increased efficiencies through integration. He has had numerous responsibilities in the Navy, spanning over 25 years, with emphasis on program direction, management, engineering, and operations. He holds a Doctor of Science in Engineering Management and Systems Engineering, George Washington University, an M.S. in Electrical and Computer Engineering, Naval Postgraduate School, and a B.A. in Physical Science, United States Naval Academy.

Dr. William Schulte is an Associate Professor in the Harry F. Byrd, Jr. School of Business of the Shenandoah University. He is also Research Professor at the Institute for Knowledge and Innovation Management of The George Washington University. He has previously taught at the Tobin College of Business of St. John's University in New York and the School of Management at George Mason University. He is on the editorial review board of the Journal of Knowledge Management, a contributing editor and reviewer to journals focused on leadership, national culture, innovation, entrepreneurship and knowledge management. His work includes scores of books, chapters, articles, proceedings, cases and presentations to international scholarly organizations including the Academy of Management, the Strategic Management Society, the International Council for Small Business, the Academy of International Business and the Decision Sciences Institute. He received his Doctorate from the School of Business and Public Management of The George Washington University and his Masters and Bachelors degrees from Louisiana State University.

Dr. Po-Jeng "Bob" Wang is currently advising political figures in Taiwan. His experiences are varied, from having worked in an international trading company to providing technical support at George Mason University (GMU) in the School of IT&E as a research assistant, doing configuration management, consulting and teaching assistant in the Computing Labs. He is a Microsoft Certified System Engineer since 1999 and also HIPAA certified. He holds a Doctor of Science degree in Engineering Management from the George Washington University; continued at GMU in the Information Technology & Engineering doctoral program; holds a M.S.I.S. at George Mason University; an M.B.A. at Old Dominion University; and a B.A. in Economics at the Chinese Culture University in Taiwan.

About the Editor

Dr. Michael A. Stankosky is the Lead Professor for Knowledge Management and co-founder/co-director of the Institute for Knowledge and Innovation at the George Washington University (GW). His experiences cover a wide range of areas, from marketing of technology to systems engineering, management science, and information technology. He has had varied careers in the military and business, covering a wide range of leadership and management positions. He is the architect of the master's, doctoral, and graduate certificate programs in Knowledge Management (KM) at GW. He has written many articles, spoken at numerous conferences worldwide, and consults to many organizations in KM. He holds a Doctor of Science in Engineering Management from GW.

Index